FIFTY YEARS OF
ENGLISH LITERATURE
1900–1950

BY THE SAME AUTHOR

LYTTON STRACHEY
THOMAS HARDY
Writers and their Work Series

FIFTY YEARS OF
ENGLISH LITERATURE
1900–1950

With a Postscript—1951 to 1955

by
R. A. SCOTT-JAMES

LONGMANS

LONGMANS, GREEN AND CO LTD
48 Grosvenor Street, London, W.1
*Associated companies, branches and representatives
throughout the world*

First published 1951
Second Edition (with a Postscript 1951–1955) 1956
Eighth Impression 1964

PRINTED IN GREAT BRITAIN BY
SPOTTISWOODE, BALLANTYNE AND CO LIMITED
LONDON AND COLCHESTER

NOTE TO THE SECOND EDITION

IN the concluding chapter of this edition, dealing with the years from 1951 to 1955, I have endeavoured to bring my survey as nearly as possible up to date. When a few years ago I was writing the opening chapters I felt that my subject was far enough away in the past to belong properly to history; but as I moved on the theme opened itself gradually as if by the natural processes of growth; and in the later chapters, though the subject matter was changing all the time, I was not acutely conscious of any great difference in my approach although I was now discussing the living and even the young. In the new section I have had to deal with many aspects of a very short period of time, which is virtually the present time; and in doing so I have tried to be as detached as I was when writing, say, about the Edwardians; to let the subject dictate to me, and not force it into a pattern of my own making. Reading and writing in this spirit I did not feel that I was winding up a story that had been left unfinished. On the contrary, I was conscious of something beginning rather than ending, of a new phase coming of which the latest books give us an inkling; the very restlessness of this period of transition may be that of a new birth. Fifty years hence some literary historian may explain why literature had to pass through its Slough of Despond on its way to the Celestial City, and the necessity of its trials and tribulations and hairbreadth escapes. We can only record the incidents as they appear at this moment, and note the signs of faith and vision which illumine them for us.

R. A. S.-J.

1956.

v

PREFACE

THE distinction between English literature and literature written in English is an important one. It is with the former only that I am concerned in this book. It is an expression of a nation's life, past and present; it is part of its history and is itself history. It is influenced by physical and social environment, and is written under the urge of ideas current at given moments. Though it may be profoundly affected by foreign literature and foreign movements of thought, whatever it gains in this way from outside will have been passed through the prism of a mind habituated to the English, or British, frame of thinking. So English literature, for all its variety, has a unity which is lacking in that vaster body of literature written in the English language.

The distinction is a simple one, but the application of it is not quite so simple. It was easy for me to decide that American literature should be excluded from my subject. American literature has its own history, its own character, its own social and scenic background, and is as distinctively the expression of the American mind and temper as English literature is the expression of the British mind and temper. Many American books are read in my country and many British books are read in America; the same or—should I say?—the similar language ensures that. Yet when an Englishman reads an American book he is conscious of stepping into an American *milieu*, and the American who reads an English book is aware of paying a visit to the older country. The only people likely to confuse the two are foreigners who know little of America or Britain; scanning the titles of books written in English in a bookshop, they are apt, too precipitately, to assume that they are British. American literature has always been different from English, even in the nineteenth century. Dickens could not have been anything but English, or Mark Twain anything but American. When Emerson and Carlyle met and conversed so laconically, they were surely conscious of themselves as two minds transcending by their greatness the greatness

of the gulf that lay between. In the distant past, it is true, the two
streams emerge from a common source; both start from the
same Shakespeare and the same Bible, and these have been potent
influences. But though the literatures of Britain and America
belong to the same family and have greatly influenced one another
they are separate members of that family and have developed each
in its own way.

It was not so easy to decide whether I ought to include authors
who, though British, have spent their lives and done their writing
in British Dominions. I decided to exclude them, partly because
my subject was in any case a vast one, and secondly because
this overseas literature emerges from a social experience which,
though complementary, is in many ways different from that of
Great Britain. In consequence, to take a single example, I have
missed the opportunity of praising that powerful South African
writer, Sarah Gertrude Millin.

The problem of Ireland was still more difficult. At the beginning of the half-century with which I am concerned Ireland was a
part of the United Kingdom; there was much coming and going
between Dublin and London, and intimate intercourse between
English and Irish writers. Bernard Shaw was born in Ireland but
did nearly all his literary work in England. Yeats was Irish, but
lived as much in the one country as in the other. In spite of the
Irish Literary Movement the literary inheritance of the two countries for most practical purposes was identical. It would certainly
have been impossible and absurd to have given an account of
English literature in the first twenty years of the century without
discussing the contributions of Irishmen. But the position was
different when southern Ireland became a Dominion and finally
ceased to be part of the United Kingdom. This separateness has
entered deeply into her life, first under the Irish Free State, afterwards under the Republican government of Eire, and has tended
to create for her writers an environment and atmosphere very
remote from that of Britain. She has held aloof from our problems
and this country from hers. Differences which at one time had
been studiously cultivated were now hardened by circumstances.
Even the customs barrier became symbolic. The temperamental
differences between English and Irish which in the past made
relations between them so interesting and profitable were less
remarked when the old close relationship ended. The people of

southern Ireland have entered upon a new phase of experience which is exclusively their own. And so, though I felt it essential to deal with the Irish contribution to literature up to 1922, it seemed proper to omit it, so far as southern Ireland is concerned, for the years that followed; and I have not discussed that powerful dramatist, Seán O'Casey, nor that brilliant novelist and critic, Seán O'Faoláin, and other contemporary writers whom I greatly esteem.

On the other hand there are some authors who were born nationals of a foreign country but adopted this country as their own, lived and worked here, absorbed our atmosphere, and contributed to our literature. Joseph Conrad, Henry James, T. S. Eliot and Arthur Koestler could not be omitted.

There are regional differences between writers who live in England, Scotland, Wales and Northern Ireland, but their works, if written in English, belong of course to English literature.

CONTENTS

Chapter One

THE TURN OF THE CENTURY

THE *race*, the *milieu*, the *moment*—the words of Taine force themselves to the surface of the mind when the critic attempts to survey a whole period of literary history, or to describe the procession of writers moving through it. In the retrospect each period acquires a distinctive character. Certain notes are struck for the first time. The instruments are new. The orchestration is original. There is something here, among the people of *that* race, in *that* unique social setting, under the momentum of ideas which were striking the racial consciousness at just *that* instant of history, which makes a given period different from any other before or after. Literature grows out of what has preceded it and holds much of its past within itself, yet it is always starting again, standing poised for an instant and then preparing for a new leap forward into the dark. The starting-points are seldom clearly visible to contemporaries, and then only to the uncannily clear-sighted. With the first significant plays of Shakespeare or Molière the history of literature turns over a new leaf, but no comet appeared suddenly in the sky to mark the change. Each century, as we look back on it, has its own shape and quality; but the seventeenth century overlaps into the eighteenth, the eighteenth into the nineteenth, the nineteenth into the twentieth; the stream is continuous, indivisible, yet each stretch of water has its unique character. From a distance we survey the centuries—and go on to subdivide them into generations, literary generations; and these, owing to the rapidity of change in this changing age, appear to become shorter and shorter as we reach our own time. I think in the last fifty years in Britain we might discern at least four generations of writers, each regarding its predecessor as outmoded and stale, though there are men still living who were writing effectively at the beginning of that period and are still writing effectively to-day.

We shall be tempted to look at these British writers who have been conspicuous in the last fifty years as products, makers and representatives of their time, changing, as Taine said, with 'the air that nourishes them'. But it will be necessary also to remember the cautionary words of Sainte-Beuve: 'in these finenesses which you admire and seem to savour so well, you are wrong to see only a *result* and a *product* of circumstances. There are always, let us hope, *des âmes délicates,* fine spirits who will seek their proper ideal, their own chosen expression'. Some will be obviously steering their craft in the very centre of the stream—the Shaws, the Wells's, the Galsworthys, the Lytton Stracheys, the T. S. Eliots—such men will by their work and influence indicate the trend of thought and literature. Others—a Conrad, a W. H. Hudson, a Max Beerbohm, a Forrest Reid, a Ruth Pitter—will not fit into a too precisely defined pattern. It is delusive to make the pattern too simple. A literary generation is what it is by virtue of the minds of persons, and what they write. The trends will exist; they will be describable—but no sooner have they been described than certain individuals will thrust themselves on us by their defiance of fashion, making nonsense of generalization. Sometimes the exceptional writer will seem to be a reviver of the past, sometimes a forerunner of the future.

To me, looking back, the year 1900 really does stand out as a turning point. It was the last year of the century, the last year but one of Queen Victoria's long reign, the last year but two of the last so-called Imperialist war in which Britain was engaged (the Boer War), and among the first of the years in which the popular daily Press, with the *Daily Mail* as its forerunner, was quickly altering the character of daily journalism. It was the beginning of the end of the supremacy of the middle classes, and middle-class standards of thought and writing. The Fabian Society, an organization of intellectuals preaching doctrinaire Socialism under the leadership of Sidney Webb and Bernard Shaw, had already established itself, and the Labour Party was starting its career as a political body led by Keir Hardie and Ramsay MacDonald. The Victorian age in England had been one of unparalleled expansion of industry, trade and wealth—of money-making tempered by charity—and active social thinking directed along the lines of *laissez-faire* Liberalism fortified by theories of organic evolution which comfortingly assured the survival of the fittest. In its middle period it had been marked by current religious and theological controversies evoked both by stresses within the Churches and by the attacks of materialists from without. Towards the end of the period religion was making its peace with philosophy, and Oxford University was dominated by the philosophy of T. H. Green, the transcendental idealist. The spectacle of sordid poverty existing side by side with great wealth had already awakened, not merely sentimental humanitarianism, but a growing desire to take organized action to improve the condition of the working classes —a movement stimulated partly by the growing power and self-consciousness of the masses and partly by disinterested endeavour. The novels of Dickens were still read by the young, but the novels of working-class life that were now being produced by such men as Gissing and Arthur Morrison and, more lightly, Pett Ridge, men by no means comparable with Dickens in range, or power, or objectivity, were none the less symptomatic as showing the feeling of bitterness and poignant suffering now aroused by contact with the poor. The poor had ceased to be just those who 'are always with us'; they had become a challenge to the social conscience, the raw material of the realistic novelist, with, or without, a purpose.

The reader of English literature is aware of a profound change of atmosphere as he moves from the mid-Victorian writers to the Edwardian. George Eliot, Dickens, Thackeray are all critical writers, but they are not critical of the fundamental bases of human society and ethics as are Shaw, Wells and, in his earlier phase, Galsworthy. George Eliot is an explorer and describer of the human soul, but for all her unorthodoxy is no rebel. Thackeray is a caustic critic of the vanities and foibles of human beings, but he moves acquiescently through the world he knows, with all its admitted absurdities. Dickens is an uncompromising critic of the cruelties of the Poor Law or the obscurantism of the law, but never was there a writer who more wholeheartedly said 'yea' to life and revelled in the portrayal of heroes and heroines, villains and monsters. The society whose abuses he attacked was the source for him of infinite delight; primarily it was his role to depict it as he saw it, with exhilaration, and his very exaggerations are a measure of the joy he experienced in recreating, and in making everything a little more than it could possibly be in real life. Such writers are the natural voices of a society which is conscious of its growing power, which is becoming aware of itself, but is not yet questioning all the fundamentals of its own life. Religion, indeed, it did question. Darwin, and the theories of natural selection and social evolution, did for a time threaten the citadels of orthodox Christianity; and no doubt the spirit of free enquiry engendered in the quarrels between science and religion did prepare the way for an attitude which was to be critical of the whole social and moral order. But the early twentieth century had for its characteristic to put everything, in every sphere of life, to the question, and secondly, in the light of this scepticism, to reform, to reconstruct—to accept the new age as new, and attempt to mould it by conscious, purposeful effort.

Of course there were harbingers of the new era, spiritual explorers who were voicing their discontents with the industrialism of Victorian Britain, the ruthlessness of social changes, the prevailing mental unrest, and the complacency of the bourgeois class. Ruskin inveighed against the hideousness which came in the train of industrialism and William Morris against the loss of beauty arising from the displacement of handicrafts by the machine; Richard Jefferies deplored the disturbance of his beloved countryside; and Samuel Butler's Erewhonians clamoured for the destruction of machines lest they should be consumed by them. Matthew Arnold, pleading for culture, exposed the Philistinism of a society too much dominated by aristocrats 'inaccessible to light and ideas' and by a populace addicted to 'bawling', 'hustling' and smashing'; and in *The Scholar Gipsy* lamented the mental feverishness of the age. Thomas Hardy went further. In a series of great novels he shows men and women who have outgrown the simpler modes of life of primitive man and have become exposed through over-developed 'emotional perceptiveness' to the assaults of a civilization for which they are unfitted. They are the too self-conscious victims of the 'social mould civilization fits us into', of the 'modern vice of unrest', the 'ache of modernism'. But Hardy's novels are saved from distressing pessimism by the nobility of the heroes and heroines whom he sends to their doom, endowed with the courage of a Prometheus afflicted by a relentless deity.

The exuberant vitality, self-confidence and objectiveness which were so evident in mid-Victorian literature were already being undermined before the century was out; the way was being prepared for something very different. But the more critical spirit of the 1880's and 1890's did not immediately lead to the new prophecy. In the last decade of the century a two-fold reaction became manifest. One took the form of an instinctive reaction against the subtler critics leading, not to less exuberance, but to more. The central figure asserting this mood of the nation was Rudyard Kipling; but before discussing the part he was to play I must say a word about a movement in quite the opposite direction, which led to a flight from all the practical issues, to taking refuge in what was known as 'æstheticism' and the escapist doctrine of 'art for art's sake'.

The so-called 'æsthetic movement' became fashionable in the universities and in some intellectual circles in the eighties and early nineties, and its adherents talked the jargon of 'art for art's sake'. Born in France, this doctrine was imported into England by Whistler and expounded in its more extreme form by Oscar Wilde and some of the contributors to the *Yellow Book*. It is a common mistake to regard Walter Pater as the originating influence in this movement. Walter Pater, it is true, owed much to French writers and especially Flaubert, and, like Wilde, turned his back on the moralism of Ruskin, who had taught that 'art must be didactic to the people'. For him the perfection of life lay in seeking experience in the spirit of the artist, in disciplined attentiveness to the 'comely', the 'gracious', the 'blithe', in fastidious receptiveness to beauty. For him the writer's aim was the transcribing 'not of the world, not of mere fact, but his sense of it'. But he was careful to say that he did not intend 'a relegation of style to the subjectivity, the mere caprice, of the individual, which must soon transform it into mannerism'. If the æsthetes who stood for 'art for art's sake' had been content to follow Pater in his demand for sincerity, for 'the finer accommodation of speech' to the vision within, for 'absolutely sincere apprehension of what is most real to him' (the artist), they would have avoided the absurdities which were soon associated with their name. But for Wilde and his fellows the artist was not merely a man with certain faculties highly developed; he was a being apart from common humanity, different in kind. For him the *subject* treated was of no importance; the artist wrote only to please himself and was not in any way concerned to communicate his vision to others. To such a one reality and truth cease to have any validity. The doctrines led inevitably to artistic anarchy. Most of the members of the school, it should be said, were not so extravagant as their theories; Wilde himself was by no means indifferent to the effect which his writings, or his personal poses, had upon others.

2

But it is only fair to writers of this school to remember that the Victorian writers, in stressing the importance of subject-matter, imagination and thought, had given far too little attention to style and form. Few of them had realized, as their contemporaries in France had done, that the utmost can only be extracted out of writing by the scrupulous study of technique, by self-discipline in the best use of words and attention to structure. But for Walter Pater literature existed to minister to beauty. It was the artist in the writer that he cared for. And that was true also for critics who absorbed something of his spirit—men like John Addington Symonds and Arthur Symons—and even those who preached 'art for art's sake' to the point sometimes of absurdity deserve the credit of helping to redress the balance in literature, reminding readers that it is an art to be studied no less carefully, no less exactly than the arts of music or painting.

The sophistication, the escapism, the weary self-consciousness which appeared among groups of painters, poets and prose-writers in the eighties perhaps indicated that literature, on the lines on which it had been pursued in Victorian England, had no more worlds to conquer. That phase of national spirit had exhausted itself, and the reaction was a sort of weariness, or nihilism, the ennui which was so aptly described as *fin de siècle*. For boisterousness and ardour there came flippancy or despair, or cynicism—the flippancy of Wilde, the despair of Ernest Dowson, the cynicism (in pictorial art) of Aubrey Beardsley.

It is almost with a sense of shock that one turns from these writers to the poetry and prose of Rudyard Kipling, who at the end of the nineteenth century was far the most popular, and potent, of those popular writers who can be taken seriously. Kipling has perhaps an even more important place in social history than in the history of literature. He, if any writer, belonged peculiarly to the time and the race, and expressed and affected the mood of the nation at a critical period. To indicate that mood of the British people which to the onlooker in the nineties appeared to be the dominant mood it is not, I think, fanciful to mention the names of three men who expressed it in their several spheres of influence—Joseph Chamberlain, Alfred Harmsworth (afterwards Lord Northcliffe) and Rudyard Kipling. Chamberlain was a Radical politician who parted from the Liberals over the issue of Irish Home Rule, and later, in his fiery advocacy of the claims and ideals of the British Empire, led the Imperialist movement which swept over the country just before and during the Boer War, denouncing opponents with the opprobrious epithet of 'Little-Englanders'. The second, Alfred Harmsworth, was a popular journalist, who holds a place in history as the first Briton who realized to the full that the largest reading public was no longer middle-class, but proletarian; that it consisted of the masses who, through elementary education, had now become literate—they were exposed to the impact of the printed word. The popular daily paper which he founded soon acquired a circulation greater than that of any five other daily papers put together. In its early days it lived upon sensation, and particularly that kind of sensationalism to which a patriotic war lends itself.

Rudyard Kipling did something which only a man of great force could have done; he took poetry off the pedestal on which it had stood so long, and wrote in language which the average commonsense Englishman read with exhilaration. What a contrast to the æsthetes! He, if anyone ever did, took verse to the people and made it a living influence among them. He and the æsthetes were poles asunder. Not for him the rarefied, the subtle, the refined. The language in which he wrote was, as it had never been for Wordsworth, though the words are his, 'the language of men'. In his ringing, rhythmic ballads he used hard, gritty words to tell the tale of ordinary men in unordinary circumstances. The emotions he touched were poignant enough, such as any man might have when moved by pity for a comrade, or homesickness, or pride in his country, or admiration for an act of physical courage. He appealed to the sense of fellowship of Englishmen when they were Englishmen together in strange lands among aliens. Tommy Atkins, the English *poilu*, for the first time became the real hero in the nation's wars; it was for him that the band played when men went out to fight for Queen and country. Kipling beat his drum loudly; it roused unpoetic Englishmen as the tom-tomming of a savage rouses the tribe. There was no lack of emotion, but it was the kind of emotion of which no man, however shy in the presence of a poet, need be ashamed. Verse as written by him became the antithesis of that unsubstantial, dreamy, fretful poetry which had marked the æsthetes; it entered the domain of ordinary life, and enlivened it with sensationalism. It breathed patriotism, the militant patriotism which came to be thought of as Imperialism.

I am speaking now of Kipling, the writer of ballads, not of Kipling the novelist and writer of short stories, because it was through his verse that his influence made itself felt most potently at a critical period. There was imagination of a much higher order in the novels, *The Light that Failed* and *Kim*, and in the short stories, and in his inimitable *Jungle Books*. The skill with which he developed a strange situation in nervous powerful language makes him one of the masters of the art of short-story writing. If Kipling had written only prose it is probable that he would have been held in higher esteem than he was by students of literature. (Respect for him has grown in recent years.) But it was through his verse that he exercised an influence in the national life in the last ten years of the century such as no English poet probably had ever done before. There were other writers whose names were household words at that time, but none left their mark as he did. The nineteenth century ends with a flourish of trumpets on the Kipling note. It was the last blast that Englishmen were ever to hear extorting that sort of sensationalism or making that sort of appeal. He himself, after 1901, though not quite a spent force—he was still to write some excellent fanciful stories and a vigorous regimental history of the first Great War—ceased to be the Kipling whose words touched the community spirit of his countrymen to the quick. In 1900 a new generation of writers was knocking at the door, men who in a very different way were to identify themselves with the Time-Spirit and introduce a new world of thought and feeling—and action.

Chapter Two

PROPHETS

'THE mass of current literature,' said Matthew Arnold, 'is so much better disregarded.' But it cannot be altogether disregarded if we would understand the atmosphere in which the choicer writers lived their intellectual lives. At the beginning of the twentieth century the old authors were still in the ascendant in the libraries; newer popular writers who reflected the more superficial fashion of the day were read and admired; popular journalism dealt out snappy trivialities to the masses in greater volume than ever before. But intelligent persons were aware of something more significant moving in the world of ideas, of new dynamic elements which were finding expression in literature. To them it must often have seemed that the mass of society was incorrigible—that it was still engulfed in pretentiousness, snobbery, sentimentalism and slavish adhesion to convention and fashion, or in crushing poverty, squalor and ignorance which was all the worse because it was being exploited by publicists.

But what is significant is that thinking people were thinking like this, that they were alive to the obsolescence of the old way of life and were demanding a new, and were actually handing on their critical or constructive ideas to others—to those who were not yet aware of Ibsen, or Karl Marx, or Nietzsche, or Samuel Butler or Bernard Shaw. A leaven was working. Society was undergoing fundamental changes, outward and inward; and there were voices proclaiming what was new in it, critical of the past, prescient of the future, already audible for those who had ears to hear.

It was impossible not to be aware of the outward transformation in the conditions of life, and the disturbing rapidity of change. The habits of the people were being modified by new mechanical inventions—the motor-car, the telephone, the gramophone, electric transport and, soon after, aeroplanes and radios. The suburbs of the big cities were stretching out further into the countryside, fed by quick trains and trams and omnibuses. Elementary education for all had produced a new generation of

9

workers more class-conscious, more aware of their potential power, more ready to insist on the satisfaction of their needs; and from the universities serious young men went to live in the East End of London to study the problems of the poor. The awareness of change taking place so rapidly and in so disorderly a way led to a demand for the conscious direction of change, for planned progress. *Laissez-faire* had exhausted itself; it had been compatible with the amassing of great wealth, but it had failed to satisfy the conscience of the community, which, in so far as it was aware of itself and articulate, was becoming more and more convinced of the need for organized action to force the pace of reform, to give to the many social security and the advantages of knowledge, art and recreation. It was scarcely possible for observant adults not to see that the world around them had changed its shape since they were children. Men were having to adjust themselves, however tentatively, however clumsily, to new inventions, new urban conditions, new arrangements of society caused by the shifting of industry or by popular education, all of these tending to induce new behaviour and new habits. To some it seemed that science and industry had run ahead of man's capacity to adjust himself to change. Hence the insistent question, what was there good in the old order, which ought to be preserved, and what was there, stale and obsolescent, that ought to be discarded and exposed as false or decaying? It was a moment when old ideas were being thrown into the melting pot, new ideas evolved and discussed. Plans for social reform were eagerly discussed, and constructive action was demanded from the political parties in the light of the ideas of the sociologists, the economists, the idealistic philosophers, and those essayists, novelists and playwrights so many of whom were assuming the character of preachers, moralists and prophets. A. G. Gardiner, editor of the *Daily News*, writing a book on the prominent personalities of the time, called it 'Prophets, Priests, and Kings'.

Before speaking of the new writers of books who were coming to the front it is worth saying a word about one distinctive characteristic of the journalism of the period. Writers in the daily and weekly Press had for the most part been anonymous, and it had usually been the collective authority of the journal as a whole which had impressed readers. But now a number of individual journalists who wrote under their own names or whose

identity was generally known were giving their own views in the
Press and attracting readers to the journals for which they wrote.
Sometimes it was the powerful individuality of an editor which
counted, sometimes one or another of his contributors. In the
nineties Bernard Shaw and Max Beerbohm had been attracting
attention by their critical writing in weekly papers, but this
influence as yet reached only a relatively small and fastidious circle.
Everyone at the turn of the century knew the name of a man of
a very different order, W. T. Stead, an energetic, exuberant,
mercurial writer who rushed in at every opportunity to expose
abuses or advertise the cause of the oppressed. He founded the
Review of Reviews. Robert Blatchford, editor of the *Clarion,*
gained the ear of the emerging intelligentzia of the working
classes in hard-hitting, unpolished but forceful articles, provocative and uncompromising. A much finer type of journalist
was H. W. Massingham, a Parliamentary sketch-writer, leader-
writer, and for a time editor of a Liberal daily paper, and for
many years editor of an outspoken weekly, the *Nation*; he was a
Radical in politics, a humanist in his general outlook, and a protagonist in the cause of freedom in all its forms, political, social,
literary.

A man of amazing promise and half-fulfilment was Charles
F. G. Masterman who, after a distinguished university career at
Cambridge, went to live in the slums of Camberwell to study the
lives of the poor. He wrote books about the condition of the
working classes, and in the columns of the *Daily News* poured
out glowing, impassioned, though often too hurriedly written
articles about current books, politics and social reform, preaching
the necessity of humane political and social action as the only
alternative to national doom. His was a strange, wayward,
tempestuous personality, plagued by a restless imagination, torn
between ambition and the ideal of service, half man of letters, half
politician, a genius who never reached his proper fulfilment.
Among his more intimate friends in journalism were G. K.
Chesterton and Hilaire Belloc; in politics, Lloyd George and
Winston Churchill. H. W. Nevinson also belonged to the same
school of writers in the Press, notable as war-correspondent,
travel-writer and literary essayist, who went through life championing the cause of oppressed peoples, whether they were subjects of the Czar in Russia, negroes in Africa, or voteless women

at home. He was a classical scholar and a writer of distinguished prose, whose *Essays in Freedom, More Changes, More Chances* and *In the Dark Backward,* imaginative, eloquent, with touches of grim humour, are abundantly worth reading to-day.

Three editors stand out among those whose personalities, mainly expressed through journalism, had much influence on public opinion during the early decades of the twentieth century. Easily first among these was C. P. Scott, editor of the *Manchester Guardian* for nearly half a century, whose paper, though a provincial one, acquired an international reputation as a model of well-informed, fair, courageous and well-written English journalism. I am not here concerned with politics, or the part which the *Manchester Guardian* played as a leader of humane Liberal thought in Great Britain. The point that concerns me now is that Scott impressed his own singular personality on his paper, making it the organ of enlightened ideas touching many spheres of life, collecting round him distinguished writers to whose individuality he gave the fullest possible scope, and not only advocating intelligent social reform, as he constantly did, and shrewd national policies, but also encouraging literature, drama, art, architecture and music, and original ideas concerning them. His staff at various times included such notable writers as Leonard Hobhouse, C. E. Montague (dramatic critic and essayist), Allan Monkhouse, Herbert Sidebotham (afterwards well known as *Scrutator* in the pages of the *Sunday Times*), and John Masefield (now Poet Laureate). Scott's name will always be associated with a highly successful attempt to retain in daily journalism the best of the old side by side with what was new and progressive.

An editor of a very different temperament was J. Alfred Spender, who edited the *Westminster Gazette* from 1896 to 1922. Throughout most of its career this journal was an evening paper, and day by day for a quarter of a century it was chiefly read for the leading article known to be written by the editor. Spender was trusted with the secrets of leading members of the Government, and kept them; readers felt that he knew things which he could reveal had he wished to, and that his circumspect judgments must be treated with respect. The articles which he wrote every day were neatly written, balanced, judicious, always on the side of the angels so far as was compatible with caution, understatement and expediency. What a contrast to another powerful editor, J. L. Garvin, who from 1908 to 1942 was editor of the Sunday *Observer*, and also editor of the evening *Pall Mall Gazette* from 1912 to 1915, a generous, impetuous, imaginative man who confidently and regularly gave advice to his country in impassioned, rhetorical, verbose articles which were the more convincing for his admirers since the policies he advocated were his own rather than those of a party. There were many writers in the first fifteen years of the century who assumed the mantle of the prophet. Garvin was one of them.

This group of prominent journalists has been mentioned early in these pages because collectively their work is peculiarly representative of a period—say from 1900 to 1914. Never, I think, before or since, has journalism been so much dominated by a number of personalities with original or receptive minds who caught up the significant ideas of their time, and communicated them to large numbers of readers. These men were propounding and arguing in public. A study of this fugitive work would make us aware of the challenge that was in the air to old-established ideas, the eagerness for controversy, the zeal for reform and planned change, the earnest desire to learn the worst about society, whether in its economic conditions, its morals, or its taste, in order that wrong might be righted. These writings, expressive of many temperaments, reveal the intellectual atmosphere in which Bernard Shaw, H. G. Wells, Arnold Bennett, John Galsworthy, G. K. Chesterton, H. Granville-Barker and R. B. Cunninghame-Graham were to find their essential and necessary *milieu*. In one sense these men were being made by their time, in another they were making it. Against this background, too, we must set quieter and more reflective spirits, like Henry James, Joseph Conrad, W. H. Hudson, Norman Douglas and a number of poets. It was an exciting age for writers—an age which marked a definite break with the past, a challenge to authority, an assertion of the right to be anarchistic in thought and in form—romantic, realistic, passionate—a self-conscious age when writers were intensely critical of the composition of society, and were beginning to be critical of the composition of the individual soul.

Chapter Three

GEORGE BERNARD SHAW

WITH the turn of the century we have entered upon the most talkative period in the history of English literature; and the two men who talked the loudest, and the most effectively, were George Bernard Shaw[1] and H. G. Wells. (I am alluding to talk when it is written rather than spoken, though Shaw was also a prolific and accomplished public speaker.) The period 1900 to 1914 is that to which they essentially belong, and though they both went on producing important work long after that time, it became less provocative, less startling, because the new generation had already assimilated their characteristic thought. From 1900 to 1914 they were the leaders in the revolution of ideas. In a period addicted to prophecy both of them, but in very different ways, were prophets (in the sense of inspired *forth-tellers* rather than *fore-tellers,* though Wells was also fond of projecting himself into the future). Both were concerned with the problems of contemporary society and its maladjustment to modern conditions and needs; with the absurdities and irrationalities which it inherited and persisted in; and with the application to it of the ideas which they thought would make it more wholesome.

Since society was changing so profoundly and quickly, and nineteenth-century conceptions of life in all its forms were under constant criticism, it was an age of incessant argument, and Shaw and Wells were foremost among the arguers. Both were in earnest, but Shaw's coruscating wit for many years made solemn people think of him as an aggressive and irresponsible paradox-monger. Wells *was* serious in manner as well as intention and his quiet humour did not detract from his persuasiveness. Shaw always liked to think of himself as a realist. He drew a distinction between two powers of the mind. 'One is the power to imagine things as they are not: this I call the romantic imagination. The other is the power to imagine things as they are without actually sensing them; and this I will call the realistic imagination'.[2] Wells was undoubtedly a romanticist, but in a much more creditable

---

[1] Born 1856. Died 1950.   [2] *Parents and Children.*

sense of the term than Shaw chose to attribute to it. The latter said that his biography would be the history of his time; and it is true that he touched the life of his time at a multitude of points, and was successful in expressing his reaction to this life in brilliant generalizations. But Wells knew it more intimately. We feel that he described it and talked about it not from observation primarily, but from his own inner experience. The world that he wrote about was an echo of the life he had lived.

Shaw, of course, was an Irishman, brought up—though he would hardly admit that he was ever brought up—in the home of an impecunious and bibulous father and a talented, musical mother; but he left Ireland for good in 1876 at the age of twenty and went to London to make his fortune. He made £6 by writing in the first nine years. The novels he wrote were rejected by the publishers. It is characteristic of him that he made his début in public life at a society known as the Zetetical, and he became an inveterate frequenter of such societies, and, as he himself reports, 'haunted all the meetings in London where debates followed lectures. I spoke in the streets, in the parks, at demonstrations, anywhere and everywhere possible.'[1] In 1884 a speech by Henry George, the American apostle of Land Nationalization, 'struck me dumb and shunted me from barren agnostic controversy to economics'. He read Karl Marx, became a Socialist, and in 1884 joined the Fabian Society, then and afterwards dominated by Sidney Webb, that singular man of encyclopædic knowledge who became the guide, philosopher and friend of statesmen behind the scenes and especially of the leaders who created the Labour Party. 'Quite the cleverest thing I ever did in my life,' Shaw is reported to have said, 'was to force my friendship on Webb, to extort his, and keep it.' 'But,' he remarks, 'as I was and am an incorrigible histrionic mountebank, and Webb was the simplest of geniuses, I was often in the centre of the stage, whilst he was invisible in the prompter's box.'[2]

But the distinctive ideas which are Shaw's do not really come from his Fabianism or even from his Socialism, which he wore rather loosely in his maturer years. His omnivorous reading at the British Museum counted for much. It took him, for one thing, to Samuel Butler, whom he described as 'in his own department, the greatest writer of the latter half of the nineteenth century'. It is

[1] *Sixteen Self Sketches* (1949).   [2] *Ibid.*

an extraordinary thing that Butler's fertile and original mind, occupied with the most vital problems of his own day, and finding expression in felicitous and by no means obscure language, won so little recognition among his contemporaries. It was partly, perhaps, because he was too far ahead of his time, partly that he had little personal ambition, and partly that he dispersed his energies too much. Now he was appearing as a critic of the Scriptures with his own theory of the Resurrection; now as a satirist of religious commentaries; now as a neo-Lamarckian criticizing Darwin and the theory of evolution; now as a student of Homer proclaiming that the author of the *Odyssey* was a young woman. Each fresh task that he attempted meant a new world to be conquered before he had secured his foot-hold in the last. What most impressed Shaw when he first discovered Butler was his dissatisfaction with the Darwinian Theory of Natural Selection; 'he realised that by banishing purpose from natural history Darwin had banished mind from the universe'. And a little later, when Butler's *The Way of All Flesh* was posthumously published, Shaw found a kindred spirit who refused to accept the shams and make-believe which so often lie behind conventional morality, and particularly that which in the nineteenth century had tended to turn family life into hypocrisy or slavery. He saw that Butler had acclaimed that 'mysterious drive towards greater power over our circumstances and deeper understanding of Nature' which Shaw was to compare with the *Élan Vital* of Bergson, the Categorical Imperative of Kant, and Shakespeare's 'divinity that shapes our ends'; and was called, in his own parlance, the Life Force.

Two other writers, one a Norwegian, the other a German, stand out among those who provoked the critical mind of Shaw in his formative period—first, Ibsen, and a little later, Friedrich Nietzsche. The latter was a strange intellectual companion for one who called himself a Socialist. He did not stop, as Butler did, at ironic criticism of the smugness and hypocrisy which often smothered nineteenth-century Christianity, but attacked it with passion and withering scorn. Christianity, as Nietzsche denounced it, was the slave morality imposed by the strong upon the weak who were willing to be the submissive instruments of their masters. But what interested Shaw in Nietzsche was not so much his contempt for a servile majority—though he shared that—as his extolling of the intellectually strong, the aristocrats of the human species—the supermen—who know their own minds, pursue their own purpose, and in pursuit of it say 'Yea' to what life can offer. The supermen were the informed and the purposeful who win the battle of life and extract from it what is worth having.

But before Shaw had come to Nietzsche he had already, thanks to his friend William Archer, the sagacious dramatic critic, been introduced to Ibsen. Archer was the English translator of Ibsen, and did more than any other man to make his work known in Great Britain. Shaw was instantly attracted to Ibsen. The exhortation, explicit in *Peer Gynt,* implicit in all his later work, to 'Be thyself', is comparable to the 'Yea to Life' of Nietzsche's superman. But Ibsen's doctrine was no mere philosophical statement. It is that which emerges from the picture of life portrayed by him with relentless realism. The middle-class people whom he showed living their genteel lives, easily shocked when reality in all its nakedness is thrust upon them, are recognized by Shaw as the same middle-class people who are to be found in Britain and France and every 'civilized' country. 'Ibsen's intensely Norwegian plays,' he says in the Preface to *Heartbreak House,* 'exactly fitted every middle and professional class suburb in Europe.' And if his plays were so often objected to by audiences in England, that, according to Shaw, was because 'his characters do not behave as ladies and gentlemen are popularly supposed to behave. If you adore Hedda Gabler in real life. . . . Ibsen's exposure of the worthlessness and meanness of her life is cruel and blasphemous to you. . . . It is not murder, not adultery, not rapine that is objected to: quite the contrary. It is an unladylike attitude towards life: in other words, a disparagement of the social ideals of the poorer middle class and of the vast reinforcement it has had from the working class.' Not that Shaw was in the least prepared to let off the upper classes any more than the poorer middle class. In an allusion to Tchekov he says: 'These intensely Russian plays fitted all the country houses in Europe in which the pleasures of music, art, literature, and the theatre had supplanted hunting, shooting, fishing, flirting, eating and drinking. The same nice people, the same utter futility. . . . The women took the only part of our society in which there was leisure for high culture, and made it an economic, political, and, as far as practicable, a moral vacuum.'

Ibsen had exposed sentimentality, romanticism, make-believe and made it his business to show men and women in society as they really are, thus evoking the tragedy that may be inherent in ordinary, humdrum life. He was a realist, in Shaw's sense of the term. His medium was the theatre, and Shaw as a dramatic critic had been studying the theatre for years. That was to be his artistic medium. He began to do all he could to discredit the 'drawing-room play' so popular in London, and with it the so-called 'well-made play' which Scribe, Sardou and others had thrust upon Paris; he laughed at the insignificance of the ingenious trifles by which interest was sustained through three Acts and the curtain neatly brought down on 'a hero slain or married'. It was to be his major business for the rest of his career to try to compel the public to listen to the significant issues of real life.

Yet the fact that Shaw made his mark upon the world in the guise of a playwright is amazing evidence of his own capacity to live up to his ideal of a superman. By sheer purposeful insistence he not only compelled himself to be an accomplished writer of plays but also compelled the world to accept him as such. Here was a man who up to the age of forty and over was mainly concerned in learning, in propagating ideas, in debating, in persuading people to accept his views about society and morals, and was already entering middle life when he determined to bring the world round to his opinions through the medium of the theatre. He deliberately set himself the task of reforming the morals of society by interesting it in action on the stage. What were his qualifications? He was a writer of forceful, nervous, simple English which anyone can understand. He got to know the stage through and through—what you could do with scenery, what you could do with moving people about dramatically, how you could make effective entrances and exits, how to build up expectation and create effects by startling surprises. He was the most skilful debater in England, and knew how to keep an audience interested in any subject. And, above all, he was witty. He was amazingly, continuously, uproariously witty—and that will carry any writer very far. Moreover there was at least one human character that he could depict to the life, and that was his own. In half of his plays there is one human being who is copied from life and appears under different disguises, and that is the infinitely various yet always the same George Bernard Shaw. Apart from that he was not skilled, as Ibsen was, in presenting individual characters; but from his judicious observation of men and women in various classes of English society he formed judgments about types, and these types became the persons of his plays. There are a few exceptions: Candida perhaps; Saint Joan, perhaps; and Captain Shotover in *Heartbreak House*. But for the most part his characters are puppets who speak the words necessary for the part they are taking in the conflict of ideas which make the play; and so much Shavian wit and agreeable absurdity emerge that an intelligent audience cannot fail to be entertained.

'My reputation has been gained by my persistent struggle to force the public to reconsider its morals,' said Shaw in the *Rejected Statement* which he presented to the Royal Commission on Dramatic Censorship. 'I write plays with the deliberate object of converting the nation to my opinion in these matters.' It would be absurd to make it an accusation against him that he used the theatre for the deliberate purpose of propaganda when he so frankly admitted that precisely this was his intention. Yet we are bound to add that any dramatist who chooses to handicap himself by combining the function of the lecturer with the function of the dramatist is likely to fall between two stools. If his characters have to be puppets standing for certain ideas, and have to speak their parts not as life but Shaw's argument dictates, then we are not likely to get the verisimilitude, still less the emotion, which the enjoyment of drama requires. If Shaw 'gets away with it' as often as he does that is because he is so witty (and when he is being witty he escapes from his own didacticism); because his stage-craft is good; and, especially, because he has prepared the minds of his audience by written Prefaces to his plays which are far more convincing than the plays themselves. This partly explains why, when his plays were produced a second or a third time, after they had been published in book form with their Prefaces, they were generally far more successful than on their first appearance.

Moreover, when a man had as much to say as Shaw had, and went on saying it persistently and cogently over so many years, in plays, in books and essays, in lectures and debates, and in letters to the papers, he was likely to win over audiences whatever the medium in which he chose to express himself. His frankness in saying things that nobody before had ever dared to say provoked, exasperated, and shocked many people, but they were compelled to listen. In *Mrs. Warren's Profession* he showed that it was society which was to blame rather than the procuress for the evils of prostitution; and in *Widowers' Houses* again it was society rather than the individual landlord who created abuses of the right to property. *Man and Superman* is one of many plays which illustrate Shaw's favourite thesis that the Life Force compels the woman to seek her victim, capture him and pin him down by marriage. *Getting Married* was written to illustrate his argument that home life as at present constituted is unnatural. 'Its grave danger to the nation lies in its narrow views, its unnaturally sustained and spitefully jealous concupiscences, its petty tyrannies, its false social pretences, its endless grudges and squabbles . . . and all the other ills, mentionable and unmentionable, that arise from excessive segregation. It sets these evils up as benefits and blessings.'

Similarly *The Doctor's Dilemma* was written to expose the superstition of medical infallibility. 'As to the honour and conscience of doctors, they have as much as any other class of men, no more and no less. And what other men dare pretend to be impartial where they have a strong pecuniary interest on one side?' *John Bull's Other Island* (which is of course Ireland, before independent Eire came into existence) has a hero who talks exactly like Shaw, and therefore very well indeed, and an Englishman, who is a type of all that Shaw conceives to be most absurd in the English character. *Cæsar and Cleopatra* does not aim at proving any general proposition, and comes much nearer to being a play than most of his works written in dramatic form. The Cabinet Ministers whom he presents in *Back to Methuselah* and in *The Apple Cart* are ineffectual caricatures; in the latter there is once again a superman who holds our attention because he has the purposefulness, the candour and the wit of Shaw. In *Saint Joan* he reaches a higher level than elsewhere because for once the grander emotions are involved and the theme is a universal one lending itself to tragic drama.

Shaw was first and foremost and all the time a propagandist—or should I say prophet? The latter is the better word, for the ideas that he wanted to promote are the ideas that he had arrived at by his own effort and insight after examining the ideas prevalent in society and finding them wanting. In the main his criticism is destructive, if it is destructive to break the chains which have held society in mental servitude. The giants at which he tilts are moral slavery, humbug, mental sloth, social apathy, superstition, sentimentalism, collective selfishness, and all the static ideas which have not been consciously subjected to the tests of real life and honest thought. His distrust of sentiment led him often to distrust of emotion, and in consequence he sometimes woefully failed to distinguish between genuine exhibitions of mass emotion and less creditable exhibitions of mass hysteria. The virtues opposed by him to the social defects which he castigates are those of the free mind—the mind of the man who has freed himself from spurious moral standards, who has discovered what he is and what he wants, and has the purposefulness to achieve his ends and make them profitable to his own spirit. Whether Shaw ought to be described as a Socialist is doubtful; it is certain that he was an aristocrat—an aristocrat in the Platonic sense, the citizen who has gold not in his purse but in his nature. His plays, being concerned with ideas, austere, logical ideas, fail to arouse emotion; the subtler, finer elements in the individual pass him by. But what he lacks in emotion to some extent he makes up in generosity and geniality. No man was ever so fierce in attack who made so few enemies. G. K. Chesterton in his *Autobiography* recalls that he began arguing with Shaw in print almost as early as he began doing anything; that he always differed from him and always thought him wrong.

> It is not easy to dispute violently with a man for twenty years, about sex, about sin, about sacraments, about personal points of honour, about all the most sacred or delicate essentials of existence, without sometimes being irritated or feeling that he hits unfair blows or employs discreditable ingenuities. And I can testify that I have never read a reply by Bernard Shaw that did not leave me in a better and not a worse temper or frame of mind; which did not seem to come out of inexhaustible fountains of fair-mindedness and intellectual geniality; which did not savour somehow of that native largeness which the philosopher attributed to the Magnanimous Man. It is necessary to disagree with him as much as I do, in order to admire him as much as I do; and I am proud of him as a foe even more than as a friend.

Those controversies are over. The gadfly who stung society to the quick in the first fourteen years of the century and compelled it to revise its ideas, went on stinging, and even in extreme old

3

age emerged from time to time to prick real or imaginary foes. But he left behind no savour of bitterness; for the young as well as the old he was the cheering, zestful, great hearted veteran who loved the smell of battle in the field of ideas; who, with an exhilarating smile on his face, was still happy to challenge and attack and attack again.

Chapter Four

EGO AND KOSMOS

H. G. Wells

HERBERT GEORGE WELLS (1866–1946) was a prolific writer. For more than fifty years a ceaseless stream of books flowed from his pen. It began in 1895, when he was twenty-nine, and continued almost to his death. As a writer, though not as an orator, he has been as much and as constantly before the public as Bernard Shaw. Many years ago, contrasting him with Shaw, I wrote of him that his life has 'represented the English life of his time', that he has been 'an integral part of it', that he 'found himself writing about that England of which he himself is symbolic', and that 'he has known it by conscious and subconscious experience, this experience being with him a kind of instinct developing into self knowledge, and so into a more objective and philosophical perception'. Wells was evidently of the same opinion, for a few years later he wrote in his *Experiment in Autobiography* (1934):—

Essentially this autobiography treats of the steady expansion of the interests and activities of a brain, emerging from what I have called a narrow-scope way of living, to a broader and broader outlook and a consequent longer reach of motive. I move from a backyard to Cosmopolis; from Atlas House to the burthen of Atlas. This theme appears and reappears in varying forms and keys; in the story of my early reading, in the story of my escape from retail trade, in the story of my student perplexities and my attempts to make my geology scientific and my physics philosophical, and so on. More and more consciously the individual adventurer, as he disentangles himself from the family association in which he was engendered, is displayed trying to make himself a citizen of the world. As his *persona* becomes lucid it takes that form. He is an individual becoming the conscious Common Man of his time and culture. He is a specimen drop from the changing ocean of general political opinion.

His account of himself, however, goes beyond mine in that he is not content to see himself as a sublimation of the common

Englishman; he expands his Ego into a sublimation of the citizen of the world. Reflectively, it may be, he achieved that aim, but I think that the consciousness which impelled him was that of his distinctively English *persona*; he was still the English writer, conditioned no doubt by his travels abroad as well as by his English experience, striving to enlarge himself to the stature of his conception of the world citizen. In any case it is a central fact about Wells's more important work that he was writing subjectively; writing about the world, that is to say, as it appeared to him by dint of his own personal experience and his own instinctive reactions to reality. That experience was very varied and let him into the secrets of many layers of English society. He was born at Bromley in Kent, and was early impressed by the changes which converted a small country town into a suburb of London. He was the son of a small tradesman and professional cricketer, and himself was apprenticed to a retail draper; so he knew the inner life of the lower middle classes. Escaping from trade, he became a teacher, studied at the Normal School of Science, South Kensington, and took a science degree; and continued teaching till 1893, when he was twenty-seven years old. Thus he acquired the bent towards science, and especially geology and biology, which was to remain with him to the end of his life. He had a variety of sex experiences which impressed themselves violently on his memory, and these were reinforced by other, later sex experiences destined to be the subject-matter of novels and the basis of his conclusions about love and marriage. When he acquired a reputation as a writer—and success came to him relatively early—he mixed with journalists, men of letters, politicians, social workers, and men of affairs generally, and did not hesitate to put these people, often mercilessly, into his books. He was quick, ingenious, imaginative, turning his scientific knowledge to account by relating it to life. With him feeling, instinctive perception, came first, and provided him with the raw material of a wider vision. He had the gift of seeing the part as part of a whole, and the whole as that which consisted of many parts. With him it was an imaginative rather than an intellectual feat to see man as a unit in a class, in a society, or ultimately in mankind as a whole. In his middle and later work he writes what he feels, but his feeling is what it is by virtue of his habit of active reflection; he feels himself in a certain environment; he creates a class or a whole society out of what he has personally experienced and felt; feeling and thought with him become one; and he projects pictures of an external world outwards from himself.

This is exactly the reverse of the Shavian procedure. Shaw starts with intellectual generalizations—these no doubt having been arrived at by a rather loose process of induction—and proceeds to set forth general ideas through characters invented to fit them. Wells starts with an instinctive feeling which becomes a perception, and builds up a world around it. He is nearer to nature, though nature may sometimes be distorted or exceptional when passed through the alembic of his whims and prejudices. Shaw's essential function was to expose the intellectual, social and moral problems of his time, to probe and clarify them. Wells's function was to give a picture of the consciousness of the changing England of his time—to describe as far as he could from his own knowledge its feelings, perceptions, desires, ambitions and intimations, with all that these appeared to involve for the present and future of the race. While Shaw claimed that his life had been the history of his time, Wells perhaps would have suggested that his life *was* his time, projected outwards from his own consciousness in the body of his writings.

The process was of course gradual. He was to grow up into and with the society around him. He began modestly and effectively with short stories and ingenious, rationalized fantasies, his method in fiction being more objective than it was later. Being something of a scientist he could turn his science to account in the manner of Jules Verne—in *The Time Machine*, *The Island of Dr. Moreau*, *The Invisible Man*, *The War of the Worlds*—but already he was interested, as Jules Verne had not been, in the social implications of the problems of space and time and evolution. The inventor in *The Time Machine* (1895) who discovered that time was a fourth dimension of space and travelled on his machine into the past and future, was interested in telling about the lives of our descendants; in presenting this imaginary picture of the future the author is criticizing the present; he is already concerned with the idea of man and society as something in a state of flux, growing, changing, becoming something for the better or worse. This process of becoming, in society, was to be a matter of perennial interest for Wells. There was no vision to him more fascinating than that of a struggling, changing world, evolving under the ruthless laws of evolution, or becoming modified, for the better, by the will and intelligence of man.

At the end of the century he was intellectually grown-up—or nearly. He was thirty-four, and was entering upon a span of years and a phase of society to which his active adult mind primarily belongs. He had come to some conclusions, provisionally, about many of the problems of that English society which he had been observing and was prepared to analyse and criticize; and he set out to enlighten his countrymen (he was always among the prophets) about the drift of the life they were leading. In books such as *Anticipations* (1901) and *Mankind in the Making* (1903) it was a rather gloomy picture he had to draw—that of a country obsessed with mean and effete class distinctions, dissipating its energies in wasteful competition and foolish rivalries, changing its shape and composition without any adequate effort to foresee and direct change—but the picture was drawn with so much gusto and ingenious criticism that it was impossible not to be exhilarated. Here at any rate was mind at work coping with the mindless. In 1905 he went one better in *A Modern Utopia*. If everything was going wrong—well, here was someone prepared to show how to put it right. Diagnosis—reform: that was the distinctive note of early twentieth-century Britain, and Wells in the theoretic sphere was a protagonist. Having shown what was wrong he was now intent upon showing how life might be ordered under modern conditions. His Utopia was to be unlike all others because his would not, like Plato's or Sir Thomas More's, contemplate a static state, set up as the ideal for all time, but an evolving, dynamic state suited to the restless nature of Man, himself changing and the director of change. In his book he used the device of a 'Voice' speaking at a sort of lantern lecture, whose owner takes the audience with him on an expedition to Utopia. He is accompanied by a botanist, a lean, grave, stupid man, whose mind was incapable of any curiosity beyond the range of the conventional and suburban. His mentality stood for everything that had to be overcome in the creating or understanding of the ideal.

We see that even at this early stage of his career Wells conceived that there could be no satisfactory State in this complex modern world unless it were a planetary State. In his Utopian planet there was one language, one State, and that a managed State. There was an abundance of labour-saving machinery, fair distribution, good transport and general opulence; the State, operating through local authorities, owned all natural products and all natural sources of power. It provided every worker with an ample minimum wage, plenty of leisure, and the best education for his children, and every opportunity for recreation and the satisfaction of his tastes; and for women it offered 'economic freedom'. Incomes for the mothers of healthy children ensured that motherhood was a 'remunerative calling for a woman'. But it must be emphasized that Wells, for all his Socialism, was intent upon making it compatible with individual freedom and even the idiosyncrasies of individuals. His State was to content itself with eliminating 'just those spend-thrift liberties that waste liberty, and not one liberty more'.

The problem of the means by which Utopia was to be brought into being was not solved in this book, though Wells did consider the problem of how, once in being, it was to be maintained. He follows Plato's example in creating a class of aristocratic rulers, whom he calls Samurai; They are a 'voluntary nobility' con-sisting of men of 'poietic' and 'kinetic' qualities prepared to sub-mit themselves to a voluntary discipline in the interests of the community. They foreshadow the higher types of men who are described in much later books, *The World of William Clissold* (1926), *The Open Conspiracy* (1928), and *The Work, Wealth and Happiness of Mankind* (1932)—those rare men endowed with exceptional, adult intellects and imagination, who are capable of subtly directing the affairs of the world along the path which will save it from destruction.

The point about such a book as *A Modern Utopia* and the other books which led up to it is this: that at a moment in British history when the mind of social workers and politicians was begin-ning to be applied as never before to the practical problems of social reform; when workers were beginning to demand security; when women were getting ready to formulate and press their claims for political and economic equality; when Socialism was developing a working programme as well as a theory; when the people of all classes were beginning to be reform-minded; at this moment Wells came in, not merely a little ahead of others in his concrete proposals, but insisting on the importance of remember-ing the intimate, imponderable things; that men in the mass are never merely a mass; that they consist of Tom and Dick and Harry, and Sarah and Jane; that all of these individuals have private lives and emotions which must be respected and remembered when we try to organize them. Much that he advocated more than forty years ago has already been achieved; much that was new then seems now a truism. But he deserves credit, not merely for being in the vanguard, but for urging the human and imaginative needs of man which, in the modern, managed world, are still in danger of being neglected.

'So much of my life has been a prolonged and enlarged adolescence,' said Wells in his *Autobiography*, 'an encounter with the world in general, that the observation of character began to play a leading part in it only in my later years. It was necessary for me to reconstruct the frame in which individual lives as a whole had to be lived, before I could concentrate upon any of the individual problems of fitting them into this frame.' For this reason it was only when he was nearly forty years old that he turned to the writing of serious novels. Even then we shall find that he is seeking to interest us in the *environment* in which his persons are placed at least as much as in the characters of those persons; and it will be the author's reactions to the scene that interest us at least as much as the action of the story. This last point was noticed by Henry James. He complained that Wells had not thought out the characters presented in the novels with sufficient care and thoroughness. In a letter James wrote to him about *Marriage* he said that he felt less interest in what was 'happening' to the husband and wife portrayed in that book than in what was happening to Wells—'these attestations of your character and behaviour, these reactions of yours as you more or less follow them. . . . I see you "behave" all along much more than I see them . . .; so that the ground of the drama is somehow most of all in the adventure for *you*. . . . Your "story", through the five hundred pages, says more to me than theirs.' From James's point of view the novels of Wells defy all the canons of art that are applicable to fiction; and yet he ends by saying that his strictures 'still leave that work more convulsed with life and more brimming with blood than any it's given me nowadays to meet'.

Wells admits the charges but not the validity of the criticism. He admits that in such a book as *Marriage* (and surely not only there) 'the writing is scamped in places. It could have been just as light and much better done. But that would have taken more time than I could afford . . . I had very many things to say.' He was content with a 'ventilation of the point at issue'. But he does not accept the limitations which James or others would impose on the novel. He will not allow that it need be restricted to describing the behaviour of individuals and watching their characters develop in a life-like way. He avowed his intention of extending the scope of the novel, getting the 'frame into the picture', and writing about everything.

We are going to write about business and finance and politics and precedence and pretentiousness and decorum and indecorum, until a thousand pretences and ten thousand impostures shrivel in the cold, clear draught of our elucidations. We are going to write of wasted opportunities and latent beauties until a thousand new ways of living open to men and women. We are going to appeal to the young and the hopeful and the curious, against the established, the dignified, and defensive. Before we have done, we will have all life within the scope of the novel.

He was later to realize that he had not done quite as much as that; but that was what he set out to do; that is the spirit we shall look for when we read the most vital of his novels, written often in such clumsy English, but for all that 'convulsed with life', as James said, 'brimming with blood'. *Kipps,* published in 1905, is the first of the real novels, written in recollection of the events of his own youth, as was *The History of Mr. Polly,* published five years later. In *Kipps* he was already feeling his way.

In 1908 came the book which I think the best of his novels, *Tono-Bungay.* This ambitious work aims at giving nothing less than a complete cross-section of contemporary English life, seen as a whole through the eyes of George Ponderevo—who is one of the many incarnations of Wells himself. George Ponderevo, the housekeeper's son, first looks out on the world through the windows of Bladesover house, a home of 'the gentry, the fine Olympians', who were still preserving the pretence of the feudal tradition, the old order, that 'fine appearance' which George was soon to see was 'already sapped'. He is still a boy when he is taken to the house of his uncle, a chemist in a small country town, a restless, ingenious, pushful man, inventor of a quack medicine called Tono-Bungay, 'slightly injurious rubbish . . . sold at one-and-three-halfpence and two-and-nine a bottle, including the Government stamp'. Mr. Ponderevo, senior, goes to London, makes a fortune out of the credulity of an exploitable public, and moves swiftly up the social ladder to the top. In *Tono-Bungay* Wells shows us the old order seeking in vain to perpetuate itself in a changing world, and the new rising assertively, chaotically in cities which grow and throw out their suburban tentacles far into the country, swarming with life that strives in vain to accommodate itself to conditions unsuited to it; chance dictates men's lives in birth, in marriage, in prosperity, in happiness or unhappiness. Bewildered 'like a man floundering in a universe of soap-suds' George Ponderevo is seen, like Wells himself, searching for 'something solid' yet linked to his mystical apprehension of an ideal, the romantic mirage which lured and eluded Wells throughout his life.

His next novel, *Ann Veronica,* was provocative in its frank treatment of sex and its apparent assertion of the rights of woman to equality with man in the domain of the passions; but the storm of criticism it raised was perhaps due as much to its lack of reticence in regard to known living persons as to its candid treatment of the sex problem. This disrespect for persons was undoubtedly the main ground of the complaints directed against his next novel, *The New Machiavelli,* a far more powerful book which was equally frank in its statement of the sex problem, and mercilessly pilloried many living men and women well-known in the spheres of politics and social reform. *Marriage,* a year later (1912), tells what might happen when 'masculine intellectual interest met feminine spending'—a study in temperaments requiring a treatment more delicate and subtle than Wells's. *The Research Magnificent* (1915) and *Mr. Britling Sees it Through* (1916) were the most successful of his war-time novels. After that, though he was to write other works of fiction, he was to devote most of his time to summing up his social philosophy or to encyclopædic exposition.

In 1918, Wells was far from having finished his work. There were many important books to follow, and these were to show continuing development of his mind and keen awareness of the post-war world and its problems. But the phase of society which provoked his critical mind, the atmosphere in which he was stirred to set the pace in the breakaway from old social servitudes and inhibitions, belong to the period 1900 to 1914. Yet it was characteristic of him that he was not to stop there or to rest in his conclusions, still less to go back a little, as Galsworthy did. He went on to draw the lessons, the conclusions, from what he had experienced, from what he had seen and foreseen. He had foreseen much. Before anyone had thought of a League of Nations or a world war he had been preaching internationalism, and the need of a world-society as the only possible satisfactory solution of the problem already inherent in the life of the world. He had foreseen the likelihood of a world war, and had foretold that when it came air supremacy would be the decisive factor. Before Fascism and its abuses had been even adumbrated he had realized that an ignorant, undirected democracy would be incapable of solving the problem of government or order, that there would be no salvation without planning and that planning demanded the leadership of superior minds. He believed that the very existence of civilization, of ordered society, was in jeopardy unless men of the highest intelligence seized the initiative, either acting themselves or, as he would have preferred, communicating their wisdom to the masses to the point where they would be capable of governing themselves.

He became more and more obsessed by the consideration that conscious human life has emerged and survived by a succession of successful adaptations to environment; that man has triumphantly conformed to nature's imperative 'adapt or perish', but is now confronted with conditions which are changing so swiftly that only the utmost exercise of his highest powers will save him from ruin. The continued evolution of civilized society seemed to him to depend on the evolution of a superior kind of man. (Shaw developed a similar idea in *Back to Methuselah*.) In *The World of William Clissold* (1926) and *The Open Conspiracy* (1928) he enunciated the doctrine that 'it is only through a conscious, frank and world-wide co-operation of the man of science, the scientific worker, the man accustomed to the direction of productive industry, the man able to control the arterial supply of credit, the man who can control newspapers and politicians, that the great system of changes that have almost inadvertently got going can be brought to any hopeful order of development'. He sees the only hope of the future in the activity and co-operation of men with 'adult' minds; in what he called an 'Open Conspiracy' among such men 'to change the laws, customs, rules and institutions of the world'.

Already, with formidable industry, he had written his *Outline of History* (1920), 'an attempt to reform history-teaching by replacing narrow nationalist history by a general review of the human record'. He followed this up with *The Science of Life* (with the co-operation of Julian Huxley and G. P. Wells; 1929) and *The Work, Wealth and Happiness of Mankind* (1932). In seeking to popularize learning he sometimes appeared to be looking forward to a new phase in world society in which all the characteristics of the aristocracy of intellect will be found among the many. But he was not always so optimistic. In his less sanguine moments he bids us consider society as composed of three primary types—the peasant, the aristocrat-soldier-robber, and the priestly-learned man. The chief enemy of the human race he finds among the sharp, clever opportunists of the world—the 'Smart Alecs', as he calls them. In the long run he looks for salvation to the 'priestly-learned' class, the aristocracy of brains and social service, who care more about their learned or professional work than carving out a career. He talks hopefully of an educated multitude, but really believes in an educated 'few'.

At the end, in his seventy-ninth year, shortly before his death, he cheerfully abandoned his optimism and concluded that it had become certain that it was beyond the powers of man to adapt himself to changing conditions; disaster confronts our species; Homo Sapiens is 'played out'. How characteristic of Wells! In his last cosmic utterance *Mind at the End of its Tether* (1946) he tells us that 'he has lived cheerfully and abundantly. Like Landor he has warmed both hands at the fire of life and now, as it sinks towards a meticulous invalidism, he is ready to depart'. It is as if, in preparing courageously for his own death, he is determined that the whole of mankind, with which in so much of his work he has identified himself, shall go with him on his journey; he does not care to think of a world surviving him; he had waited for this penultimate moment to discover that 'this world is at the end of its tether'. What amazing egoism, egoism on a cosmic scale! With this confidence in himself as a living embodiment of the human species—and, at the end, so much an embodiment that it lives and dies with him—Wells succeeded in impressing himself and his views on the book-reading public effectually; before he was dead, his views had been absorbed and digested so thoroughly that they became truisms—the younger generation was inclined to pass him by as a man talking platitudes. That gives us the measure of his success. Just as the British Liberal Party taught all Britons to be Liberals and all but perished because its work was done, so with Wells. He was one of the moulders of opinion in Edwardian and Georgian Britain, and for the historian at least he will be among the greatest of the revolutionaries. But his work may date; for all the vigour of his writing, he had no polished style to support it. In the future he may or may not get the credit for what he has done, but the mark he left on the mind of the nation cannot be effaced.

Chapter Five

BENNETT AND GALSWORTHY

NEVER was there a time in English history when the novel was taken more seriously than in the first fourteen years of the present century. It was a common saying in those days that anyone who had anything to say was likely to say it in the form of a novel —we have seen that H. G. Wells fought hard to extend its boundaries. How many and how diverse were the important men of letters who gave of their best in fiction during that short period —Henry James, Wells, Bennett, Galsworthy, Conrad and E. M. Forster—and many others who produced notable books. They fall into two broadly distinguishable groups: those who, like James or Conrad, were concerned primarily with the art of letters, without paying much attention to the problems of the age in which they lived; and those who made it their business to project that age and the significant problems with which, for them, it was burdened—men who were deeply influenced by the Time-Spirit, and by their work left their imprint on the mental outlook of their own and and the succeeding generation. The former, with some variations of technique, might perhaps belong to any age; the latter could not possibly belong to any but their own, though they may transcend and outlive it.

Wells, as we have seen, belongs to this category. With qualifications, we must put in it Arnold Bennett and John Galsworthy. I say 'with qualifications', for both Bennett and Galsworthy were very much concerned about the craft of fiction; Wells was not. The first of these was never disposed to preach when he was writing fiction, and the second always endeavoured to conceal his preaching. Both were obsessed, as Wells was, by the sense of the persistence of change, which was altering not only the outward shape of England but having also its potent effect on character and moral values. But whereas Wells was primarily interested in the larger unit of society, with men as its ingredients—as seen through the eyes of one man, himself—Bennett and Galsworthy were interested in the effects which society had in shaping the character and destiny of individuals. They are in the main tradition of

English fiction when they concentrate on character, though their treatment of the social setting and the background of criticism were new. Both were much influenced by the contemporary prophets; but Bennett consistently refrained from prophecy, Galsworthy often.

Bennett's posthumous reputation has been adversely affected by the inequality of his output. It has been damaged by the vast mass of the competent but second-rate work which issued from his pen not only before the production of his best novels, but later, in the intervals between them. It was damaged also by his own much-advertised belief in the importance of worldly success. His earliest work was pot-boiling; also a great deal of his later writing, when he was well-off, could only have been justified to himself by the large profits it brought him. He was extravagant and ostentatious, proud of the fact that his writing could bring him wealth, and of his ability to drive a hard bargain, thus demonstrating, as he liked to do, that a man of letters could be a successful business man, even standing up to and associating with captains of industry. To many critics it seemed impossible to believe that such a man could ever have been quite sincere, and hence they have been led to attribute to patience, industry and imitativeness what in fact was due to his genius.

The 'Five Towns' of the ugly, sprawling industrial region of the Potteries, the most 'provincial' of all the provincial areas of England, were the scene of his boyhood and early manhood. The twenty-one years which he spent there (from his birth in 1867 till he went to London to seek his fortune as a clerk in a solicitor's office in 1888) were years of dullness and frustration, in which he saw the towns grow bigger, blacker and more prosperous, but not more urbane; they were spent under the shadow of an exacting Puritanism, which he grew to detest, and a sombre paternal authority against which he rebelled. Residence in London meant for him escape—escape from the drabness and the dull social restrictions of the Five Towns, and opportunity to make money and enjoy all the things that had been denied him. He soon found that he could make a living by writing—articles, stories, gossip-features—and from 1893 to 1900 found a stand-by in a journal called *Woman,* of which he was first assistant-editor, then editor. But he was under no illusions about the trivial nature of such work. This was his means of livelihood—it was not what he was

going to do. He had the pertinacity, the practicality, of his
ancestors, along with other qualities which they had not. Industrious in his writing, he was no less industrious in his reading.
He read the English novelists, including of course his contemporaries, and particularly admired George Moore. He applied himself to French, and studied the style and technique of Maupassant,
the Goncourts, Huysmans, Balzac and, later, with special devotion, Stendhal. In 1903 he settled in Paris, married a Frenchwoman
Marguerite Soulié, in 1907, and spent much of his time till 1912
in a house in Fontainebleau. By that time the hack-writer had
turned into a novelist admitted, in England and America, to be of
the first rank.

How was such a transition possible? I think it is probable that
he began in ignorance. In his early twenties, when he was still
poorly read and had no real standards, he gratified his instinctive
desire to write and wrote anything. A little later, when his ambition to be a serious writer had been awakened, he was content to
regard his hack journalism as a mere means of subsistence—it was
like any other routine occupation which provided a livelihood, to
be pursued so far as was expedient, but completely differentiated
from the literary work which he had set his mind on doing, and
was to be his ultimate *raison d'être* as a writer. His first published
novel, *A Man from the North* (1898), was autobiographical, slight,
and lacking in high distinction. But it was well-written; it was
seriously meant; it was Arnold Bennett feeling his way at the age
of thirty. He wrote several ephemeral novels and several unsuccessful plays—he had no success with a play till he wrote *Milestones*
(1912), in collaboration with Edward Knoblock. In fiction he had
no considerable achievement to his credit till he wrote *Anna of the
Five Towns* (1902), in which he looked back upon the scenes of his
youth and began to discover how much lay there that might be
used and worked upon by the novelist surveying the past in the
light of the present.

It was not till he was forty-one years old that he completed the
first novel which revealed his real power. He began *The Old
Wives' Tale* in Fontainebleau in 1907 shortly after his marriage.
Nearly twenty years had elapsed since he left the Potteries and
went to London, and in the interval he had explored the literary
life of London and Paris, had travelled considerably, had read and
written much, and cultivated a style. He was far enough away

from the dull streets and chimney pots of the Five Towns and the custom-bound routine of their inhabitants to be free from the pain of suffering them, and detached enough to be able to look back on the scene and the people, and see them as he could not when he had been among them. He remembered how old-fashioned they were, how imperceptive of the nature of the changes which had been gradually transforming the outer scene —the electric trains, the electric light, the superior baths—and the more subtle chemistry of ideas which even then was affecting their manners and conduct. The young people he had known as a youth were older now, and another set of young people were growing up. The adventurous were becoming sedate, the sedate were becoming aged or were dead. Having decided to write about this unexploited field, the home-land of his youth, rich in material that a realist might turn to account, it was inevitable that he should be acutely aware of the changes that had come over industrial England, and the effect upon people of the passage of time. Inevitably he felt, as Wells felt, the swift flow in the outer shape of our civilization, so little perceived at any given moment by the average human being; and he felt also, more subtly than Wells, the tragedy of the spectacle of men and women growing old without the power of adaptation.

'Every novel,' said Bennett in one of his later newspaper articles, 'should have a main theme that can be stated in ten words.' Could the theme of *The Old Wives' Tale* be thus simply stated? 'Two provincial women, differently affected by change, suffer and grow old.' I have used eleven words, and am not satisfied with the sum-mary. But there, perhaps, is the gist of the matter. The story opens in the sixties of the last century. The centre of the scene is the draper's shop in the square of the growing provincial town. The old order, sure of itself, stereotyped, is personified in the elder Baineses—Mr. Baines, now become a paralytic, and Mrs. Baines, ruler of the household, strict guardian of the proprieties and right relations between daughters, shop-assistant, servant-girl, customers. In the daughters, Constance and Sophia, we have the beginnings or at least the possibilities of the new order—Constance progress-ing only a little way in her challenge to authority, breaking the rules, but prudently, by marrying Mr. Povey, the assistant, and then settling down in her turn to live the respectable life of the Five Towns—Sophia, the younger, more spirited, wilful,

4

passionate, who runs away with a commercial traveller to Paris, is jilted, meets Gerald; but her bourgeois upbringing and Teutonic ancestry prevail against the challenge of romance and adventure. In the end she comes back to the Five Towns and joins her sister. The two, who had been first seen as girls 'rather like racehorses, quivering with delicate, sensitive, and luxuriant life; exquisite, enchanting proof of the circulation of the blood,' are last seen, growing old, withered, scarcely reflecting that time has passed over them stealthily, imperceptibly, blackening the air around them, quickening the pace of the traffic, removing father, mother, husbands and son, and leaving them, unaware of the strangeness, to die in the twentieth century.

Bennett has evoked this sense of the seemingly permanent, the normal, in the midst of the relentless flux, with men and women arrogantly and rather foolishly pursuing their routine as if it belonged to the order of eternity; and he has been content himself to move slowly, to risk dullness, in the attempt to present dullness, drabness, fatuity with objective fidelity. The characters come to life under his hand; the description of the setting is masterly; sentimentality is revealed without sentimentality. Bennett had learnt from his French and Russian masters how to detach the author from his theme, to stand aloof and watch his victims struggling. He shows himself to have been a careful, a meticulous observer of life—but how much more! Life accurately described is nothing till the imagination has seen it in perspective. To deny, as some critics have done, that Bennett had imagination is to deny the palpable issue of his work.

Clayhanger (1910), the first novel of the Clayhanger trilogy, is in some ways a greater book than *The Old Wives' Tale*. Once again the scene is that of the Five Towns, and again we are to watch the succession of generations, and the conflict between them. But here we have a more magnificent, a more universal theme, the conflict being not only between personalities, and all that they stand for, but between warring elements in the spirit of the hero. Edwin Clayhanger is a character who will hold his place among the great figures of imaginative literature—this strange, uncouth, unsophisticated man, with the instincts of an artist struggling against the Puritanism of his upbringing. In portraying this character and writing this book Bennett has amplified a theme which has had a grim fascination for several imaginative writers

during the last century, the conflict between father and son. Such
a conflict was described, though not once and for all, in Butler's
The Way of All Flesh; revealed, much more gently, in Edmund
Gosse's best book, his autobiographical *Father and Son* (1907); and
more recently in *The Backward Son* (1940), Stephen Spender's
novel. But for Bennett this theme is subordinate to a vaster
theme, and I do not think he has ever been given full credit for
the far-extending and profound vision which make this book so
significant and subtle. It has sometimes been said that he lacked
philosophic background. It is true, it was not his habit to write
or think philosophically; but as a novelist it was not necessarily
his function to do so. Much that is implicit in a work of art and
constitutes its background may be produced, as Coleridge pointed
out, by an unconscious activity, which is part of the activity of
genius. For Bennett, in *Clayhanger*, it is sufficient to describe what
he has seen, and all the implications emerge for us when we study
his vision—the dull, squalid environment of the Five Towns of
the Potteries, the people who inhabited them with marked
characteristics handed on from generation to generation, the
father, Darius Clayhanger, who from humble origins had
worked his way up to be the owner of a successful printing shop,
hard, obstinate, conscientious, unimaginative, entrenched in
his Methodism and his fixed ways of life; and on the other side
the son, Edwin Clayhanger, in whom 'a flame burnt that was like
an altar-fire', with his hatred of the cramped life, his groping
ambition to be an architect, shy, awkward, persistent like his
father, but without the persistence of genius.

The conflict which emerges is no simple one. For Edwin it is in
part a struggle against the habitual drabness of the Five Towns and
the opposing will of his father. But it is much more than that.
Bennett perceives that a man cannot be a Clayhanger and suddenly escape from his ancestry, his environment, his reluctantly
acquired habits of thought—something of the mind of Darius
persists in Edwin himself, the Puritanism, the fear of the flesh and
the devil, the ingrained respect for hard professional work. Thus
the conflict, which had been that between father and son, assumes
another form, a conflict between the released Edwin, aflame with
his love for Hilda, and the repressed Edwin, who is still a Clayhanger, a man of the Five Towns. And so we reach a third phase
of the conflict, that between the ambiguous Edwin and the

spirited Hilda, who suddenly, incomprehensibly, jilts him, and disappears, leaving him to resume the routine of his life in the printing shop, and to succeed his father; nor is it resolved when, after the lapse of years, in the third volume of the trilogy, *These Twain,* he rediscovers Hilda and marries her. The conflict between Hilda and Edwin continues till 'death do them part'.

The second volume of the trilogy, *Hilda Lessways* (1911), is less important than *Clayhanger,* and really adds little to the significance of its theme; but it is a good novel. It is free from the surplusage which encumbers both *The Old Wives' Tale* and *Clayhanger,* and we can pursue the narrative without dissipation of interest. In an attempt to get inside the feminine mind of Hilda, to state her case, to justify her, the author abandons the aloofness, the divine detachment which was so effective in *Clayhanger,* and becomes a partisan. But he has made highly skilful use of the reader's acquaintance with the story as already told in *Clayhanger,* so that wherever the lives of Hilda and Edwin touch we are conscious of the background—these same events, thus experienced by Hilda, had been seen, but under what a different perspective, by Edwin. Such a device was to be used later by an American writer, in *The Bridge of San Luis Rey.*

There was to be only one other book by Bennett on the grand scale of *The Old Wives' Tale* and *Clayhanger—Riceyman Steps* (1923)—and in this he was to show that a place, other than that of the Potteries, could be made to cast its witchery over his story and its persons. Not that the dingy neighbourhood of Clerkenwell (in London) brings to us in this book the awareness of a whole society of human beings born to live just there; yet we are made to feel that this grim story could only have happened quite like this in the vicinity of that musty book-shop and the house opposite, with the children playing on the steps, and Elsie the servant going to and fro. How slowly the story moves, but how could it be otherwise? How else could we come to know this slow-moving, indolent, kindly man, sinking further and further into habits which could scarcely have been developed elsewhere than in this second-hand bookseller's shop, bracing himself to the one infinitely bold step, that of asking Mrs. Arb to marry him, and struggling quite in vain against the miserliness which in the end destroys him. There are only two considerable characters in the book, Earlforward and the girl Elsie. Against great odds Bennett succeeds in making both of them real.

Without these major books Bennett would have been a conspicuous and deservedly notable literary figure of his time, but not a great one. He was amazingly active. We have seen that he wrote plays, and one that had a great success, *Milestones* (1912), in which the process of change and growing old was again his theme. He easily turned out articles and short stories, and for several years contributed a weekly causerie on new books to the *Evening Standard*, pluming himself on his flair for spotting winners—he respected his own works and others the more when they became best-sellers. With the surface of his mind he was able to produce books which were competent and entertaining. Later, when he had successfully cultivated the acquaintance of politicians and Press-potentates, he turned his experience to good account in the brilliant satire of *Lord Raingo* (1926). In later life (1930) he threw his undiminished zest and all that remained of his imagination into a *tour de force*, *Imperial Palace*. Here his theme was not, as it had been in his greatest works, a distinctively English one. Indeed it would be hard to think of a concern more international in its character than that of a great luxury hotel such as he here describes, splendidly organized to cater for the material comforts of the rich, exploiting all the inventiveness of modern research, enlisting the interest of big business men on the one side, and on the other touching the private and occupational lives of an army of individuals engaged in greasing the wheels. There are hundreds of pages of elaborate description glowing with the movement of things directed and happening. The conflict which Bennett usually seeks to excite is, in this case, between the vast, organized mechanism of Imperial Palace and the centrifugal private emotions of human beings. The book is magnificent, but it is hard, metallic. There are no lovable or even very interesting characters, nothing to enlist our affections; but, like the hotel, it is colossal; it is admirable.

Often we are disposed to think about Bennett—What a pity he squandered himself so much on vanity and vanities, on money-making, display and pot-boiling! But without these diverse elements in his make-up he would not have been what he was, and we may doubt if he could have produced more masterpieces —he was amazingly sagacious in judging his own power. It would be a mistake to suppose that the merely clever books which he turned out so often and easily are the essential Bennett; for a time, by sheer force of numbers, these trifles, these parerga, tended to obscure the view of his greater achievements and led critics to forget or underrate them. The experience which we derive from reading *The Old Wives' Tale* or *Clayhanger* or *Riceyman Steps* carries its own evidence. Time will sweep away the by-products—the vain, the mean, the vulgar, the meretricious—and leave the genuine, the memorable thing, which exists for literature.

Galsworthy was exactly contemporary with Bennett, born in the same year, 1867, and destined to observe and react to the same ferment of ideas about society which were in the air from 1900 to 1914. Both were to have their successes by writing about the particular spheres of society known to them, recalling Victorian memories, observing the passage of the years and contrasting the successive generations. Both went on writing and consolidated their reputations in the period following the first Great War. But there the resemblance ends. Galsworthy belonged to the so-called upper classes, and was most at his ease in describing the life of the country gentry or people of inherited wealth living in London. Bennett belonged to the humbler middle class and was most successful when writing of people who belonged to it. The latter spent much of his life writing for money; Galsworthy had private means which enabled him to be quite indifferent to the earnings of his work. Bennett from natural disposition looked upon the spectacle of life with detachment—it was interesting, and that was enough; Galsworthy was a suffering participant in the sentiments and emotions engendered by life, and had to discipline himself by the adoption of a rigid technique to keep the novelist in his proper place. Bennett never wrote books 'with a purpose'; he had no bent for moralizing; but in Galsworthy the reformer was never far behind. In his play *Strife* (1909), he was intent upon showing the inhumanity and waste involved in the opposite extremes of prejudice—that of unyielding employers on the one hand, and that of strike-leaders on the other. His play *Justice* (1912) was an appeal for the more humane administration of the law—'They've forgot what human nature's like', says Sweedle, speaking of the upholders of the letter of the law and the prison system of the time. (This play so moved Winston Churchill that he soon after initiated reformist legislation.)

Galsworthy was of a Devonshire family. He was taught early to ride and hunt; was educated at Harrow and New College, Oxford, and at the latter was known for his immaculate dress and slightly dandified manners. He read law between 1890 and 1894, travelled, and on a ship met and became friendly with Joseph Conrad without the least idea that the latter was shaping to become a writer. When he first began to discover his bent for authorship he was without any clear conception of those large social and moral problems which dominate most of his mature work. Under the excitement induced in him by Kipling's prose he wrote the short stories and the novel, *Jocelyn,* which were published in 1897 and 1898; and then came Flaubert and the Russian writers, especially Turgenev, under whose influence he wrote his first really notable book, *Villa Rubein* (1900).

At this stage he was thinking above all of literary technique—how to transplant into English that wonderful air of detachment which distinguished Flaubert and Turgenev—how to present the spectacle of life with gracious impartiality without obtruding the personality of the writer. *Villa Rubein* has a charm and restraint which, were we speaking the language of pictorial art, might make us say that it was an admirable example of the school of Turgenev. It was worth reading, and in addition the writing of it was valuable to the author. It was only by such restraints of technique that he could hope to keep under control that tender sentiment of his for all things living—including animals—and his strong natural poetic feeling, which was not supported by capacity for successful expression in verse. It was fortunate for Galsworthy the novelist that he had submitted himself to the discipline of art before he, too, was to be numbered among the prophets. He had acquired a literary conscience and a technique, adaptable to his purpose, when his interest turned more and more to moral and social questions. If he could no longer fully sustain the air of sublime aloofness, he could create some illusion of it by the method he deliberately adopted—that of presenting the spectacle of life and its contending forces, himself standing in the middle, like Fate holding the balance. 'We find ourselves,' he wrote in the Preface to the revised edition of *The Island Pharisees,* where he contrasts opposite elements in society, 'so near that thing which has no breadth, the middle line, that we can watch them both, and positively smile to see the fun.'

Thenceforward, Galsworthy was always to be on the middle line, observing what lay to the left and the right of it, in his earlier days laying the emphasis of blame on the right, later shifting it to the left. 'The Institutions of this country,' he writes in the Preface from which I have just quoted, 'like the Institutions of all other countries, are but half-truths; they are the working, daily clothing of the nation; no more the body's permanent dress than is a baby's frock.' Already he has guarded himself—'half-truths'. Later we shall be asked to see more of that half of the truth which resides in the surviving past. But at present, in *The Island Pharisees*, little sympathy is asked for the ninety who 'desire peace and comfort for their spirit', who 'will have it that the fashions need not change, that morality is fixed, . . . that every one will always marry, play, and worship in the way that they themselves are marrying, playing, worshipping', who 'have no speculation, and hate with a deep hatred those who speculate with thought'. To the left of the line are the other ten, 'the yeasty stuff . . . chafed by all things that are, desirous ever of new forms and moulds'.

In book after book we observe him holding the balance between opposed ideas or between characters with opposite tendencies; in *The Man of Property* (1906), the first novel of *The Forsyte Saga*, between the mechanical mind of Soames Forsyte and the impulsive Irene; in *The Country House* (1907), which many will think the most attractive of his novels, between the unimaginative Squire and his perceptive, compassionate wife; in *Fraternity* (1909); in *The Patrician* (1911); and in the plays *Justice* (between Sweedle and the advocates of 'an eye for an eye') and *Strife* (between the viewpoints of employer and employed). There, in his younger and more fruitful period we see him standing, discreetly, it is true, on the 'middle line', but enlisting all our sympathy for the young in mind, the generous, the rash, the wilful, and exposing in his satire the inflexible, habit-ridden, soul-drugged survivors of an old and out-worn order. That is how he impressed the young of that time who were to be in middle life when he wrote his last book— so different—which was to come under the judgment of a yet younger generation.

The changes in Galsworthy (changes consisting mainly in his diminishing ability to change) are apparent within the range of

The Forsyte Saga itself, the first volume of which was written in his earlier period. The *Saga* consists of *The Man of Property* (1906), *In Chancery* (1920) and *To Let* (1921), and was followed by a 'second Trilogy of the Forsyte Chronicles', *A Modern Comedy*, containing *The White Monkey* (1924), *The Silver Spoon* (1926) and *Swan Song* (1928). Finally there was *On Forsyte-Change* in 1930. There were also two 'Interludes' which belong to *The Forsyte Saga* and two in *A Modern Comedy*. A formidable total.

Writing of *The Forsyte Saga*, the first Trilogy,[1] Galsworthy said that its 'first word was written on Campden Hill, London, of a May morning in 1903' and its 'last word was written at Hampstead on August 15, 1920'. In his Preface to the second Trilogy, *A Modern Comedy*, he writes of the author's intentions: 'To render the forms and colours of an epoch is beyond the powers of any novelist: but to try and express a little of its spirit was undoubtedly at the back of his mind.' As with Bennett, the epoch whose chances and changes he reflects covers several generations. The Chronicles look back on the Early Victorianism of the old Forsytes, which he tells us was 'already on the wane in 1886'. 'What has survived, and potently, is the Victorianism of Soames and his generation, more self-conscious, but not sufficiently self-conscious to be either self-destructive or self-forgetful. It is against the background of this more or less fixed quantity that we can best see the shape and colour of the present intensely self-conscious and all-questioning generation.'

He strikes his individual note firmly and truly in *The Man of Property*, where it rings freshly, and there already we have the essentials of his style and method. This book has more in common with his earlier work in general than it has with the rest of the Forsyte Chronicles, except that it shares with the latter many of the same leading characters. Reading it, and the other books of that period, young Edwardians were disposed to think of Galsworthy as one of the advanced writers engaged in the war upon obsolescent ideas and the tyranny of habit, leading the world on to a more elastic, freer, more humane way of life. But in later years it was as if he had reversed the engines. The Great War had come and gone, and left its disturbing changes in the temper of society and fantastic innovations in taste and behaviour. Soames is now more sympathetic to him. He came to regard with respect and even tenderness those older men who, having formed

[1] See *The Life and Letters of John Galsworthy*, by H. V. Marrot. (1935).

habits, sought to conserve the social standards of a more rigid age; he looked askance at those young, restless, troublous spirits in whose lives he could discern no aim or purpose, who needed, as he thought, the sheet-anchor of tradition to restrain their wandering impulses.

In spite of his efforts to keep on the middle line, to look with tender sympathy on all that was human, it seemed to many that Galsworthy the pioneer and humanist had been replaced by Galsworthy the moralist and disciplinarian, himself a little set, almost a Forsyte—an Institution. In the later phases of the Forsyte Chronicles he still wears that garment of impartiality; he is still surveying the ages as they pass, and the men and women, old and young, who stood for the old order and the new. But the Galsworthy who had once looked forward so eagerly to a young, assertive, generous future, began to shrink back almost in horror when it came into being and took possession of a post-war world. He became uneasy at a society filled with the Irenes and Fleurs who were once his real heroines; and Soames, the possessive 'man of property', whom he had castigated for his irresponsiveness to the call of life, became transformed, ennobled almost, into a reflective elder critic of our time, a guardian of the Samurai honour and dignity of the past. And so it happened, in the period between the wars, that critics who in their youth had drawn upon the ideas of the younger Galsworthy, and assimilated them, became impatient with the old Galsworthy, now a pillar, it seemed, of just that constitution which he himself had laboured to undermine. More than any other then living man of letters he himself had become an English Institution; and as such respected by the multitude, praised by the correct, and derided by young originals.

But to-day it is easier to see him as a whole—to recognize that for a dozen years he was an active force in awakening Edwardian England from intellectual lethargy; a man of letters devoted to the conception of literature as an art, yet equally convinced that it has a social function to fulfil; a man of great strength of purpose, of generous impulses, modest in his thought and in his manner to others; chivalrous in his sympathy for the weak, but with the good sense never to confine his sympathies to a class. Before his death he had reached that last stage of success at which a man's work has been so much read, and become so familiar, that it is apt to be looked upon as *passé*. It was then that he was awarded the Nobel Prize for literature.

Chapter Six

CHESTERTON AND OTHER ESSAYISTS

*Hilaire Belloc—Dean Inge—G. K. Chesterton—Max Beerbohm—
Robert Lynd*

THOSE who speak bitterly of the confusion and uncertainty of
the present age sometimes look back nostalgically upon the
years before the first Great War as if that had been a time of
settled order and calm. It was not so. It was an age of unease and
restlessness, conscious of glaring inequalities in the social system,
an age when political passions ran high, when women suffragists
turned to militancy, labour to strike movements, and Irish
politicians to preparations for violence. In literature the spirit of
the time manifested itself in debate and controversy. We have
considered the cases of Shaw and Wells, ever conspicuous in
the debate, and Bennett and Galsworthy, contemplating it—the
latter sometimes joining in. There were many others, like G. K.
Chesterton and Hilaire Belloc, essayists primarily whether they
were writing short essays, or books in the spirit of essayists. And
there was Charles Masterman, who was discontented with the
present because it was not changing fast enough, unlike his friend
Chesterton, who idealized the past, and sought to restore the
spirit of an order which had vanished.

One thing was common to Wells, Galsworthy, Chesterton,
Belloc, Masterman and many other writers of this period—a disbelief in the efficacy of pure Reason, and a tendency to glorify
intuition, instinct and human passion; and in this respect they
participated in a world movement, which was exemplified in the
pragmatism of William James, the American, in Henri Bergson,
the French exponent of Vitalism, in Maeterlinck, the Belgian,
whose mystical books were much read in Britain, and the English
philosophical humanist, Schiller. Yet the history of religion has
shown that, however firmly the foundations of belief may be held
to transcend the logical, controversy is not on that account in any
way diminished. Men will argue more passionately in defence of
a view which they claim to be beyond argument than about a

47

thesis which is provable. Chesterton, a romanticist who came to identify his romanticism with what he believed to be the teachings of Catholicism, spent his life in attacking the conclusions of intellectuals and defending the claims of inspired credulity. Hilaire Belloc (born 1870) also a champion of Catholic tradition, retired into himself occasionally in lyric poetry, which in *The South Country* and a few other poems touched a high level of feeling and expression; but in most of his work he usually had the air of one contending against an adversary, and bent upon exposing him. Much of his most effective verse was satire, and his delightful Nonsense verses tended to be slightly combative. We are frequently conscious of a note of challenge in his biographical, historical and descriptive-discursive writings. There is an engaging pugnacity even in his positive, inconsequent light essays. In a long and distinguished literary life Belloc, for all his masculinity, was like some jealous she-bear fiercely defending her young.

In this connection it is appropriate to speak of another important writer who was a militant, if not perhaps wholly orthodox, defender of Christian dogma. W. R. Inge became a dignitary of the Anglican Church, a Dean. He was born earlier than Chesterton and Belloc (1860), and in the days when they were at their best (1900–1914) was occupied mainly in academic studies and the writing of books the most notable of which were concerned with various aspects of the history and practice of mysticism; but strangely enough, at the time when their energies were flagging, he entered upon a new phase of activity and descended into the arena of controversial essay-writing, and in the third and fourth decades of the century poured forth series of brilliant, combative essays in the best Edwardian manner, proving that no style is out of date when it is backed by learning, sense for language and sympathy with the living. His conservatism, his respect for tradition, his dislike of demagogy, were expressed with a dour frankness that won for him the sobriquet of 'the gloomy Dean'.

G. K. Chesterton, to be himself, had to be young. Born in 1874, he was the mischievous boy of the Edwardian period, plunging among the disputants in the market-place, pulling the coat-tails of the sophists. He wrote nonsense verses; he wrote nonsensical novels like *The Napoleon of Notting Hill* (1904), *The Man who was Thursday* (1908), and *Manalive* (1912); he wrote hilarious essays and books like *Heretics* (1905), *Orthodoxy* (1908), *What's Wrong with the World?* (1910)—yet all of these in spite of their levity expressed the fundamentally serious point of view of the essential, unique Chesterton. In his book *Dickens* (1906) he showed that he could be a very good appreciator of an author whom he both esteemed and had taken the trouble to read. When he was over forty he seemed to lose, alas, much of his gusto. A great part of what he produced in later life was dulled, repetitive, having the air of good sayings that have lost their goodness by being said too often; and these later lapses have injured his reputation, and caused him to be ranked far below his real worth. But once at least in later life, in his *Autobiography* (1936), the old gusto returned in its original force. In going back to his own past, his first enthusiasms and friendships, his earliest controversies, he was evidently stirred by the joy of fighting his battles over again; the delight of re-collection energized him to the writing of another book in his youthful, his best, style.

But even at his best his genius was not of the kind that was acceptable to the generation that followed. Shaw and Wells in the twenties and early thirties were not outmoded, as he was; the young intellectuals of the twenties, not content to dismiss him as Edwardian, were inclined to relegate him to the Victorian category—the limbo of unmentionable literature. Had he not been an incorrigible optimist, an unscholarly doctrinaire, a punster, a paradox-monger, devoid of fastidiousness, and *au fond* a sentimentalist? A damning list of charges—to all of which Chesterton himself would have cheerfully and proudly pleaded guilty; had he been put on trial, like his brother, it might have been said of him, as he said of Cecil, that he 'stood in the dock at the Old Bailey and was found guilty of patriotism and public spirit'.

It was natural that he should be accused of Victorianism, since, writing in Edwardian times, he refused to embrace novel ideas for novelty's sake, and became a praiser of times past, and not merely the past, but the near past, the age of his father and grandfather—and that when it had already become fashionable to abuse one's immediate forbears. He refused to be up to date except in the fact that the doctrines he attacked were the latest doctrines and that he armed himself with the latest verbal weapons of precision. Bernard Shaw was the typical iconoclast of the time; Chesterton became the champion anti-iconoclast. Shaw was absolutely indispensable to him, for Shaw was the fighting embodiment of all the things that he existed to fight. 'Shaw is seen at his best,' he wrote, 'when he is antagonistic. I might say that he is seen at his best when he is wrong. I might also add that he generally is wrong. Or rather, everything is wrong about him but himself.' Shaw appeared to be always attacking to destroy; Chesterton was always counter-attacking to defend. He attacked Socialism because he believed in the sanctity of individuals and the joy of craftsmanship; the principle of community life, because he believed in the home; stark realism, because he was a romantic; the theory of the superman, because he preferred the 'common man'; rationalism, both because it threatened orthodox religion and the enchantment of the irrational, and also because it led to those awful conclusions which 'tend to make a man lose his wits'—the unrestricted self-sacrifice of Tolstoy, for example, or the unrestricted egoism of Nietzsche. But in one respect Shaw and Chesterton were alike. They both detested shams, and especially sham persons. They could not bear hypocrites. On that point they might have shaken hands and seen that they were fighting on the same side.

His devout clinging to his Victorian ideals was due no doubt to his extraordinarily happy Victorian childhood. His grandparents were desirable grandparents. His father and mother were exactly the father and mother he would have chosen. His account of his father cutting out cardboard figures for a toy theatre reveals him as a man who, like the son, 'never left off playing', or at any rate always wished there were more time for the 'serious, constructive work' of play. Chesterton's eulogy of childhood is almost unqualified. For him it does not imply the Stevensonian world of make-believe. 'It is only the grown man who lives a life of make-believe and pretending; and it is he who has his head in a cloud.' He affirms that he delighted in the toy theatre because he knew it was illusion produced by artifice. His imagination had been precise and factual. 'I liked to see a fire lit more than to imagine faces in the fire.' His childish perceptions, so far from being vague, were clear and positive. In his *Autobiography* he recalls experiences of his childhood with the conviction that that was his real life and the beginning of what should have been a more real life, and that it is man who afterwards darkens the vision with dreams, or 'goes astray from it in self-deception'.

With this romantic conviction of the rightness of childhood it is not surprising that Chesterton should have gone on upholding the rightness of the childlike faith and the childlike point of view, and that it should even have coloured his conception of God, till God was seen as a Being endowed with the superbly exaggerated qualities of a child. 'Because children,' he said in *Orthodoxy*, 'have abounding vitality, because they are in spirit fierce and free, therefore they want things repeated and unchanged. They always say, "Do it again"; and the grown-up person does it again until he is nearly dead. For grown-up people are not strong enough to exult in monotony. But perhaps God is strong enough to exult in monotony. It is possible that God says every morning, "Do it again" to the sun, and every evening, "Do it again" to the moon. . . . Repetition may go on for millions of years, by mere choice, and at any instant it may stop.'

For the self-conscious period of boyhood, as opposed to childhood, he had none of the same reverence. Writing of his art-student days he tells, as another might tell of amorous escapades and secret lusts, of the horrible crimes of indulging in the decadence of rationalism and the vanity of thinking about thought; from which sinful morbidity he at last freed himself under 'a fiery resolution to write against the Decadents and the Pessimists who ruled the culture of the age'.

Above all things he disliked 'fussy culture', pretentious academicism, posturing well-doing, and organizations for reforming the world. Yet he was like a moth attracted to the very things which, if he mingled with them too closely, he knew would destroy him. He could not steer clear of political and sociological groups, queer societies and mystic sects, which too insistently thrust themselves into his controversial writings. During the Boer War he felt compelled to be a pro-Boer Liberal, but he instinctively disliked pro-Boers. He hobnobbed with Theosophists, but 'disliked them because they had shiny pebbly eyes and patient smiles'. He built up a working philosophy based on a faith which admitted no scepticism and rejected nothing because absurd; on a patriotism which began in love of home; on a sense of humour; on affection for friends; and hatred of priggishness. His judgment of life was profoundly influenced by his instinctive regard for certain persons and his instinctive shrinking from certain others. He spent the dozen best years of his literary life arguing with the intellectual busybodies, laughing at them, hitting or missing as luck would have it, defining and redefining his own exuberant Yes to the simpler articles of faith. His real time—1900 to 1914—would be scarcely thinkable without him. He helped to keep that very earnest period sane by his exuberance, his vivacity, and the charm and inspired wisdom of his fooling.

But it would be a mistake, as we shall see, to attempt to discover homogeneity in the great mass of Edwardian literature, which in fact was infinitely various. I can think of nothing further away from prophecy or controversy than the exquisite writings of Sir Max Beerbohm (born 1872), with their simple but elegant diction, their dry wit, their aroma of subtle humour and sweetness. Oxford was a pervading influence throughout his life. His undergraduate experiences in the nineties remained the magic background of all that came to him; he was one of those, in his youth, to whom things seemed to *come*, as if unsought. Oxford left its unmistakable imprint upon him, not to be effaced—with its elegance, its learned ease, its friendships, its conversations, its precocious seriousness and frivolity, and the unforgettable atmosphere such that even its railway station 'whispers [to the tourist] the last enchantments of the Middle Age'. Beerbohm took what he had loved in Oxford with him into the literary and artistic life of London, where he began doing his inimitable cartoons in the *Yellow Book*, and was allowed to 'have his fling' as a writer in the *Saturday Review*. He knew most of the authors and artists and theatre people and was on bowing terms with the politicians, continuing the inquisitive undergraduate life in what the undergraduate had thought of as the great world; to encounter it was for him a perpetual delight.

He had the art of extracting honey from experience, and giving it back again for the enjoyment of others in his drawings and writings. The same economy of line and character-sketching which distinguished his cartoons reappeared in another form in his essays, which were piercingly critical without ever being unkindly, delicately subtle yet as simple as the Bible. His excursion into gently ironic fiction in the novel *Zuleika Dobson* (1911) and the fanciful satiric stories called *Seven Men* (1919) revealed the same talents. Oxford, his first love, provided the setting for the delightful novel in which that 'lithe and radiant creature', Zuleika, takes the undergraduate world by storm; all the undergraduates follow the example of that leader of fashion, the Duke of Dorset, by drowning themselves in the Isis for love of her;

and Zuleika, touched, indulges the dutiful notion of entering a convent; but changes her mind, and, instead, takes the next train to Cambridge.

We must not call this book a satire; the author corrected the misnomer, in 1946; he himself 'had supposed it was just a fantasy'. There is fancy, and the precision that it needs, in all his work, including that done in reminiscent vein. Max Beerbohm brushes lightly, delicately, wittily, over the surface of life, with great tenderness for all that he has enjoyed, and unfailing humour. In his observations, and in his style, there is 'nothing too much', but there is always just enough. His occasional broadcasts in the Third Programme of the B.B.C. are talks that fastidious listeners do not willingly miss. His is the kind of writing which English literature is supposed not to have; though in fact there is every kind of writing in English.

Much of the work of Alice Meynell (1847–1922), and nearly all her poems, were of the last century, but many of her reflective and graceful essays belong to the Edwardian period. The essays of E. V. Lucas enjoyed immense popularity, and were informed by a keen relish for literature and, somewhat in excess, for Charles Lamb. A more philosophic and keenly critical writer of this period, who deserved more attention than she received, was Violet Paget, better known as Vernon Lee.

Finally, as essayist, a word in praise of Robert Lynd (1879–1949), an Ulsterman, acclimatized in England, attached to all the nobler causes, but oppressed by none of them. His genial disposition shines benevolently through the twinkling humour of his essays, which have something of Lamb in them, something of Chesterton. Half in earnest, half in jest, they have charmed readers for forty years. He was 'Y. Y.' in the *New Statesman*, and literary editor of the *Daily News*, which in 1930 became the *News Chronicle*.

Chapter Seven

ABOVE THE BATTLE

Henry James—Joseph Conrad—George Moore—Ford Madox Ford (Hueffer)—E. M. Forster—Norman Douglas—W. H. Hudson

WE have now reached a point in our consideration of English literature when it seems to become necessary to begin all over again. Hitherto, in the main, I have been discussing writers whom I felt justified in regarding as representative of, and expressive of, the age and the society to which they belonged; who lived in a time of social progress, and wrote about progress; who tended to rush into the contemporary fray as prophets, moralists, reformers, or who were at least intensely interested spectators. Having said so much, I have to draw back and point to something which defies these categories—What about Henry James, Joseph Conrad, George Moore, W. H. Hudson, Ford Madox Ford (Hueffer), and Norman Douglas, to say nothing of some of the poets? Or E. M. Forster, for that matter, who has no liking for the vatic style? Here I have named no fewer than seven writers of high distinction all of whom, with the possible exception of George Moore, did much of their best work during the first twenty years of the century, and five of them during the first fourteen. This was a period, strangely enough, when contemporary critics were wont to denounce its barrenness; but in the retrospect we see it as one of extraordinary fertility, and not merely fertile, but richly diversified. Writers belonging to opposite extremes flourished side by side, men who thought little of style and left it to take care of itself, and men who lived for style. This period witnessed a revolution in the literary approach to social ideas, and another revolution in literary technique and taste.

The latter was beginning, of course, in the nineteenth century. It would be unfair to overlook the influence of the Pre-Raphaelites, and especially Rossetti, with their devotion to art, or even the affected votaries of 'art for art's sake', who at least encouraged the growing disposition to study the art and literature of France. And especially I would insist on the importance of Walter Pater, who had something of the spirit of Winckelmann in his devotion to Hellenism, but showed himself also a writer of the new age by absorbing the doctrines of Flaubert and the best French literature of the nineteenth century. But his direct influence on other writers was less than might have been expected, and I think the main consequence of his writing, apart from the pleasure it gave and will give, was that it made fastidious readers aware of new possibilities of language, and ready to be attentive to the subtle tones of a James, a Moore, or a Conrad. Actually these writers went for inspiration not, as they might have done, to Pater, but to the French originals, Stendhal, Maupassant, Flaubert, the Goncourts, and to the Russian Turgenev. George Moore (1852–1933), who studied art in Paris in the seventies, but soon found his *métier* in writing, had the avowed aim of writing novels in English in the French manner—though I hardly think that his early novel *A Mummer's Wife* (1885) written under this impulse, justifies the claim so well as his much later book, *The Brook Kerith,* produced in 1916—when he had perhaps forgotten his early ambition. Ford Madox Ford used to say amusingly about Joseph Conrad—the story was significant, but not necessarily true—that he decided to make English and not French his adopted language because the French had so many stylists, the English none. It was George Moore, I believe, who mockingly remarked that Henry James went to Europe to study Maupassant while W. D. Howells remained in America to study James.

Be that as it may, in the early years of the twentieth century it became customary among the élite in England, as in New England, to speak with reverence of French literature and indeed of all things French. There was a *mystique* in being French which was almost the opposite of the mystical; it meant intellectual curiosity; it meant light, clarity, verve, *le Beau dans le Vrai*—a kind of conscience born in a man for whom it is pain to deviate from the rules of art. Such a conscience had been rare among nineteenth-century writers of English prose, and in fiction it had been conspicuously absent. There had been vitality, gusto, rich inventiveness, and delight in the representation of characters among the mid-Victorian novelists, but little regard for form and technique, little evocation of beauty by perfection of language. It was by the grand simplicity of his nature and his themes that Thomas Hardy had been able to touch tragic splendour, in spite of the clumsiness which too often marred his style. Henry James was among the first of the Anglo-Saxons to come under the spell of the French, and to realize that it was the proper destiny of the novel, in English no less than French, to become a form of art not only by holding the mirror up to nature, not only, or necessarily, by greatness of theme, but by so subtle a choice of natural elements and of the words to be employed that the story will be beautiful as a whole and in all its parts.

I think it is justifiable to claim Henry James (1843–1916) for English literature at least as much as for American. He was born in New York in 1843 in a family whose ancestors were Scots and Irish; was often in Europe when he was between twelve and seventeen years of age; and had his education in New York, London, Paris and Geneva. After 1868 he lived principally in Europe, first in London, then in Paris, and after 1875 England became his home. He lived for many years in London, and in 1898 bought a house in the congenial old-world town of Rye, in Sussex. In 1915 he was naturalized as a British subject. England had long been his spiritual home. There he found the social ease and the manners which pleased him; the dignified houses and the traditional life of an upper class which he felt qualified to describe. There was the atmosphere whose aroma he savoured, lending itself to delicate and sufficiently complicated human relationships which piqued his curiosity and provided him with his themes.

No doubt just because he had been born in America he was capable of seeing the scene with greater detachment, with just that aloofness which accorded with his technique. He was to wander over the world like an inquisitive god, observing with passionless curiosity the strange behaviour of its inhabitants, and especially of those who 'behaved' according to the rites and ceremonies of their class, staying when his attention was held to study the characteristic antics of some group of people at the moment when their behaviour became interesting. His art was to be, in the proper sense of the term, disinterested—that is to say, it was to be concerned exclusively with the matter in hand, to show, to exhibit, a chosen tract of life, to present a theme just for what it was worth as an interesting distillation of reality, untouched, unprejudiced by any consideration except that of presenting it perfectly; the artist so concerned cannot want to make his readers better, or to teach them a lesson, or to persuade them to any view about morality or politics or religion or anything whatsoever that does not spring of itself out of the situation described. To deal with real life in its more interesting relations—that and nothing more was his object. 'Art,' he said, 'is the one corner of human life in which we may take our ease. To justify our presence there the only thing demanded of us is that we shall have felt the representational impulse.' Art means an escape from embarrassing convictions and prejudices. 'Wherever her shining standard floats the need for apology and compromise is over; there it is enough simply that we please or are pleased. There the tree is judged only by its fruits. If these are sweet the tree is justified—and not less so the consumer. . . . We are not under theological government.'

James has left us in no doubt concerning the processes by which he found his themes and afterwards developed them. We may say that they started in each case with an intuition, with the sudden sensing of a situation full of possibilities waiting to be explored and developed. I have already quoted Arnold Bennett's dictum: 'Every novel should have a main theme that can be stated in ten words.' Long before, Goethe had said: 'The true power of a poem consists in the situation—in the *Motive*.' James in like manner recalls words that he heard fall from the lips of Ivan Turgenev 'in regard to his own experience of the usual origin of the fictive picture'. 'It began for him almost always with the vision of some person or persons, who hovered before him, soliciting him, as the active or passive figure, interesting him and appealing to him just as they were and by what they were. He saw them, in that fashion, as *disponibles*, saw them subject to the chances, the complications of existence, and saw them vividly, but then had to find for them the right relations, those that would most bring them out.' Joseph Conrad, too, tells that his stories generally began with a strongly imagined vision, as when he conceived the idea of the skipper looking over the side of the ship, tempted to desert his crew—the focal point of his book, *Lord Jim*.

For James himself the focal points were similar. Words spoken by a friend at dinner gave him his idea for *The Spoils of Poynton* (1897). 'There had been but ten words, yet I had recognized in them, as in a flash, all the possibilities of the little drama of my *Spoils*, which glimmered there and then into life.' His friend had been saying that 'a good lady in the north, always well looked on, was at daggers drawn with her only son, ever hitherto exemplary, over the ownership of the valuable furniture of a fine old house just accruing to the young man by his father's death.' With James's 'sense for the subject', that single touch was enough. It only remained for him to find the right relations between the mother, the son, the daughter-in-law, and to exploit to the full the character of the house itself, the pride and possessiveness of the mother and the tangle of vanities in which the persons were involved. He had a situation, an affair in which the characters were involved. It was his task to show, to exhibit the evolution and involution of its unfolding.

To achieve his end of 'showing', of letting the life of his story speak for itself, James was no more willing to let the author appear in his novel than a dramatist would put himself upon the stage. Infinite care was needed to keep the author superbly aloof; sometimes a narrator was chosen, through whose eyes the scenes are described; sometimes the action is presented as it appeared to one of the characters—to Maisie, for example, in *What Maisie Knew* (1897), though in that case, since Maisie was a child, and could not have been fully aware of all the coarseness of her worthless parents and the implications of the scenes in which she was involved, the author had to stretch his method, giving 'the whole situation surrounding her', but 'giving it only through the occasions and connexions of her proximity and her attention'. No doubt it is mainly because he was so detached from his subjects, so ruthless, or should I say faithful, in presenting what he called 'clumsy Life again at her stupid work', in showing human life as something in the long run rather comic, that he has been thought of as one utterly pitiless, and devoid of human sympathy. This impression has perhaps been intensified by the meticulous care with which he used language, so intent, in his exact analysis of each situation, upon describing it without possibility of error, and therefore refining upon his words, qualifying them, dotting the i's parenthetically, that he added, by such coldness of refinement, to our feeling of his heartlessness. This habit of writing with qualifications and parentheses grew upon him as he got older. His early tales and novels are quite simple. *What Maisie Knew* and *The Spoils of Poynton* (1897) are still comparatively direct in their writing. *The Awkward Age* (1899) is somewhat more involved, and the style reaches the height of its obscurity (I say 'height' and not 'depth', since in this case the novel could hardly have been what it was without these difficulties of style) in *The Golden Bowl* (1905), one of the most intriguing and at the same time most baffling of his works. In the novel on which he was engaged near the end of his life, left unfinished, *The Sense of the Past,* such obscurity as there is in the writing gradually disappears for the reader who is ready to open his mind and his sensibility to the infinitely subtle fascination of the adventure, to enter with Ralph Pendrel that dignified house in Berkeley Square (called Mansfield Square in the novel), to shut the door behind him, and in its 'inimitably quiet' atmosphere become aware of and join the company of Pendrel's well-bred ancestors. For me this unfinished book is the most delicate, the most gracious and exquisite of his works.

A great part of human society is ignored by Henry James. He is not interested in the 'common herd', and the vulgar people who may be depicted are there as a foil to those who are of 'finer grain'. He can produce an effect of terror, as in *The Turn of the Screw* (1898), but he is seldom concerned with tragic passion. He prefers to move lightly, delicately, curiously among the lesser incidents of life, searching as with a microscope for small essences hidden to the naked eye, but so contriving the accumulation of small things as to reveal life in a strange aspect whose strangeness he purposed to evoke. His writing became more and more mannered as he went on, and his habit of verbal refinement led too often to unrewarding obscurity. Preciosity could go no further. But he brought something new into English fiction. After him there is no excuse for judging the novel otherwise than as a fine art. With him English fiction starts again.

From James we turn to another writer of English, Joseph Conrad (1857-1924), who also was not of English origin, but adopted England for his country, having a difficulty which James had not—that of mastering the English language. He was born of Polish parents in the Ukraine, and his full name was Teodor Jozef Konrad Korzeniowski. In *Some Reminiscences,* published in 1912, he gave striking pictures of his childhood and of some members of the noble Polish family to which he belonged, with a few indicative words about his mother, 'wide-browed, silent . . . whose eyes had a sort of commanding sweetness', who accompanied his father into exile. Over all 'hung the oppressive shadow of the great Russian Empire—the shadow lowering with the darkness of a new-born national hatred fostered by the Moscow school of journalists against the Poles after the ill-omened rising of 1863'. At the age of nine he put his finger on a map in the blank space round the Upper Congo and said: 'When I grow up I shall go *there*.' He did, and out of that grim experience sprang the most wonderful of all his stories, *Heart of Darkness*, published with two other long short stories in *Youth* (1902). In 1873 he enjoyed a 'jolly holiday' travelling about Europe with a tutor, and a year later his boyish ambition to go to sea was ful-filled when he signed on as a member of the crew of a French vessel. For four years he served in the French marine and read much French literature; but in 1878 he joined an English ship, and in 1884 became a British subject and was certified as a Master Mariner of the British Mercantile Marine. When he left the service in 1894 he had in his kit a tattered manuscript, the product of four years of much-interrupted work. It was *Almayer's Folly* whose publication in 1895, thanks to the perspicacity of Edward Garnett, confirmed him in the resolve to be a writer. He settled in Kent, and lived in England till his death in 1924.

'Poetry and the language proper for it,' said Dante, 'are an elaborate and painful toil.' If it was toil and pain for Dante to write in his own Illustrious Vernacular how much harder for Conrad, whose prose was the prose of a poet, to express the infinite subtleties of his impressions in a language he had had to acquire. Flaubert was described by Walter Pater as 'the one martyr to style'. For Conrad no less writing was a prolonged martyrdom in which he suffered anguish of body and spirit in his efforts to find the expressive words. *Almayer's Folly* and *The Outcast of the Islands* (1896) were written in his years of appren-ticeship; in the writing of *The Inheritors* (1901) and *Romance* (1903) he sought the collaboration of Ford Madox Hueffer, and un-doubtedly each rendered services to the other. In *Lord Jim* (1900), he had felt his way to the language appropriate to him and come into his own. The motley shipload of Moslem pilgrims from all the East, the cosmopolitan crew, the movements and sinister stillness of the tropical sea, the abandoned ship, the inquiry, the tormented conscience of the delinquent—here was a theme after Conrad's own heart, giving utmost scope to a luxuriant imagination probing the secrets of reality. 'What is a novel,' he said, 'if not a conviction of our fellow-men's existence strong enough to take upon itself a form of imagined life clearer than reality and whose accumulated verisimilitude of selected episodes puts to shame the pride of documentary history?' *Typhoon* (1903) was a *tour de force* of imaginative re-creation in which the savage, concrete realities of a tempest of seemingly supernatural fury is rendered in terms of spiritual reception—the only weakness of this terrific book is that it prolongs the moments of highest tension beyond bearing and thus tends to lose some of its force.

In *The Mirror of the Sea* (1906), which is among the best and perhaps the best of his books, he distils the essence of his experience and memories of the sea. He dwells insistently on the proper use of nautical terms which for him have ritual significance; on the physiognomy of gales, which you 'remember by your own feelings'; on the 'intimacy with which a seaman had to live with a ship of yesterday' such that 'his senses were like her senses, that the stress upon his body made him judge of the strain upon the ship's masts'; on the East Wind, and the West Wind, who 'keeps faith with his brother, the King of the Easterly Weather'—in him the primeval and the intensely self-conscious meet—we feel the elements personified, the gods and the devils returning in pristine reality to assail the spirit of perceptive modern man. Even his language recalls the tones of the sea, in sentences short and sharp like small breakers, or in long voluminous sentences like ocean rollers.

In the *Secret Agent* (1907) and *Under Western Eyes* (1911) he attempted other themes with a power one might not have suspected, though these books scarcely belong to the essential Conrad. *Chance* in 1914 brought him the popular success which he had so long deserved and missed; he retained his power to the end. *Suspense* was published in 1925 after his death.

It had been in English ships that he had sailed and sojourned in the tropics, and explored that Eastern archipelago which was first fixed for readers and for him in *Almayer's Folly,* and is like the background of a sunset to all that he wrote later. It was a two-fold experience that he gained there, experience for which he was temperamentally prepared. He learnt to use his hands, to know the parts of a ship, to appreciate those exact, definite, hard facts which are necessary to the navigation of dangerous waters, to think in terms of ordinary men and ordinary things, to live under circumstances where common sense must prevail, where cant must be detected, where impracticality must be ruinous. He learnt, in fact, that the physical and concrete, the bodily, the ordinary, the touchable, are root realities, indispensable to safety and sanity; and he qualified to become a Master Mariner. But that was not all. In his travels he had had also another kind of experience, which may have belonged to 'youth', or 'romance', or 'folly', but whatever it was he was fortunate, in that period of his life, to light upon so sumptuous a scene and have his vision filled by those bright and dark seas, those luxuriant, fantastic shores, the coming and going of queer ships, by things variable yet in a sense constant in their variety, bright and multi-coloured as he saw them in the retrospect. In his books all became harmonized to one rich tone, deriving from his personality, which dominates his sentences, his portraits of persons, his descriptions of scenes and fearful, dramatic crises.

Here is something strange which belongs to English literature yet comes from Poland, from a Slav temperament which has accommodated itself to devices learnt from the French, and has given a heart to prose that might have been French if it had not been fortified with the gritty words of the English language, words corresponding to qualities which, perhaps, give surface protection against a climate of mist and sentiment. Conrad owed much to the French and their literature. Every literary Slav admires them because Frenchmen could be dry and precise and gay, and because they taught Russians how to behave in society and how to write books. Conrad learnt from them, yet he is further removed from the Gallic temperament than from the British. The mixture of French manner and Slav feeling, of classicism and mysticism, of order and unrest, of hardness and fineness—the earth-bound and the other-worldly—this at the last appealed to the romantic yet practical English when they had learnt to appreciate his subtle, nervous, expressive style.

George Moore was born in Ireland in 1852 (died 1933), but at the age of eighteen, provided with ample means, went to study

art in Paris, mixed with artists and men of letters, and set himself
to press all the arts into the service of literature. He wrote poems,
short stories, novels, critical studies and reminiscences, and his
chief virtue lies in the limpidity and directness of his style. He was
an æsthete imbued with a desire to be a realist, the victim of a
fluid temperament which led him to alternate between naturalism
and romanticism, ingenuous seriousness and amusing satire. The
novels which he wrote between 1884 and 1905, including *A
Mummer's Wife* (1884), *Esther Waters* (1894), *Evelyn Innes* (1898),
Sister Teresa (1901) and *The Lake* (1905), gained him the ear of a
wide public, because they had exciting straight stories, and the
respect of critics, because they were well written and extraneously
supported by his graceful if rather pretentious critical writings. In
Memoirs of my Dead Life (1906) he set down in sensuous, elegant
prose so much of his past as he could turn into pen-pictures, poems,
symphonies for the present. His later books of recollections,
Ave (1911), *Salve* (1912) and *Vale* (1914), collectively entitled
Hail and Farewell, are far more readable and more likely to survive
by reason of their malicious and witty allusions to persons he had
known, especially some of the protagonists of the Irish Literary
Movement which he himself in certain moods had chosen to
decorate. *The Brook Kerith* (1916) is a highly ingenious reconstruction of the Gospel story in fiction. George Moore was a man
of immense talent who fell short of great achievement because he
was fundamentally, in his art, insincere, and never emerged from
dilettantism.

There were some who feared that the same fate might befall
Ford Madox Hueffer (1873–1939. In middle life he changed his
last name to Ford). He was the son of a well-known musical
critic, Dr. Hueffer, and through his mother inherited a place
in the Pre-Raphaelite circle. In the 1880's Madox Brown, the
Rossetti brothers, Holman Hunt, Watts-Dunton and the rest
were accustomed to patting the head of that nice, tractable but
unpromising little boy known as 'Fordie', and a little later were
all very much surprised when he precociously started writing and
publishing books. One after another these appeared when he was
still in his twenties—novels, critical studies of the Pre-Raphaelites,
and works written in collaboration with Conrad—and at the age

of thirty he had made some impression upon fastidious readers by the ease and charm of his style and his individual, unconventional approach to any subject he handled. Certainly he was an impressionist. 'It preaches no particular sermon,' he said of *The Heart of the Country* (1906) which succeeded *The Soul of London* (1905); 'it announces no particular message; it is practically no more than a number of impressions arranged after a certain pattern and in a certain order.' That was to be his method always—a number of impressions arranged after a certain pattern—and to many of the critics (including Garnett), who looked severely or indulgently upon him at this time and for long after, it seemed that he was a talented trifler, enjoying a little reading, a little music, a little theatre-going, and cards and golf and society, setting down in sometimes quite exquisite language the fanciful impressions of one whose world was all fancy, unrelated to reality.

But Ford was not to be deterred by any sort of pontifical criticism—the pontiff in any case he detested—and went on in his own way, praising Flaubert and Henry James as the greatest of artists, and their technique as the only right one. Not that he appeared to have much in common with either of these writers when he produced a series of novels on an historical theme: *The Fifth Queen* (1906), *Privy Seal* (1907), and *The Fifth Queen Crowned* (1908); they were romantic; they were like tapestries, embroidered with a wealth of realistic description, and full of details which anyone ignorant of history might have believed to come from laborious research. These were followed by several other clever novels written in lighter vein and, in 1911, an admirable series of essays entitled *The Critical Attitude* in which he set forth some of the principles of writing which explained both his literary creed and his practice. Here he held up the banner of an art which was to be uncontaminated by any ulterior motive—by any desire to preach or teach or moralize—and should be devoted to the expression of 'those ideas which are a part of ourselves, which are our very selves'. For the novelist, it will be his function to present the world as he sees it, simply registering the picture of life in accordance with the pattern which it must assume for him. Words are his material, and the search for the right word and the use of the appropriate rhythm will be of the essence of his art. He himself seemed to have inherited a sense for words and for cadence, and his exuberant fancy provided the material; long before middle age writing ceased for him to be a toil, and his facility, though it made for freedom and a sort of elegant colloquialism, also tended sometimes to prolixity and extravagance.

In 1908 he founded the *English Review* which he edited for a year with high literary distinction and complete disregard for what was financially feasible. Its economic failure under him, and perhaps its continuance under a more practical editor, Austin Harrison, who enjoyed the support of a millionaire, Alfred Mond, chagrined him; and to this disappointment was added, a few years later, a succession of worries arising from his alliance with the novelist, Violet Hunt, his law-suits with his wife, and his break with Violet Hunt. Characteristically, in the course of these troubles, he contrived to get sent to prison for contempt of court. During the war, though over military age, he succeeded in getting a commission, and served for about three years in the Army, at home and in France, and saw just enough of the front line to give him the experience he wanted.

When the war was over and he had shaken himself free from his more harassing entanglements, though it would not be true to say he had learnt to distinguish between fact and fancy, or had lost his love of a gesture, or his joy in imagining vain things, he had at least gained the 'experience' which he had thought essential to the artist; he was no more to be accused of dilettantism. Out of these experiences, which were not such that they could be just romanticized, came the series of war-novels on which his reputation will mainly rest (though *The Good Soldier,* written just before the war, is of comparable merit)—*Some Do Not* (1924), *No More Parades* (1925), *A Man Could Stand Up* (1926) and *The Last Post* (1928). Here, seen through the eyes of the principal actor, Christopher Tietjens, whom he liked to think of, and described as 'the last English Tory, omniscient, slightly contemptuous—and sentimental in his human contacts', he presents a wide tract of English life as it had come under his ken in a few crowded, exciting years in a period of national crisis, before and during the first Great War. It is a tragi-comic picture of Vanity Fair on a huge scale, with the personal tragedy of Tietjens torn between his supposed duty to a self-indulgent, worthless wife and his repressed passion for another woman, and his long conflict with the inanities of spurious artistic circles and the humbug of officialdom in Government departments and in military headquarters—which made no sense when he contemplated the patient soldiers who were cannon-fodder in war. 'I hope,' he wrote in a Preface, 'that this series of books, for what it is worth, may make war seem undesirable.' Yet, knowing Ford, observing his method, we may be sure that at the time of writing he had no ulterior end—no end beyond presenting the rich images of life as they crowded upon him in the complex picture he had formed in his mind. Not all of the characters are convincing—even the hero, Tietjens, has in him too much of Ford's preconceived idea of what an English gentleman should be—yet the total effect is one of life, in its passion, its puerilities, its waste and its beauty, springing out of the canvas on which it is brightly painted.

Just before and during that war Ford wrote some moving poems in free verse, and liked to surround himself with very young writers, Ezra Pound among them, whom he constantly spoke of as *mes jeunes*. During his later years, when he lived mostly either in France or America, he went on writing assiduously, and completed a voluminous impressionistic history of the literature of the world shortly before his death. In the 1920's and 1930's he had considerable success in the United States, and in his latter years he had the solace of knowing that he was esteemed in Great Britain by younger critics who in general were little disposed to tolerate Edwardians. They accepted him as belonging to their own species.

Those who listen from time to time to excellent talks on the radio given by E. M. Forster (born 1879), or have heard him speaking at gatherings of literary persons at the International P.E.N. Club, or at least know how often he is mentioned as one of the major living novelists of to-day, may wonder why I introduce him at this stage of my survey. The answer is simple; his important novels, with one exception, were written before the first Great War, and even *A Passage to India* was published as long ago as 1924. His delightful book of critical essays—or rather lectures, for they were written for oral delivery—*Aspects of the Novel,* was published in 1927. Let me note the dates of the earlier books, which quickly brought him fame. *Where Angels Fear to Tread* appeared in 1905 (when Forster was twenty-six years old); *The Longest Journey* in 1907; *A Room with a View* in 1908; *Howard's End* in 1910. Most of his best novels, then, had been written when he was in his twenties or early thirties, and when *A Passage to India* appeared he was still only forty-five. The memorable collection of short stories, *The Celestial Omnibus*, which contains his little masterpiece, *Other Kingdom*, was published in 1911. His admirers have to try to remember that as a creative writer he must be numbered, a youth, among the Edwardians; and unless something happens, as it might, they may go on wondering how it is that a mind which is so evidently alive to the modern world is content to add so little of substance to his published work.

It would not be very profitable to look for literary 'influences' and 'origins' in such a case as his. Certainly I do not see him as deeply moved by Shaw or Wells, though he would not have been inattentive to *The Way of All Flesh*. He was versed in Greek poetry, and the fanciful element in him which appears so often in his writing was attracted to the magic of Greek legend and the union he found there of physical beauty and immortal strangeness. Perhaps the English novelist who gave him greatest pleasure was Jane Austen. There are times when Forster's simple narration and the way in which he sets people talking, or gossiping, remind us of that lively and exquisite author; but we are soon aware that it is not just delight in the characters for their own sake, or the entangling them in the necessities of a plain plot, that is carrying Forster's story along; the strange is about to emerge, the tragic perhaps, a situation tense and taut which will be a reflection upon the lives of men in relation to the gods. He is not in the least, as I have suggested, among the 'prophets' of the period; but he is not uninfluenced by those social incongruities which produced the prophets, though he, like the writers who were to appear a decade or two later, turned his criticism, not upon society, but inwards. He is acutely aware of the falsities of social convention which desiccated English middle-class life; of the aridity of superficial culture and its judgment of what is spontaneous, instinctive and sincere. When a clash comes—and he contrives that it always should—it arises from actions determined by character, from human incompatibilities, differences arising from nature—nature in its simplicity, and nature overlaid by maxims or prejudice.

His earliest novel *Where Angels Fear to Tread* has none of the signs of immaturity. But it bears the signs of youth. It is charmingly written and has a well-constructed plot. But the supreme power of the novel comes from the amazing portrayal of the handsome young Italian, 'the son of an Italian dentist, with a pretty face'. Apart from his handsomeness, his naturalness, his gaiety, Gino appears to have nothing to recommend him. He is crude in his manners. He spits. His morals are loose. He is boastful, spendthrift of his wife's means, and to English eyes vulgar. Yet such is the cunning of Forster's craft that Gino becomes the very incarnation of pagan youth and high spirits and delight in life and puts to shame the fussy English people who, owing to an English girl's rash marriage with him, become entangled in his inconsequent career. The Italian village of Monteriano, to which Gino belongs, becomes a commentary on Sawston, the Surrey village which breeds Mrs. Herriton, narrow, strong-willed, her daughter, narrow, spiteful, her son, sterile specialist in Italian culture; and the connecting link is that plain Miss Abbot, with so little to recommend her but her primitive response to the pitiful, the physically beautiful and the passionate—to the playboy, Gino. Only a young man could create such a dance of enchanted youth as Forster has created here, yet only maturity could thus relate it to the habit-ridden world of Victorian or Edwardian England. This book is the amazing product of percipient, tremulous youth which by some miracle of precocity is also mature.

Forster's next novel, *The Longest Journey*, is a far more ambitious work, though not well constructed. We note the recurrence of the physically primitive type, shown here twice—in the bully, Gerald, who, whatever else he might lack, had the certitude of passion which wins; and Stephen, a much more admirable type, who surely illustrates what the young philosopher Ansell talking to a friend called 'the Spirit of Life'—the indefinable quality for which Ansell searches in persons and in life. 'Myself I've found it in books. Some people find it out of doors or in each other. Never mind. It's the same spirit. . . .' The Spirit of Life is not lacking in the talk of undergraduates, or later of 'two philosophic youths repining in the British Museum', or the tale of the hero, Rickie, struggling to endure an unsatisfactory marriage, and the descriptions of Mr. Pembroke, the cruelly egotistic schoolmaster, and Rickie's aunt at Cadover House, and Gerald, and Stephen. There are people in this book, and places, which in their several ways evoke the Spirit, and its magic. Magic, pagan magic, is never far away in Forster's stories.

Certainly not in *A Room with a View*, a perfectly constructed little comedy, where irony and magic are blended in the 'melody and movement' of this thwarted and happily ending love affair. Pan himself is not absent. At the famous picnic party in the hills near Florence he 'had been amongst them—not the great god Pan, who has been buried these two thousand years, but the little god Pan, who presides over social contretemps and unsuccessful picnics'. Yet it was surely the great god Pan who returned to life when Lucy escaping from dullness plunged through the wood and fell at the edge of the promontory.

At the same moment the ground gave way, and with a cry she fell out of the wood. Light and beauty enveloped her. She had fallen on to a little open terrace, which was covered with violets from end to end. . . . From her feet the ground sloped sharply into the view, and violets ran down in rivulets and streams and cataracts, irrigating the hill-side with blue, eddying round the tree stems, collecting into pools in the hollows, covering the grass with spots of azure foam. . . . This terrace was the well-head, the primal source whence beauty gushed out to water the earth.

It was then that the unspeakable George 'stepped quickly forward and kissed her'. And that correct, unwanted lady, Miss Bartlett, saw.

'Passion should believe itself irresistible.' Perhaps that, in five words, is the theme of *A Room with a View*. If Forster in his novels preaches anything at all, it is belief in the natural, the spontaneous, the unashamed, the body as the tenement of the spirit, as opposed to the inhibitions of false culture and the respectable superstitions. That is one element in the kernel of conviction which underlies all his novels. And another is similar and follows from it. He believes in the genius of place. Every hillside in his mythology has its Pan, every wood its dryad, and every natural man has his proper abode —the abode that belongs to him, his ancestors, his kind. If the body is the tenement of the spirit, the room, the house, the village or township is the tenement of the human being who is part of a human society; and deprived of it human beings are restless, dis-embodied creatures, gibbering souls, bereft of humanity. This is the tragedy of modern life exposed in *Howard's End*, where the house which Mrs. Wilcox loved remains as a symbol of perman-ence in a world whose curse it is that it has no fixed home, no anchorage, no respite from continuous change and flux. The new

6

buildings with their new and constantly changing tenants grow up like weeds in a day and come nearer and nearer to the garden and wych-elm of *Howard's End*. The personal, the individual, is seen bravely holding on to what links it with tradition and the enchantment of the past under the assaults of soulless undirected change.

During the first ten years of his literary life Italy, among foreign countries, held the first place in Forster's affections. But before the first Great War India and Indian society were already claiming his attention, and his first writings, I think, on India appeared in 1914 in *The New Weekly* as a series of articles entitled 'Adrift in India'. But ten years were to elapse before the appearance of his novel *A Passage to India*. The tragedy in this story arises from the incompatibility of temperament between the English ruling class in India and the people of India; or rather, the seeming incompatibility, expressed, presumably falsely, by the narrow-minded official who said: 'I have never known anything but disaster result when English people and Indians attempt to be intimate socially. Intercourse, yes. Courtesy, by all means. Intimacy—never, never.' The dramatic and indeed terrifying situation which Forster creates arises from this habitually cultivated prejudice of caste and race. Miss Quested, a newcomer, does not believe in this incompatibility. She is friendly with the sensitive, shy, upright Dr. Aziz, and the tragedy begins in that dramatic scene at the Marabar Caves, which the author has the skill to make tense, eerie, oppressive with portent; and reaches its second high point in the trial scene in which all India seems pitted against all official Britain, and justice is done to the Indian through the evidence of an English girl and an Indian magistrate administering British law. Between English and Indian Forster endeavours not to take sides. The tribal spirit keeps them apart; but in each camp those who have individuality are persons first; to the artist their tribalism is irrelevant.

More than twenty-five years have elapsed since the appearance of *A Passage to India*, and in the whole of that period no major work has been produced by him. There have been several volumes, including *Aspects of the Novel*, *Goldsworthy Lowes Dickinson* (1934) and *Abinger Harvest* (1936), and occasional more recent writings which indicate no loss of power, but on the contrary the same capacity to see things in a fine light with artistic precision, and to expose them unconventionally, intimately, fearlessly, in language choice, direct, free from affectation. His work is still that of a man mature but by no means old, from whom much might be expected. Yet all that he has done in the last half-century seems, in comparison with his earlier work, in the nature of parerga. Why? His silence is one of the literary puzzles of our time. He himself has explained it by saying that the novel as he conceives it demands a society with some stability, resting on something fixed not only in manners but in place—how can there be a society without homes, without neighbourhoods, without foci? We remember how important the *genius loci* is in nearly all his novels.

But is that all? Have we not seen that he excels when he is portraying the physical vitality, the paganism, the exuberant passion of youth, and that he himself in his early maturity was a very young man who wrote of the feelings of youth as only a young man could write, and that he could no more have produced a Gino or a George Emerson in his middle age than Shelley, had he lived to be old, could have written 'The Skylark'? The best that he had in him to say he wrote then, forty years ago, when all that was lyrical in him could give magic to his realism; and if he is conscious that he cannot do just that again, well, why should he write something else, of a world in which his Pan is dead? Perhaps that is why the most considerable living English novelist chooses to keep silence. *Favete linguis.*

I can think of no living writer who is further from the Edward-ian prophets, or nearer to the pagans—say, the Greek pagans under the early Roman Empire—than Norman Douglas. He was born in 1868, and as lately as 1946 produced a little book, charac-teristic enough, called *Late Harvest.* 'Alas, how have you spent your days!' he quotes from a poem by Platen which he had read fifty-seven years ago. 'Now,' he replies, 'having reached nearly twice the age at which Platen died, I no longer complain of how I squandered my days; my one regret is that I have not many more of them to squander.' Douglas is the complete if not the perfect Epicurean, and he might have belonged to almost any civilized period of history—except, perhaps, the present, which he has spent his life in evading, seeking the soft airs of the Mediterranean where ancient paganism still lingers, or another civilization, that of the Arabs, a thousand years away from our own. *South Wind* was the novel which, to his surprise, brought him fame and a small modicum of fortune, and led collectors to pay huge prices for first editions of his earlier works. This book, he wrote, 'was the result of my craving to escape from the wearisome actualities of life'. 'To picture yourself living in a society of such instability, of such "jovial immoderation" and "frolicsome perversity" that even a respectable bishop can be persuaded to approve of a murder —this was my aim.'

Nearer, I think, to his real character are such books as *Siren Land*, which gives the very savour of the island of Capri as it must have been before the tourists came; *Fountains in the Sand*, conceived in the smoke-begrimed recesses of an Arab café in Tunisia, and mainly written in 1910; and *Old Calabria*, published in 1915, the fruit of many journeys on foot and several years of research and writing. *They Went* (1921) illustrates as well as anything the bizarre devilry which is an important element in his humour. Douglas has an erudite, flexible and pungent style which reflects the genuine man—one frankly bent on pursuing a life of pleasure, whose pleasures consist in savouring all the good things of life, sensuous and imaginative, among congenial and unaffected friends, or in solitude, among objects agreeable to the eye, in literature and in odd recesses of learning. Some readers may be shocked by his Mephistophelian love of shocking and the seeming cruelty of his perverse humour, but no one sensitive to style can fail to admire the virility of his writing, so expressive of all that he found lovable or detestable in an enchanted or grossly practical world.

In the first page of the first book he ever wrote—*The Purple Land* (1885)—W. H. Hudson makes his hero comment on the duration of life. 'What soul in this wonderful various world would wish to depart before ninety! The dark as well as the light, its sweet and its bitter, make me love it.' Born in 1841, he lived to the age of eighty-one, and in spite of a life which contained more than its share of dismalness, he did not recant his optimism. His joyous childhood among the farmlands of the Rio de la Plata is described in that glowing autobiography, *Far Away and Long Ago*, which he wrote when he was seventy-seven (1918). He has told how the serious illness at the age of fifteen which long affected his health turned his mind to study and grave reflection upon life and death. In 1869 he went to England and lived in near-poverty for all the rest of his life, though he was given a small Civil List pension in 1901. It was a grim irony of fate which decreed that this man whose subject was Nature and wild life, whose heart was among countrymen and country scenes, should have been condemned to live most of his years in a dreary London region, the home of his unimaginative wife. The feeling of the mass, the 'monstrous organism', he wrote in that best of his books, *A Shepherd's Life* (1910), 'troubles and confuses my mind when I am in London, where we live "too thick"; but quitting it I am absolutely free; it has not entered my soul and coloured me with its colour or shut me out from those who have never known it, even of the simplest dwellers on the soil who, to our sophisticated minds, may seem like beings of another species. This is my happiness—to feel, in all places, that I am one with them.'

This sense of 'oneness' with places he loved lies at the root of Hudson's communicative power. As a naturalist he made some contribution to knowledge, not through exhaustive scientific study, but by his loving and patient observation of wild life, and especially of birds; when he was in London, the birds of Kensington Gardens were his joy and consolation. But in those parts of rural England which he made his own, the southern counties, and especially Sussex, Hampshire and Wiltshire, where he would sleep in cottages and walk and loiter in fields or on downs, we feel that he has entered into the whole life of each place with senses alert to the lesser and greater things in it. He has been attentively watching birds and four-footed animals and flowers; he has been talking to the labourers and the working-women and children with natural ease; and the place itself—cottages, church, fields, downs, skies—is the setting to this composite life of men and creatures. As we read we become aware of the many elements which constitute the harmony of place, including the ancestors of men now living and the graves of the dead.

His kinship with nature may be compared with Thomas Hardy's, but he does not, as Hardy did, dramatize nature; and, unlike Hardy, in the presence of nature he feels no bitterness, no sense of the cruel operations of an indifferent Providence, though he is aware of the solemn procession of life and death. Not that he is by any means unreflective. He resents the mass life of the towns and modern sophistication, but finds in nature a sufficient purgation—the interest he discovers in all the small significant things he records and comments on gives a clue to his valuation of life. In that early book, *A Crystal Age* (1887), he presented in Utopian form his antidote to the growing town-mindedness of the world; and in that charming allegorical romance, *Green Mansions* (1904), he let his fancy loose in the story of Rima, half girl, half bird. But he deserves most to be remembered by his autobiography and the books in which he set down his actual observations of places and living things as in *Nature in Downland* (1900), *Hampshire Days* (1903), *A Shepherd's Life* (1910), and his many books about birds. His range was not broad—he had not Hardy's all-embracing vision. His imagination had not a multitude of facets; his moods were not various; but within his range there was intensity and serenity. He has created awareness of a certain relationship with Nature which is not Wordsworth's, not Hardy's, which we shall always think of as Hudson's.

Chapter Eight

DRAMATIS PERSONAE

FOR the purpose of this bird's-eye view I should like to consider the situation of any intelligent young man who was just becoming adult in the Edwardian period and was entering upon his life-work, possibly in the sphere of literature. We should appreciate his position better if it were possible to draw a full picture of the social, intellectual and imaginative forces which surrounded, assailed, and stimulated or repelled him. The twentieth-century mind must have been peculiarly affected by the sheer multiplicity of the intellectual, imaginative and sensory influences that are brought to bear on it; a man's power of absorbing this and rejecting that will be of profound importance in determining his personality and the character of his work. To draw such a picture in its completeness is obviously beyond the scope of the present book—perhaps of any book. I can do no more than hint at the multifarious voices which the young man in the early years of the century, intently listening, might have heard around him, bombarding him, clamouring for his attention —the voices of the writers whom we have already been discussing, the voices of the social reformers and politicians, the scientists achieving miracles in the world around, the philosophers and theologians and agnostics, the scholars, pursuing art and letters, the pioneers of those new movements, in art, in the theatre, in poetry, and, not to be ignored, the merely popular authors who reflect the mind of the literate masses and provide them with entertainment. What a shop-window, inviting the literary aspirant to enter and explore and equip his mind for the modern adventure! Some of these influences would be predominant; others would permeate the atmosphere which surrounds him and affect him indirectly. The sum-total determines the character of the age.

Much of the genius of this period went into science, but the influence of science upon literature came rather from the impact of inventions upon the imagination than directly from the writings of scientists. Would it be proper to regard *The Golden*

Bough of Sir James Frazer (1854–1941) which appeared in twelve volumes between 1890 and 1915 as an exception? This massive and wonderful account of primitive customs and beliefs springs in part from the science of anthropology, in part from classical and historical studies, and in part from the reconstructive imagination of a man who was scientist, scholar, historian and man of letters. Philosophy through the work of some of its exponents touches literature more nearly than science does. T. H. Green with his neo-Hegelianism had profoundly affected the thought of Oxford towards the end of the nineteenth century, and Bernard Bosanquet (1848–1923) pursued a similar path in the late nineteenth and early twentieth century. F. H. Bradley (1846–1924) is one of those few philosophers who charm by their style no less than stimulate by thought. The remorselessness with which he destroys one illusion after another and leaves the reader at one stage gasping at the apparent completeness of the ruin is no less stimulating than the skill with which he then turns and re-builds the foundations of reality. But it seemed that philosophy along these lines had gone as far as it could go. Raiders, bent on giving it a more practical and human significance (perhaps at the expense of intellectual consistency), like the American pragmatist, William James, and the English humanist, Schiller, fortified the conscience of reformers who believed in justification by works. But the time had now come when science, no longer at war with theology, and mathematics should join hands with philosophy. It is significant that the first published book of Alfred North Whitehead (1861–1947) who has so deeply influenced contemporary British philosophy, should have been *A Treatise on Universal Algebra*. Bertrand Russell (Earl Russell), has flung his philosophic net very widely, and though born in 1872 is still one of the most potent thinkers of our time. He too started as a mathematician, and indeed collaborated with Whitehead in the writing of *Principia Mathematica* (1910). He is one of the few greater philosophers who have descended into the arena of common life, turning from speculative study to write about practical questions—social, moral and even political in lively, sardonic English.

English literature has been rich in historians, but it was only towards the end of the nineteenth century that history was systematically studied at the universities, where it has been pursued as one of the humaner branches of learning, and holds its own (where the classics are retreating) against the encroachments of science, economics and other modern studies. In the last fifty years there have been no writers of history whom we can put in the company of the greatest, unless we include James Bryce (1838–1922), whose more important literary work, however, belongs to the last century. But the period has been distinguished by team-work, respect for sources, and thoroughness, and also by the willingness of historians, trained in historical method, to apply this method to recent events.

Some of them have been drawn into active life in politics or journalism. Thus H. A. L. Fisher (1865–1940) went into Parliament in 1916 and became President of the Board of Education. J. L. Hammond (1872–1949), whose most important contributions to history were *The Village Labourer, 1760–1832* (in which his wife collaborated), *The Town Labourer* and *The Skilled Labourer* (produced between 1911 and 1919), was also at one time editor of a weekly political journal, the *Speaker,* and subsequently a leader-writer on the *Manchester Guardian* and other daily papers, and an active participant in political and social life. G. P. Gooch (born 1873), a learned and wise historian of political ideas and recent international politics was from 1906 to 1910 a Member of Parliament and has been for many years joint-editor of the *Contemporary Review*. With H. W. V. Temperley (1879–1939) he edited *British Documents on the Origins of the War, 1898–1914.* Sir Alfred Zimmern (born 1879) and Arnold Toynbee (born 1889) are distinguished students who have devoted a great part of their work to historical or analytical study of modern European affairs. R. W. Seton-Watson (born 1879) brings humanity and imagination to his studies of Central European and especially Slavonic affairs both as historian and exponent of the present. It is interesting to note that the best and most reliable book on recent English history, *England 1870–1914* (1936) was written by a scholar who devoted the greater part of his life to daily work on a newspaper, R. C. K. Ensor (born 1877).

These are only a few outstanding examples which go to show how closely the study of modern events in the spirit of the historian and the study of history in the light of knowledge of modern life have been pursued side by side in the last fifty years.

George Macaulay Trevelyan (born 1876) is a little more aloof from contemporary affairs than the writers whom I have mentioned though he has taken a keen interest in the National Trust and the preservation of natural and architectural beauty. His three books on Garibaldi (1907–11) at once put him in the front rank of living historians, and since then, after service in the first Great War, he has been continuously active in producing historical works and biographies. His *English Social History* (1944), illuminates history by that sort of interest in the social life of the people only possible to one who also takes an interest in the social life of his own time. Also keenly interested in contemporary life is a younger historian, A. L. Rowse (born 1903).[1]

The young man whom I have been considering, becoming adult in the early years of the century, would find a bewildering profusion of well-known novelists inviting but not always meriting his attention. What would he make of those two idols of the less fastidious middle classes, the sensational, mouthing prophetess, Marie Corelli (1855–1924), or Hall Caine (1853–1931) whose fevered descriptions of the Isle of Man and spurious romance thrilled hundreds of thousands of readers? A little later a much less pretentious and wholly undistinguished writer, Charles Garvice, enjoyed the favour of the million; and he in turn was succeeded by a writer of thrillers, Edgar Wallace (1875–1932), who was not without real talent and imagination, but for the most part squandered his powers in carelessly written sensational novels which were devoured by his numerous and not always ignorant readers. For a few years in the first decade of the century Katherine Cecil Thurston was in the top rank of best-sellers with a number of tasteless, melodramatic society novels. Robert Hichens (1864–1950), whose popularity lasted longer, was a better writer not without literary sensibility; he exhibited some neatness of satire in his earliest novels and later some talent for evoking atmosphere from the strange or the macabre; but always one heard the machinery creaking; his escapism, as

[1] For further comment on Rowse see p. 205.

exemplified in *The Garden of Allah* (1905), led only to the vapid. With Hichens perhaps one might rank William J. Locke (1863–1930), a self-conscious, sententious, pseudo-romantic moralist who sometimes lamentably attempted realism, and had popular successes with *The Morals of Marcus Ordeyne* (1905) and *The Beloved Vagabond* (1906). He also wrote plays.

In the same category I am disposed to include Sir James M. Barrie (1860–1937), though he had some considerable powers denied to those whom I have just mentioned, and his vogue lasted much longer; indeed it continues to-day. Even reputable critics have taken him seriously. He was first welcomed in the last century as one of the Scottish 'kail-yard'[1] school of writers, which included Ian Maclaren and S. R. Crockett, and he never lost his fondness for introducing, as with a twinkle of the eye, expressions from the Scottish vernacular. He appealed alike in novels, light essays and plays to the great heart of the people by his whimsicality, his sententiousness, his modest earnestness and, in the case of the plays, by his sense for the theatre and his talent in construction. His sentimental play for children, *Peter Pan* (1904) is spoken of as a classic, and its fantasy still pleases children. Apart from this *Quality Street* (1901) remains the most popular of his plays, while *The Admirable Crichton* (1902) which is the most free from his characteristic defects is not so much in favour. In the main his success has been due to his skilful mingling of smiles and tears, whimsy and earnestness, and his belief in himself.

Our intelligent young adult might or might not be attracted to Barrie, but he would be in no danger of losing his heart to the other best-sellers I have mentioned. But there were some popular writers who might afford him genuine entertainment. A prince among them was W. W. Jacobs (1863–1943) who had an inimitable vein of humour all his own in describing sea-captains on shore, night watchmen, etc., and their women-folk in simple, well-constructed short stories.[2] Before and after the turn of the century Pett Ridge was depicting East End London characters with a sly humour; he was a serious and sympathetic observer of the London working classes. It was in this period that the detective story came into its own. Already in the last century Conan

---

[1] A cottager's cabbage patch.
[2] Collected in such books as *The Skipper's Wooing* (1897), *Odd Craft* (1903), *Night Watches* (1914).

Doyle (1859–1930) had written his Sherlock Holmes stories. The famous Holmes, with his unerring eye for the revealing clue, and his naïve companion, Dr. Watson, belong now to the world of legend. Conan Doyle had no effective successor till E. C. Bentley (born 1875) produced *Trent's Last Case* (1912), a skilfully devised thriller which set a fashion, prescribed the rules of the game, and, in fact, created a new kind of literary sport of which the modern public shows no sign of tiring. It may be observed that though there is a death in almost every detective story there is seldom any evocation of the gruesome or the uncanny. For uncanniness we might turn to that adept in stories of the supernatural, Algernon Blackwood (born 1869), or to the masterly *Ghost Stories of an Antiquary* (1905), the work of a distinguished scholar and mediævalist, for long Provost of Eton, Montagu Rhodes James (1862–1936). For pure fantasy in books designed to interest children I know nothing better in this century than *The Wind in the Willows* (1908), by Kenneth Grahame (1859–1932), a story in which the persons—Mr. Toad and others—are creatures who live their daily lives on the banks of the Thames.

Such were some of the writers whose books were filling the bookshops when our young adult was looking for inspiration—signs of the times, no doubt, yet so many of them not rich in significance. The older generation was still holding its own in the formidable person of Mrs. Humphry Ward (1851–1920), who had won fame with her religious novel, *Robert Elsmere*, in 1888, and continued to combine an air of high seriousness with lightness in *The Marriage of William Ashe* (1905) and in *The Case of Richard Meynell* (1911). Israel Zangwill (1864–1926) was still writing with power and imagination about Jewish people and Jewish life, and in later life became a protagonist in the cause of Zionism. Eden Phillpotts (born 1862) was a sincere but rather perfervid writer about Devon scenes and Devon people who zestfully and regularly produced novels, stories, plays and poems for the greater part of half a century. At the age of sixty-seven William De Morgan (1839–1917) began to take the town by storm with a series of lively novels,[1] which proved that Victorian humour and expansiveness were still acceptable.

It is strange to recall that William Somerset Maugham (born

---

[1] *Joseph Vance* (1906), *Alice-for-Short* (1907), *Somehow Good* (1908) and several others.

1874), who is still actively producing books at the rate of about one a year, was already appreciated by discriminating critics in the first decade of the century. Indeed his first book, *Liza of Lambeth*, received and deserved praise more than fifty years ago (1897). He could reveal with a few touches the essentials of character and evoke feeling for place, had a sense for the crisis of situation which is so necessary to a short-story writer, and could produce telling effects with economy of language. In middle life he developed a facility for writing highly actable society plays which, for some time, probably diverted him from working on more subtle if less profitable books. Fineness of perception, skill in management, deftness of writing mark most of Maugham's novels and stories.

Our young adult, searching the review columns or listening to talk in Soho restaurants, would observe how earnestly the critics discussed the character-drawing in the psychological novels of the time—many of which were conscientiously realistic and severaly analytical. Lucas Malet (Mary St. Leger Harrison, 1852–1931) could be mordantly clever in describing the meanness of life and earnest in setting it against a background of idealism, as in *The History of Sir Richard Calmady* (1901) or *The Far Horizon* (1906). May Sinclair (died 1946), a highly talented, spirited and intellectual writer, suddenly sprang into fame with her novel *The Divine Fire* (1904), a story of passion whose unguarded writing was no handicap to its popularity. During the next ten years it was followed by much more subtle studies of feminine character in novels such as *The Helpmate* (1907), *Kitty Tailleur* (1908), *The Combined Maze* (1913) and *The Three Sisters* (1914). During the Great War and after her mind was much occupied by philosophy and mystical studies. (*A Defence of Idealism*, produced in 1917, showed how well equipped she was to discuss contemporary philosophy.) But in her study of mysticism she lacked the balance and steady insight of a remarkable woman, her friend, Evelyn Underhill (Mrs. Stuart Moore, 1875–1941) whose *Mysticism, a Study in the Nature and Development of Man's Spiritual Consciousness* (1911) revealed the learning, understanding and spirituality which in her were so rarely combined, and gave to the poems which she wrote from time to time depth and beauty. Another writer who was producing novels of distinction at this time and continued to do so at a high level between the World Wars was Mrs. Henry

Dudeney (died 1945).[1] She wrote with delicate perception and a sensitive style about Sussex people and Sussex scenes. Too seldom read or remembered to-day is a young writer, who could scarcely have belonged to any period but the decade before 1914, and died young—Stephen Reynolds (1881–1919). Consumptive, he found health in living as a fisherman in a fisherman's family in Sidmouth, and described the home and life of his friends in strong, simple, masculine language in *A Poor Man's Home* and *Seems So*.

There were many other books, of many kinds, calling for attention. That versatile writer, John Buchan (1875–1940) afterwards Lord Tweedsmuir and Governor-General of Canada, produced his first novel when he was an undergraduate at Oxford in 1898, and from his pen a stream of novels, histories, biographies and other books poured for thirty years, *Greenmantle* (1916) being perhaps the most pleasing of his adventure stories, and *Oliver Cromwell* (1934) the most distinguished of his biographies. How do justice in a few lines to Maurice Baring (1874–1945), that fastidious, piquant, versatile writer of poems, novels, plays, travel books and much besides who believed that practice in the art of living was the pre-requisite of success in the art of writing? In the realm of fantasy and dream the tales of Arthur Machen (1863–1947) were written with distinction and some charm, though he did not always escape the sentimental or the far-fetched. Conal O'Riordan (1874–1948), for a time better known as Norreys Connell, suffered throughout most of his life from spinal trouble caused by a fall from his horse. He was an interesting, romantic personality who produced many ambitious novels, plays and poems which seldom quite achieved their aim. Exceptions were his powerful short play *The Piper* and his novel *Adam of Dublin* (1920) which, with its sequels, had a considerable success. John Davys Beresford (1873–1947) made his reputation with *The Early History of Jacob Stahl* (1911), and maintained it with *The House in Demetrius Road* (1914) and *These Lynnekers* (1916), realistic novels written with much delicacy and skill; and wrote many subsequent books, but less effective. Compton Mackenzie (born 1883) gained distinction with *Carnival* (1912) and *Sinister Street* (1913–14), a book which shocked some

---

[1] Author of *The Orchard Thief* (1907), *Maid's Money* (1911), *The Secret Son* (1915), *Quince Alley* (1926), *The House in the High Street* (1931), and other excellent books.

readers and caused admiration in others by its frank dissection of youthful emotions. Since then he has written books of many kinds, forceful and highly individual, though he has scarcely fulfilled the promise of earlier days. Gilbert Cannan (born 1884) produced a romantic, passionate, but formless novel *Round the Corner* (1913) and two or three plays, and seemed to have qualities which might be those of a D. H. Lawrence in the making; but he never matured. W. L. George (1882–1926) with *The Second Blooming* (1914) might be taken as a precursor of the clever, flippant, satiric writers who were to be so much in evidence after the first Great war. No literary person in the first twenty years of the century could be unaware of the personality of Violet Hunt (died 1942), who wrote rather garish novels such as *White Rose of Weary Leaf* (1908) and macabre stories such as *Tales of the Uneasy* (1910); but her chief distinction lay in her social relations with the literary and artistic personalities of her time.

There was much activity in literary scholarship and much acute literary criticism during the first twenty years of the century, and some of the ablest practitioners have continued to work during the whole or a great part of the last fifty years. These two branches of study should not be identified, as they too often are, though they overlap. Literary historians are often indifferent judges of literature; a critic need not be one who has devoted himself to exhaustive factual research. Woe to him if he lays claim to a scholarship he does not possess! Sir Edmund Gosse (1849–1928) was widely read and a lively writer on literary subjects, and did much to arouse interest in Ibsen. When in a course of lectures *From Shakespeare to Pope* (1885) he ventured to cross swords with Churton Collins (1848–1908) on questions of fact he was judged to have had much the worst of it. His literary causeries in the *Sunday Times* for some years after the war were discreet adventures in contemporary criticism which added much to the liveliness of that journal. The career of George Saintsbury (1845–1933) on the other hand illustrates the discrepancies that may exist between scholarship and criticism. Saintsbury was a man of omnivorous reading, with a colossal memory and an untiring zest for literature, but his literary judgment was sometimes execrable. His *History of Criticism* (1900–04), his *History of English Prosody*

(1906–10) and other historical treatises and studies are mines of information still indispensable to students, and written with a gusto which makes them enjoyable. Sir Sidney Lee (1859–1926), who made no claims to be a critic, will probably always be remembered for his *Life of William Shakespeare* (first edition 1898) and his other Elizabethan studies. No less distinguished work in Elizabethan research was done by men like Sir Edmund K. Chambers (born 1866), author of *The Medieval Stage* (1903) and *The Elizabethan Stage* (1923), and that very able writer, W. J. Lawrence (1862–1940), whose researches shed light on the stage and the background of the Elizabethans. William Paton Ker (1855–1923) was both scholar and discerning critic.[1] Andrew Cecil Bradley (1851–1935) brought an acute critical mind to the study of Shakespeare in *Shakespearean Tragedy* (1904) and other books; and Sir Walter Raleigh (1861–1922) while ranking as a scholar, is memorable as a man of fine taste and humane appreciation who illuminated all that he touched.[2] The most distinguished Shakespearean scholar of to-day, still actively engaged in editorial work, is John Dover Wilson (born 1881), whose literary judgment and taste match his learning. Sir Arthur Quiller-Couch (1863–1944), who made his reputation in the last century as an historical novelist, and in later life (from 1912) was King Edward VII Professor of English Literature at Cambridge, brought taste and fine discrimination to his critical judgments of poetry and other literature. For half a century Gilbert Murray (born 1866. Regius Professor of Greek at Oxford University 1908–1936) has held a unique place as a humane interpreter of Greek life, a successful translator of Greek plays, and an inspiring defender of liberal causes. I regret that I can give no more than a sentence to that self-effacing man and faithful servant of literature, Ernest Rhys (1859–1946), who as the editor of *Everyman's Library*, backed by the publishers J. M. Dent, made the classics of all countries available to English readers in volumes issued at a popular price.

Some of the students I have just mentioned—to whom I should add Thomas Seccombe (1866–1923), a man of learning who poured forth what he knew with gusto and an engaging humanity—turned their attention, often or occasionally, to contemporary literature. They contribute their quota to the literary

[1] Author of *The Dark Ages* (1904), and *Essays on Medieval Literature* (1905).
[2] *Milton* (1900), *Wordsworth* (1903) and especially *Shakespeare* (1907).

background of the period. In the foreground were other critics, wrestling with the problems and controversies of their own age. There was William Archer (1856–1924), translator of Ibsen, pressing the claims of realism in the theatre before and after the turn of the century, himself writing one successful play, *The Green Goddess*. With Granville-Barker he worked out a scheme for a National Theatre (1907) which gave impetus to a movement enthusiastically started in 1908, drearily preserved for forty years, but now likely to achieve its end with the promise of Government support. A. B. Walkley (1855–1926) was a more lively and accomplished critic of contemporary drama, who first threw his weight on the side of Ibsen and his English disciples, but later, insisting that the theatre was a place for pleasure, refused to submit to the mesmerism of Shaw and those who would turn the stage into a battleground of ideas. Charles Edward Montague (1867–1928) was a versatile and perceptive writer whose criticisms of literature and drama adorned the *Manchester Guardian* for many years.

A ubiquitous intellectual influence behind the literary scene in London was Edward Garnett (1868–1937), a publisher's reader, reviewer, and writer of carefully considered 'intellectual' plays. The considerable influence he exerted was due rather to his persuasive conversation than to his writing, which was stilted and dull, and to the reputation he acquired as the discoverer of literary genius. It was undoubtedly he who first pushed the claims of Joseph Conrad. He was among the first to give encouragement to Galsworthy, D. H. Lawrence and, in late life, to H. E. Bates; but, since it was with him a cardinal element of faith that 'the muddle-headed British public' never recognizes a genius till he is dead, he was apt to be less enthusiastic in his regard for his 'discoveries' if they attained fame and fortune. Worldly success was for him the hall-mark of literary failure. His wife Constance as a translator and he as a critic did much to promote the appreciation of the greater Russian novelists in Britain. He preached incessantly that fiction should turn its back on the cant and false romanticism of the nineteenth century, and should face the harsher or more passionate realities of life with frankness and courage. Lawrence absorbed his words with devout and hungry attention. When asked by a too curious inquirer what was his own special subject in literature, 'The passions', Garnett replied, austerely.

7

The air was very full of 'movements' in the days when the young adult was feeling his way. We have already noted the voices of the prophets and the social or moral reformers, and the quieter tones of those who would give fiction its place among the arts. There were realists demanding a more exact correspondence between literature and all the facts of life, psychologists demanding a more minute analysis of human character, and intellectuals who insisted that art should not address itself to pleasure, but to the improvement of the human mind with important ideas. Hence what was called 'intellectual drama' as well as realistic fiction, and realistic or didactic poetry. And to prove, in that many-sided age, that nothing human was alien to them, the supporters of these doctrines gladly gave their attention to the protagonists of the Irish Literary Movement, who throughout the British Isles were proclaiming the advent of a Celtic Revival.

It would indeed have been strange if, in this lively period, men of ideas had not attempted to energize the theatre and to associate it with the literary and graphic or decorative arts. Already before the end of the nineteenth century Ibsen had been introduced to the English theatre, Oscar Wilde could get an audience, and Sir A. W. Pinero (1855–1934) had made his reputation with *The Second Mrs. Tanqueray* and other serious plays. William Poel (1852–1934), an actor, producer and authority on the Elizabethan stage, revealed new potentialities in the theatre when, with wonderful simplicity and dramatic restraint, he produced the old Morality Play, *Everyman* (1903); and with example and literary precept went on for many years advocating his ideas for the presentation of drama. Edward Gordon Craig (born 1872), a brilliant designer for the theatre and a powerful, though rather rhetorical, writer, throughout the whole of his life preached the necessity of treating the theatre as a temple of all the arts—the literary art, the scenic art, the art of movement or dancing, and music. In fact as designer and producer he was more active in Italy, Germany and Russia than in England; but his ideas and his example have had considerable influence on the English theatre for the last forty years.

In Ireland the identification of the literary and dramatic arts became a living reality at the Abbey Theatre, Dublin, the founding of which was financed by that imaginative Lancashire woman, Annie Elizabeth Horniman, in 1904. In 1908 she acquired the Gaiety Theatre in Manchester, which for several years provided a distinguished example of what could be done with a repertory theatre devoted to serious plays. There were produced the plays, including *Hindle Wakes* (1912) of that promising Lancashire dramatist, William Stanley Houghton who, born in 1881, died in Paris in 1913 at the age of thirty-two.

But it was in London, in 1904, at about the same time as the Abbey Theatre was being started in Dublin, that the young actor, producer and playwright, Harley Granville-Barker (1877–1946), financially assisted by Vedrenne, started his series of dramatic adventures at the Court Theatre in Sloane Square. This for some years was to be the home of what was known as 'intellectual drama' where the best literary men available who were ready to apply their talents to drama were to have an opportunity of seeing their work intelligently presented on the stage. Bernard Shaw provided the *pièces de résistance* of the programmes. One or two of Barker's own plays were produced there. *The Voysey Inheritance* (1905), *Waste* (1907) and subsequent plays *The Madras House* (1910) and *The Secret Life* (1923) showed him much under the influence of Bernard Shaw, but with an interest in his characters as individuals no less than as types, which in Shaw was rare. Plays by Galsworthy, John Masefield, St. John Hankin and many other notable writers were produced under the direction of Granville-Barker. The Court Theatre became a principal subject of discussion in literary circles, though the complaint was sometimes heard that the 'intellectual drama' which was staged there suffered from too much intellect and too little drama.

For Granville-Barker himself it was to be a stepping-stone to greater things. In other theatres later he was to have opportunities of showing how Shakespeare, studied by a man with some scholarship, himself endowed with creative imagination and taste, an actor experienced in the stage, who understood also the value of appropriate scenic embellishment, could be made to appeal freshly to the heart and imagination of a modern audience. In later years, having unfortunately fallen out with Shaw, he abandoned the living theatre, and went to live for the most part in Paris, where for two years before the last World War he was Director of the British Institute. But those later years of retirement from theatrical life were not wasted, even in the interests of the theatre itself. For Granville-Barker devoted himself to an intensive study of what he called 'dramatic method' (*On Dramatic Method,* 1930), and in particular to the plays of Shakespeare. His *Prefaces* to individual plays are illuminating studies in criticism, and are almost indispensable to intelligent actors. His *Preface* to *Hamlet* (1936), to take a single example, is a full-length study of the play based upon the consideration that Shakespeare was an actor-dramatist versed in the art of the theatre. He starts from the assumption that competent producers and actors must understand the whole movement of the play, must enter into the playwright's rendering of the characters, must appreciate his use of poetry and prose, and, in fact, be students of his complete art. The difficulties of dealing with a seventeenth-century play, which arise from different social conditions and also from over-familiarity, are, he finds, to some extent resolved by getting down to the acting side of the play; by remembering that an actor, Elizabethan or modern, is always an actor; that what we read in the text is put to the proof in actual production. Granville-Barker achieved something that had never been done before in the study of Shakespeare by virtue of the happy union in him of practical stage experience and a capacity, inborn and trained, to understand the mind and imagination of Shakespeare. His influence on drama and the production of drama has been profound and perhaps lasting. He has shown that the centuries-old gap between literature and drama can be bridged—that the theatre has no valid excuse for being unliterary and that dramatic literature requires for its fulfilment stage, actors, scene and audience.

But for our young adult embarking on the literary life in Edwardian England all the world's a stage, and the scenes are numerous, various and perhaps bewildering. Before we pass on to the next Act two more scenes must be presented, introducing other actors. There is the Irish 'Literary Revival', with W. B. Yeats as the principal person, destined to be in the lime-light almost to the end of the play. And secondly, there is a pageant of purely English poets whose verses to-day are like a swan song of the old order, a requiem to a tradition which, as some have thought, was to die with them.

Chapter Nine

THE IRISH LITERARY MOVEMENT

Yeats—Synge

A FEW years before the end of the last century a breath of wind blew from the west over England and made English readers aware of something new, strange and alluring, as novel in its way as the romanticism of Wordsworth and Coleridge had seemed a century earlier. Borne on this western breeze were voices, as if heard from afar, of minstrels singing songs of old times cherished in the minds of a living people. It was the beginning of the 'Celtic revival' and for Englishmen of new awareness of 'the Celtic Twilight', an expression derived from the title of Yeats's book published in 1893. For some time these words were used, often by people who had not read the book, to indicate something vague, misty, unsubstantial, like the romantical outpourings of the Highland Scottish poet, Fiona Macleod, who on his death was discovered to have been William Sharp. But this Irish literature, which was destined to make so deep an impression on the English as well as the Irish mind between 1900 and 1914, was to take on clear lineaments; it was to be at its best an expression of the Irish character in a unique moment of Irish history, when the more scholarly and more imaginative of the Irish nationalists were rediscovering the ancient history of their race and seeking both to revive its language and literature and write a new literature in the spirit and as far as possible in the language of the old.

Henry W. Nevinson, writing in the *London Mercury* in March 1939, just after Yeats's death, spoke of the effect which the young Irish writers had on Englishmen in the 1890's:

At that time there was something in the real Irish or Celtic nature that was wanting to our souls. It had been hinted to me a few years earlier by the great Celtic scholar, Kuno Meyer, who went about Ireland searching for old Irish manuscripts, long obscured in the peaty smoke of Irish cabins. And I had known the distinguished Fenian, old John O'Leary, when he was an exile in Paris, where I induced him to talk to me almost every night upon Ireland while we drank the innocent *mazagram* in a little café on the Left Bank. ' AE '[1] and Douglas Hyde, just then becoming a little known, helped our enthusiasm. But, true poets as both were, it was Yeats who fulfilled our vague and undefinable desire for something outside the limits of even the finest English thought and language in those days.

The Irish Literary Movement must not be identified with the political movement for Home Rule, but both came from the same impulse. It should be remembered that the political movement evoked widespread sympathy in Great Britain, and had the open backing of the official Liberal Party which ultimately passed a Home Rule Bill through Parliament and had it put on the Statute Book. But the literary movement, which early won the esteem of British readers, was watched through all its phases with intense interest without any intrusion of political feeling. Englishmen followed the activities of the Irish National Literary Society (founded in 1892), the Gaelic League (founded in 1893, under the presidency of Douglas Hyde, that indefatigable Gaelic scholar who strove hard if in vain to restore the use of the ancient Irish tongue) and the Irish National Theatre Society (1903); and it was an Englishwoman, Miss Horniman, who provided the money for founding the Abbey Theatre in 1904. Under the ægis of Yeats, Lady Gregory, Edward Martyn and a company of actors attuned to their spirit, the Abbey Theatre became the home of a distinguished drama which, if both drama and acting were taken into account, could scarcely be equalled anywhere else in the English-speaking world.

The men and the women who were protagonists in this movement were united by the sense of a mission—a mission to unearth what was inherent both in Ireland's memory of her past and in the life of the simple, unspoilt peasants of to-day; to reclothe the ancient heroes and make them live again in prose or verse; to penetrate to the beliefs and half-hidden secrets which lie behind the customs and superstitions of the folk; to submit to the romance which romantic stories engender and to reconcile this, if need be, with gritty realism—for perhaps Ireland was the one place in the world where the actual and the ideal were inseparable, or at least always contiguous. The language, too, was to be simple and racy of the folk. Since the old Gaelic was too difficult and too rarely

---

[1] Pseudonym of George William Russell (1867-1935).

understood, then a vernacular should be found which would be in essentials that of the folk, but slightly conventionalized for the purposes of literature. Lady Gregory (1852–1932) and J. M. Synge (1871–1909) laboured successfully to develop such a language, the one using it with rare humour and charm in her short plays, the other to more tragic purpose in such plays as *Riders to the Sea* (1903), or the tragi-comedy of *The Playboy of the Western World* (1907). George Russell (AE) felt the inspiration and was carried along by it in his lyric poetry, and in his play *Deirdre* which, produced in 1902, marks the beginning of the Irish Theatre movement. For AE the legends of Ireland stirred in every Irish scene, and his feeling for them, combined with his love of the occult and his mystic studies, led him as often to pantheistic imagery as to other-worldliness. Lady Gregory's *Gods and Fighting Men* (1904) and other records of Ireland's legendary past thrilled Yeats and peopled his mind with heroic figures. They moved in his imagination side by side with those of the recently living whom he added to the heroes. We can hardly think of Yeats without Lady Gregory and AE, or any of these without Synge, whom Yeats had first met in 1896 when Synge was a student in Paris. Around them were others—George Moore, first friendly and co-operative, afterwards hostile—many lesser poets and playwrights, and the players of the Abbey Theatre. But these four were the nucleus of what became a sacred company, a priesthood; they were guardians of the gods and fighting men and the mystical communion between a splendid past and the folk of to-day in whom they believed its spirit to be preserved; they had charged themselves with the duty of rendering the life and spirit of a race in a language which, while inspired by Ireland, would also lend itself to universal literature.

Synge was twenty-five years old, studying in Paris, when Yeats first met him. Yeats, thinking too much, perhaps, of Arthur Symons and other friends among the French Symbolists, recommended Synge to make a thorough study of contemporary French literature; but a little later, knowing him better, urged him to give up France and 'seek in the Aran islands a life that had never yet been expressed in literature'.[1] The advice was taken. He

[1] See *W. B. Yeats, 1865–1939*, by Joseph Hone (1942).

went to the Aran Islands, and to the Irish counties of Wicklow
and Kerry, and to the Congested Districts. He listened to the folk;
he studied their manners and speech; and out of this material,
though he had only eleven years of life remaining, wrote two
books descriptive of the places and people he had visited, some
poems and translations, and six plays by virtue of which he ranks
as a major dramatist.

The last of these, *Deirdre of the Sorrows* (1909), is the least satisfactory, because here he left the common folk whom he knew so
well and turned to the ready-made tale of the old heroic Saga
whose conventional trappings had inspired AE and Yeats, just as
the familiar tales of ancient heroes suited the genius of the Greek
tragedians; but for Synge they were an embarrassment, restricting
his fancy, and affording no scope for the grim humour which was
of his essence. It was Synge's forte, not to turn the heroes of
tradition into living men, but to make ordinary men into heroes;
to show the lives of common peasants with unsparing realism,
speaking their common speech racily, evoking the humorous
together with the intensely emotional, laughter moving side by
side with horror. Modestly, and no doubt rightly, in his Prefaces to
The Tinker's Wedding (1909) and *The Playboy of the Western World*,
he attributes half his success to the people of the time and place in
which he lived.

> Anyone who has lived in real intimacy with the Irish peasantry
> will know that the wildest sayings and ideas in this play[1] are tame
> indeed, compared with the fancies one may hear in any little
> hillside cabin in Geesala, or Carraroe, or Dingle Bay. All art is
> a collaboration; and there is little doubt that in the happy ages
> of literature, striking and beautiful phrases were as ready to
> the story-teller's or the play-wright's hand, as the rich cloaks
> and dresses of his time. It is probable that when the Elizabethan
> dramatist took his ink-horn and sat down to his work he used
> many phrases that he had just heard, as he sat at dinner, from his
> mother or his children. In Ireland, those of us who know the
> people have the same privilege. . . . In a good play every speech
> should be as fully flavoured as a nut or apple.

But his success sprang not only from the fact that in Ireland he
found 'a popular imagination that is fiery, and magnificent, and
tender'. He found that, and used it; but other Irishmen have

---

[1] Preface to *The Playboy of the Western World* (1907).

known it, too, and been led astray by it. Even Yeats, at times, in his youth, was seduced by its sweetness, its strangeness, its fancy. But Synge discovered also something else that lies at the very core of his genius and gives it strength. 'It may almost be said,' he wrote, 'that before verse can be human again it must learn to be brutal.' If I may quote words that I have used before, 'he does not mean the brutality of our English or French realists, or ugliness, sheer fact, miscalled truth, without beauty; what he wants is fidelity to *common* truth, a realization of the root, primitive facts— the most grim primitive facts—that hard basis of fact which must be accepted before the imagination can bear fruit'. In his greatest play, *The Playboy of the Western World*, there is a certain brutality of frankness even in the choice of theme, in which the audience at the Abbey Theatre, violently protesting, were not wrong in detecting a criticism of the Irish character. Who can say that to describe the romanticizing of a supposed murderer who boasts that he has killed his father, and the scorn that follows when it is found that the father was not killed, is not a criticism of a quality of the Irish? ('There's a great gap,' Pegeen alone perceives, 'between a gallous story and a dirty deed.') But who will say, on the other hand, that he is not as lavish with his praise when he shows the Playboy at the end driven on by the fire of imagination to display the very courage he is supposed to lack? The poetic spirit, after all, could be the spur to action. Pegeen perceives it. 'Oh my grief,' she cries, 'I've lost him surely. I've lost the only Playboy of the Western World.'

But it is something more than purely Irish character that Synge displays in the poetry and humour of his dialogue and the tense dramatic situations in which his persons behave. In *Riders to the Sea* (produced 1904), the whole of human nature is in Maurya, the 'old woman with one thing and she saying it over', who, lamenting the death of four sons by drowning, and becoming almost demented from fear that a similar fate will befall her remaining sons, hears of the death of the last of them with fortitude and is reconciled to her fate.

Michael has a clean burial in the far north, by the grace of the Almighty God. Bartley will have a fine coffin out of the white boards, and a deep grave surely. What more can we want than that? No man at all can be living for ever, and we must be satisfied.

It is an ending in the manner of Greek tragedy, and as universal.

William Butler Yeats (1865-1939) was at the centre of the Irish Literary Movement, and indispensable to its existence; it was fruitful in inspiration for him. But he transcended it, and lived long, at his best, after it had faded. The early influences in his life were not exclusively Irish. For twelve of his first fifteen years his parents' home was in London, though his most cherished memories were of the long holidays spent at the home of the Pollexfens in the Irish County of Sligo. In 1880 his father, John Butler Yeats, took his family back to Ireland, but again settled in England in 1887; and a few years later W. B. took a flat for himself in Woburn Buildings in Bloomsbury, and retained it for twenty-four years. This is not to say that in youth and middle age Yeats was not constantly in Ireland. He went to and fro between London and Dublin, and Dublin and Sligo and the western counties. His earlier literary friends were poets who lived in London, English and Irish—Dowson, Arthur Symons, Lionel Johnson, AE, John Davidson, Selwyn Image and Ernest Rhys—it was the last who, recognizing his sense for Irish lore, set him to compile a book of Irish fairy tales. It was in Ireland of course that he developed his enduring interest in legends, fairy tales and the supernatural, and his Irish friend AE encouraged his instinct towards the mystical. It was in Dublin that he joined the Hermetic Society, which was started to promote oriental religions and theosophy, but equally in London he pursued his inquiries into Buddhism, Spiritualism, and the occult in many forms, including astrology, and other researches that were to earn him a reputation for being a magician. But though an interest in the occult and in spiritualism remained with him throughout his life, and he was wont, like Blake, to talk familiarly about his spirit acquaintances, he kept such things in their place. His official biographer, J. M. Hone, asking whether he really believed in the occult, or was playing with fantastic images, replies that 'his poetic genius halted half-way between faith and simile, so as to preserve the sibylline quality of his own experience'.

But it was at least with enduring passion that he pursued his dream of Ireland, and his intellectual arguments about his dream; it was an element in his romantic relationship with Maud Gonne, the beautiful woman who loved political notoriety and adventure among revolutionaries in all the capitals of Europe; but it was

with a devotion practical as well as passionate that he set himself
to build up an Irish theatre in Dublin. The seduction of his
language and his romantic themes and the sweet distillation of
emotional experience moved English no less than Irish readers in
the nineties and made them aware of a new lyrical voice that had
a fay quality, a wild tenderness, something which, in Nevinson's
words, 'was wanting to their souls'. They heard him chaunting
(not chanting) 'a tongue men do not know'. They became
familiar with the 'Rose' symbolism which first appeared in

> Red Rose, proud Rose, sad rose of all my days!
> Come near me, while I sing the ancient ways.

and the deeper notes of Innisfree, and the sad lyrics of old age:

> When you are old and grey and full of sleep

and the eeriness they felt

> When we bent down among the fading coals
> And talked of the dark folk who live in souls
> Of passionate men, like bats in the dead trees.

and the wild love poems of *The Wind among the Reeds* (1899).

Here in one person seemed to be the bard of ancient times and
the accomplished poet who, while he was absorbing old Irish lore,
was moved also for a short time by the verse forms of Rossetti,
was enchanted by the ritual enjoined by Pater, and was giving
much of his mind then, as always, to William Blake. But at that
stage it was the Blake of *The Songs of Innocence* rather than of the
Prophetic Books who influenced his verse, as we may see in such
lyrics as *Never Give all the Heart*, which contains the same idea and
many of the words of Blake's:

> Never seek to tell thy love.

The ending

> For he gave all his heart and lost

lacks the poignancy of Blake's

> Ah, she did depart.

It is interesting that Robert Bridges, who wrote his best poems
in old age, should have advised the young Yeats to devote himself

more exclusively to verse, on the ground that youth is the time for poetry. It is true that the poetic vein which yielded *Innisfree* and the beautiful idealistic play, *The Countess Cathleen*, would never appear in the later years with the same softness and assonance. Yet as it turned out not only was Yeats to go on writing poetry all his life, but the best was to be at the last. It has been pointed out that his poetic career divides into three parts, like a Greek tragedy, with a beginning, a middle and an end. If so, the middle is less clearly definable than the beginning or the end. The practical activities in which he engaged, at the time when Irish drama was being put to the test at the Abbey Theatre, undoubtedly had much effect on his character. He was compelled to concern himself with the material details of the theatre (not excluding its finance), the training of actors and teaching them how to speak verse, and the political prejudices and frequent obstruction of societies and cliques in Dublin, some of them led by narrow-minded fanatics. Maud Gonne, too, often dragged him into a political atmosphere from which he would have preferred to stand aloof. When he experienced the pettiness of men in whom he might have expected comradeship and the excesses of some of the leaders of Sinn Fein he suffered disillusion, or rather release from illusion, and at the same time acquired a sort of worldly-wisdom, a capacity for judging life realistically, yet without loss to his imagination. He knew where his own strength lay, and was not to be easily diverted from his proper work—though we must remember that for him full living was always the necessary experience for the poetic life. When someone in the war period asked him for a war poem he replied:

> I think it better that in times like these
> A poet's mouth be silent, for in truth
> We have no gift to set a statesman right.

Yet when some men for whom previously he had had no great regard died in the Easter Rebellion of 1916 he could not but be profoundly moved, however little he agreed with their politics. Out of their sacrifice, however misguided, he was constrained to feel that 'a terrible beauty is born'. The spectacle of war in Europe and war in Ireland and quarrels between well-meaning men induced bitter reflection:

Things fall apart; the centre cannot hold;
Mere anarchy is loosed upon the world,
The blood-dimmed tide is loosed, and everywhere
The ceremony of innocence is drowned;
The best lack all conviction, while the worst
Are full of passionate intensity.

I cannot here discuss the part that Yeats played as a Senator, as eloquent public speaker, as defender of the lost cause of freedom from censorship in Eire, and an honoured elder in the State. In his later years he withdrew from public life, travelled, saw those friends he cared to see and pursued his vocation. Poetry meant not less to him now, but even more. He wrote with no less passion, no less imagination, but with far greater force. His gentleness gave place to a sort of ironic fierceness and grim frankness. Something hard and earthy was substituted for the softness of the romantic lyricism of his youth. This later thing had a sterner ring of truth, a virility, a grip on experience as a whole, and he found a new idiom and a new imagery with which to express it. He had not given up his dreams, or even his spirits, or his wilder flights of imagination; but it was now the imagination of a man who had trodden the earth, had known men and been undeceived about women (without ceasing to love them). His poetical excitement remains.

Never had I more
Excited, passionate, fantastical
Imagination, nor an ear and eye
That more expected the impossible.

In the last year of his life he was writing:

When a man grows old his joy
Grows more deep day after day.

He does not shrink from 'the foul rag and bone shop of the heart'. He compares himself to the Stilt-Jack who walks on high stilts in procession:

Malachi Stilt-Jack am I, whatever I learned has run wild,
From collar to collar, from stilt to stilt, from father to child,
All metaphor, Malachi, stilts and all. A barnacle goose
Far up in the stretches of night; splits and the dawn breaks loose;
I, through the terrible novelty of light, stalk on, stalk on;
Those great sea-horses bare their teeth and laugh at the dawn.

He read the younger modern poets, and was eager to understand what they were doing and seeking. But he insisted that great subjects were needed for great poetry, and that its true function was to evoke joy and minister to the emotions. 'The arts are all the bridal chambers of joy', he wrote in *On the Boiler*, and he even added that artists should praise or represent 'great or happy people'. 'To me it is a fundamental defect in modern art,' he said in 1938 to the present writer, 'that it too much provokes to thought; classical art engenders feeling.' For this reason it seemed to him that Ibsen was a sign of decadence and Bernard Shaw more so. He delighted in theorizing about art, but he had no patience with art which begins in theory—it will begin, he said, 'with the thing seen, and felt, the dream, it may be, the poetical facts'. Even in his youth

> Players and painted stage took all my love
> And not those things that they were emblems of.

The old man with his 'eagle eye', rejoicing in 'an old man's frenzy' went on to the end living his poetical life, looking askance at 'the cavern of the mind', peopling his world with images

> those images
> That constitute the wild,
> The lion and the virgin,
> The harlot and the child

writing with irony and measured vehemence, still respecting 'the aristocracy who are above fear, the poor who are beneath it, and the artists whom God has made reckless'. The whole of Yeats's life was the life of poetry, and each part enriched and added splendour to that which followed.

Chapter Ten

SOME ELDER POETS

Thomas Hardy — Charles Doughty — Robert Bridges — A. E. Housman—Gordon Bottomley

WE have seen that Ireland and the Irish literary movement provided inspiration for Yeats's poetry. Can we discern any corresponding influence in the work of purely English poets at the beginning of the century? Can we see any driving-force operative among the poets comparable with that which so evidently affected certain novelists and playwrights? Anyone looking round in 1900 or for several years after might have been at a loss for an answer. Of greater Victorian poets Browning and Tennyson were recently dead. The robust ballads of Kipling were still in men's ears, but he was to write nothing more of that kind to stir the rising generation. The *Yellow Book* writers were dead or *passés,* and their prestige had fallen. Robert Bridges was already admired for his accomplished verse, but no one could have guessed that, like that far greater poet, Yeats, he was to write his best work in extreme old age. Nor would anyone at that time have supposed that Thomas Hardy as poet might come to be ranked even higher than Hardy the novelist. It might almost seem that the taste of the age was reflected in the exorbitant praise that was showered on the artificial, grandiloquent and rather sickly verse of Stephen Phillips (1864–1915) exemplified in his poetic dramas, *Paolo and Francesca* (1899) and *Ulysses* (1902). The Poet Laureate, appointed in 1896, was Alfred Austin (1835–1913) than whom none of the versifiers who have demeaned that office wrote meaner verse. True, there was A. E. Housman (1859–1936), a lyric poet of a high order, but at that time he had produced only one volume of verse, *The Shropshire Lad* (1896).

And yet, as it turned out, the next twenty years were to be by no means deficient in remarkable poetry, and some of the best of it was to be written by old or elderly men—Hardy, Bridges

99

and Charles Doughty. Thomas Hardy (1840–1928) wrote all of
his great Wessex novels in the nineteenth century, and as a
novelist is outside the scope of the present work. But though he
wrote poems in his early youth, and at intervals during his novel-
writing period, it was in his last thirty years that he turned his
back on prose-fiction and devoted himself to his first love,
poetry, to whom in spirit he had always remained true. His
admirers are divided into those who rank his novels higher and
those who prefer his poetry. He himself is on the side of the
latter. To be a poet, to give his life to poetry, that had always
been his desire, and if he had been quite free to choose it is likely
that he would have written no novels at all. In later life he spoke
with the utmost impatience of those who insisted on regarding
him as a novelist rather than a poet, complaining of American
visitors who were wont to interrupt any remark about his
poems with: 'And now, Mr. Hardy, tell us something about
your *real* work.'

It is worth asking what Hardy was supremely qualified to do
in literature, whether prose or verse, and how far he achieved it
in either form. After examining his novels alone, and before his
best verse had been written or published, that very competent
critic, Lionel Johnson, writing in 1896, felt constrained to compare
Hardy, not with another novelist, but with a great poet—with
Wordsworth. That was a testimony to the poetic quality of his
mind, revealed in prose, by one who had never known that
Hardy could write poetry of a very high order in metrical form.
Poetic feeling and power are evinced in all the more moving
passages in the novels; Marty South's lament in *The Woodlanders*,
though written as prose, may stand as one of the superb, the most
moving, lyrics of the English language; and there are scores
of passages in the novels which have a comparable effect on our
minds. In spite of his own preference, we cannot lightly conclude
that the main work of his middle life was devoted to a second-
best; and I think it more likely we shall find that in the case of
a person so single-minded, so consistent as Hardy his poetry
sprang from the same impulse as that which inspired the best of
his novels. If we agree that the greatest works of any writer are
those which bear the most distinctive and ineffaceable imprint of
what is most essential in his mind and imagination, then we have
a touchstone by which to test Hardy's works. What are the

essentials that make him what he is? Arthur McDowall, writing
a critical study of Thomas Hardy in 1931, points to them, I
think, successfully. Alluding to that 'momentous opening chapter'
in *The Return of the Native*, which he justifiably describes as 'the
fullest achievement of Hardy's prose and, in its evocation of the
spirit of a place, unexcelled by any English prose', he says:

> These few pages have the gradual march of a symphony. Three
> strands are intertwined in it; a living sense of the heath, an ex-
> pression of Hardy's mind and a reflection of the lot of humanity.

There, then, are three elements which Hardy is supremely
qualified to show, which are found, separately or in combination,
in his best work—Nature, in her sweeter or her wilder moods;
Humanity, breathing and passionate; and Destiny, presiding over
all, cruel in its blindness. In his epic drama, *The Dynasts*, the
third element only is revealed with all Hardy's power, and we
shall expect some loss through the absence of the first and the
second. Even the Pities in this epic can never speak for humanity
with the sure voice of Marty South, nor does Nature reach us,
here, as it does through the spaces of Egdon Heath and the
forest-world of *The Woodlanders*. We must seek compensation
in the majesty of the impression which he has created in exhibiting
mankind in moments of crisis tossed hither and thither under the
presidency of the Unconscious Will.

But the sweeter and more human life comes before us again
and again in the short lyrical poems which Hardy went on writing
to the end of his life, and with more grip, more distinctiveness
as he got older. In his earlier poems he had been content to write
as the spirit moved, adopting the measures and something of the
manner of that other Wessex poet, Barnes, or using metrical
forms which clung to his memory from the reading of other
poets, Shelley or Tennyson or Hood or Browning. But in the
later lyrical poems there is a greater weight of experience, and
emotion arising from experience, a deeper undercurrent of
thought, and a variety and richness of diction. He uses common
words to convey uncommon ideas, and is not afraid of uncommon,
even uncouth words, if they serve his purpose, and still employs
West Country words which Barnes in his way had used just as
Burns used Scottish words. His lyrics do not all bear the mark of
a master of poetic language, and sometimes he is telling a short

8

story in verse where the significance of the story seems to count for more than the metrical manner of its telling. When he is writing under the impulse of strong feeling, of the 'vision' which evoked

> Certain starry thoughts that threw a magic light
> On the worktimes and the soundless hours of rest
> In the seventies

we see his mind calling upon new romance or stirring the embers of dead passion in a world still lit for him by imagination, warmed by sympathy, and turned by his sense of cosmic tragedy to pity or irony. When the feeling was less strong he had no sure tact in the use of words to preserve felicity of diction. Lionel Johnson pointed out that Hardy and Wordsworth 'both go lumbering over low ground, when they relinquish their accustomed heights'; but he might have added that much low ground that was too deliberately chosen by Wordsworth was for Hardy familiar and cherished soil which he could tread with unaffected joy.

> Any little old song
> Will do for me

he sang in one of his gayer moods—for Hardy could be gay, as Wordsworth never could. With that sort of freedom he approached many of his lyrical poems, with 'spontaneous utterance' (sought too unspontaneously by Wordsworth), moving from the low ground to the high. His 'vision' still came to him in his extreme old age.

> In the seventies naught could darken or destroy it,
> Locked in me,
> Though as delicate as lamp-worm's lucency;
> Neither mist nor murk could weaken or alloy it
> In the seventies!—could not darken or destroy it,
> Locked in me.

It has become customary to regard *The Dynasts* (published in three Parts in 1904, in 1906 and 1908) as the greatest of Hardy's works. In this long epic-drama, mostly written in verse, but with some passages of description and dialogue in prose, we have the grand summing up of his philosophy or vision of the world, its terrestrial denizens and its super-terrestrial rulers and onlookers. Hardy was not a trained philosopher, but he had read much philosophy and much history, and arrived at conclusions which alone, for him, seemed to fit the facts. This philosophy, this vision of the universe, was implicit in his novels and his shorter poems. Already in *Jude the Obscure* he had shown Sue Fawley imagining 'that the First Cause worked automatically like a somnambulist, and not reflectively like a sage; that at the framing of the terrestrial conditions there seemed never to have been contemplated such a development of emotional perceptiveness among the creatures subject to those conditions as that reached by thinking and educated humanity.' Everywhere percipient men and women were becoming aware, as they had not been in simpler ages, of an 'Unfulfilled Intention', or an 'unsympathetic First Cause'. This general vision of life dominates all Hardy's adult work; but he had started, as a creative artist should do, by showing us life first, the implication of life appearing from the picture as it develops; and the life through which he showed it in his novels had been that of the simple country people of Wessex, close to the soil, living much as their ancestors had lived for centuries. In *The Dynasts* he has the same vision to unfold, but the life through which it is to be seen is that of mankind in a momentous period of world history engaged in its terrestrial conflict, subject to 'It', the 'Immanent Will', the 'Inadvertent Mind', the 'Great Foresightless', and observed by the Spirits of the Years, of the Pities, of Rumour, the Spirits Sinister and Ironic, the Shade of the Earth and Recording Angels. *The Dynasts* is an epic-drama on a vast scale telling the whole story of the Napoleonic wars in so far as that struggle was between England and Napoleon; but it is not a story out of which a philosophy emerges, but rather a philosophy unfolded through the tragic events of this story. Thus it is essentially didactic; but it is not in consequence inartistic, for it proceeds by the method not of expounding, but of revealing through action and choral comment on action. Inevitably one compares it with Tolstoy's *War and Peace*; and instantly one observes that though Tolstoy is showing the stupidity of war and ambition the supreme interest of the work lies in a number of individual persons who are the victims of war rather than in the philosophic thesis. The reverse is the case in *The Dynasts*. There the cosmic theme is everything. The Napoleons, the Pitts, the greater and lesser characters who come on and off the stage are puppets; they exist only to prove the tragic, the ironic circumstance of pitiful mortals struggling against an irresistible and senseless Destiny.

I have suggested that of the three elements that give power to Hardy's work—his handling of Nature, of Humanity (as individuals), and the sense of Destiny—*The Dynasts* from the nature of the work affords little scope for the two first, and depends for its effect mainly upon the third. It must be impressive to succeed, and shock us into acquiescence. Many things go to make its impressiveness. Hardy has studied his historical material with meticulous care, and on that score he can stand up to the historians. He had pondered this historical material for half a lifetime, and had lived in it imaginatively. In his native county of Dorset he had talked to men who remembered the days when they were waiting for the Napoleonic invasion. He is intensely patriotic, in that he loves the people of his native land, yet he is singularly objective in his treatment of the protagonists, whether Napoleon or Vi'leneuve, or Nelson or Pitt, who are presented with biographical disinterestedness. He has welded together typical incidents in this long war into a complete, continuous epic story; and a story it is essentially, conveyed in a succession of scenes (described) and dialogue passages, with the constant comments of the Spirit onlookers who look aloofly, or pitifully, or ironically on the human puppets vainly defying the pattern imposed on them by the immanent Will.

It may be read as a story, and as a story it is not without compelling power. It is told mainly in verse, but by no means all of the verse reaches a high poetic level, though it never lacks vigour. There is much low ground over which it 'lumbers'. But the theme as a whole has been imaginatively seized, and the cosmic spirits of which Hardy is so conscious are never far away; and he has invented a language with which to make them speak, a language full of strange words, full of images which crowd fast one upon another with cumulative suggestive strength; as thus, in an early passage where the Spirit of the Years speaks:

Of our great-hearted young Compassionates,
Forgetting the Prime Mover of the gear,
As puppet-watchers him who pull the strings.—
You'll mark the twitchings of this Bonaparte
As he with other figures foots his reel,
Until he twitch him into his lonely grave;
Also regard the frail ones that his flings
Have made gyrate like animalcula
In tepid pools.—Hence to the precinct, then,
And count as framework to the stagery
Your architraves of sunbeam-smitten cloud.—
So may ye judge Earth's jackaclocks to be
Not fugled by one Will, but function-free.

There was no nineteenth-century poet, except possibly Hopkins, who employed imagery like that.

There are plains and peaks in *The Dynasts*—long stretches of dusty plain, but rewarding heights. There is humanity in the comic passages, but one misses humanity in his heroes. Nature, too, is seldom here as it is in his novels and lyrics; yet there are passages which only Hardy, the friend of Nature, could have written, even if Nature is taken out of its context. It is introduced with grim effect into the lines given to the Chorus of the Years, contemplating the field of Waterloo before the battle.

Yea, the coneys are scared by the thud of hoofs,
And their white scuts flash at their vanishing heels,
And swallows abandon the hamlet-roofs.

The mole's tunnelled chambers are crushed by wheels,
The lark's eggs scattered, their owners fled;
And the hedgehog's household the sapper unseals.

The snail draws in at the terrible tread,
But in vain; he is crushed by the felloe-rim;
The worm asks what can be overhead,

And wriggles deep from a scene so grim,
And guesses him safe; for he does not know
What a foul red flood will be soaking him!

> Beaten about by the heel and toe
> Are butterflies, sick of the day's long rheum,
> To die of a worse than the weather-foe.
>
> Trodden and bruised to a miry tomb
> Are ears that have greened but will never be gold,
> And flowers in the bud that will never bloom.

One might suppose that Hardy had felt beforehand the Great Wars that were to come, and that the Pities, foreseeing them, were praying that the unconscious Will should waken, and rouse Itself to 'fashion all things fair'. *The Dynasts,* for all its faults, is an imaginative conception of unique strength, necessary to the completion of Hardy's work. The wonder of that work is its completeness, rounded to his life.

Doughty (1843–1926) as a poet has been too little read, in his own life-time or since; there is gold in his poetry for those who will dig to extract it. Like Hardy, he resolved in early manhood to be a poet, and only in later years devoted himself to verse. In all that he did we seem to find him endeavouring to get to the rock-bottom of the realities which lay behind his studies—literally to the 'rock-bottom' in the study which engaged him as an undergraduate at Cambridge; it was geology; he went off alone for nine months to study glacier action in Norway. He laboured to probe the English language to its depths, learning Teutonic languages, mastering Early English, becoming versed in the poetry of Chaucer and Spenser and the contemporaries of Spenser; but not as a grammarian; his interest in what he regarded as the most virile period of English literature led him to study its subject-matter, and track down the sources of civilization, first among the antiquities of Europe, and then in the Holy Land and Arabia; everywhere studying the people and their way of life— geologist, antiquarian, humanist. The literary result of his long travels in Arabia—he went always dressed as an Arab Christian, being unwilling to pretend to be a Moslem—was his book *Travels in Arabia Deserta,* first published in 1888. It was at once recognized by William Morris and Robert Bridges as one of the great travel books of the world but was little heeded by the general

public till Garnett prepared an abridged edition in 1908. For
T. E. Lawrence this book was as a Bible, and inspired him to go
and do likewise.

But it is not with *Arabia Deserta,* which belongs to the last
century, that I am here concerned, but with Doughty, the poet.
On his return from the East he lived for some years on the
Riviera, and in 1899 settled down in the south-east of England.
His long epic poem, *The Dawn in Britain,* which he had first
conceived when he was living among the Arabs, appeared in
six volumes in 1906-07, and was followed by *Adam Cast
Forth* in 1908, *The Cliffs* (1909), *The Clouds* (1912), *The Titans*
(1916), and *Mansoul, or The Riddle of the World* (1920).

Of *The Dawn in Britain* he writes that 'its Anglecism, or
linguistic horizon, is that nearly of the days of Spenser'. To the
ordinary reader his language will seem a little less modern than
Shakespeare's, but more so than Chaucer's. His vocabulary is full
of strong, shaggy, Saxon words, but his use of archaisms and
expressive exotic words present no real difficulties to an interested
reader. The metre he employs is blank verse, strangely stressed
and rugged, marvellously responsive to the changes in his theme.
His subjects are always the simple, the elemental, or the vast, and
the abundant imagery which lifts them into poetry is concrete and
startling by its rare combinations. Even when the speakers are
spirits, as in *Adam Cast Forth* and *The Cliffs,* the words they use
are earthy, though perhaps unearthly in their significance.

The language he employs is something all his own, in which
you can feel the days of Chaucer or Spenser, though it is neither
Chaucer's nor Spenser's. I do not mean that it is an invention such
as Joyce used in *Finnegans Wake,* evolved out of his own inner
consciousness primarily for himself alone; it is a language perfectly intelligible, arrived at by one who has deliberately turned
from a literary language which he feels is losing its potency, and
has, firstly, soaked himself in sixteenth-century literature and the
Authorized Version of the Bible, and, secondly, transplanted
himself into the life of a half-primitive community by living
among Arab nomads, people dwelling to-day in the desert like
the children of Israel. He knew the ways and thoughts of simple
people, and the language fitted to express the actions and fundamental emotions of which they are capable. He was fully conscious
of what he was doing; he knew in his own way what T. S. Eliot

was to discover later, that the language and imagery of contemporary poetry had become stale from imitation and repetition. The enemy of the British is made to say, in *The Cliffs*, concerning English writers:

> They imitate now each other, till they dwindle,
> Like the images of opposed looking-glasses,
> Barocco too! to inane nothingness.
> 'Tis nigh not credible, how they are untaught,
> In their own tongue. They seem to think it hath,
> Nor dignity nor honour!

And elsewhere he speaks of a bardism 'like Abana and Pharpar, nearly run-out to the dregs, and unwholesome pools in the desert'. His own ideal is expressed in the *Post Illa* to *The Dawn in Britain*:

> It is idle to imagine, that any man not a well-taught lover of his tongue, can enter into the Garden of the Muses.
>   Further, it is the prerogative of every lover of his country, to use the instrument of his thought, which is the Mother-tongue, with propriety and distinction; to keep that reverently clean and bright, which lies at the root of his mental life, and so, by extension, of the life of the Community; putting away all impotent and disloyal vility of speech, which is no uncertain token of a people's decadence.

Never did writer adhere more faithfully to his own standards. Moreover his themes were as splendid as his language. In *The Dawn in Britain* he has no less an aim than the unfolding of the drama of Britain's life from the fourth century B.C. to the time of the destruction of Jerusalem—in all, about 450 years. It is the work of a man of simple Christian faith, of inexhaustible patriotism, with a warm sympathy for folk groping towards civilization, whether Christian or heathen, and in all cases faithfully rendering scenes and action as he conceives them to have happened. It is an epic narrative of heroes and great events, told in language which never fails to be virile and arresting and at moments of crises reaches poetic heights. No less ambitious is *Adam Cast Forth*, a poetic drama of about the length of an ordinary play, in which his theme is taken from the Judæo-Arabian legend of Adam and Eve (Adama) who, cast forth from Paradise, meet after long wanderings upon a mountain. Adam tells Eve the story of his sufferings:

> Still seeking thee, shut up
> Mine heart in anguish, I like worm, crept forth;
> Till lean my flesh and dry was, as a leaf.
> I cried to heaven, loud calling, by their names,
> Angels of Succour, which we knew in Eden:
> But void returned my voice to me again!
> I asked of wide-spread ground, dim glowing rocks;
> And whirling fiery blast, which full of shrieks
> Was in my peaceful ears! where Adama was?
> And was there none that answered. Day and night-time,
> I hearkened, and I might not hear thy voice.
> I saw thee oft, in sorrow of vast Night,
> The swoon of sleep, I wist not whither, pass;
> In sun-beat and most desolate wilderness!
> Thy form beheld; but seldwhiles thy loved face.

In his poetic drama *The Cliffs* Doughty did not shrink from dealing with contemporary Britain at a time (1909) when some were already thinking in terms of a possible German invasion; and we see in one vision the country people of Norfolk, sophisticated rulers in Parliament, and celestial beings (Sirion, 'divine shining One from Heaven', Truth, and a company of Light Elves) who are no more out of place in this setting than are Puck and Oberon in the Shakespearean play or the spirits in *The Dynasts*. This book is full of memorable expressions: 'men-rocks, harder than granite'—'skew-eyed, wall-eyed men, venemouss'—'catterpillar-crinkled leaves in Spring'—'Men's rushlight wisdom'. The word *rock* best conveys the character of all Doughty's work—his mind is like a rock; he quarries in a mine of rocky facts and rocky words; and the result is like something sculptured out of intractable granite—a thing of the past and the present, and the past in the present, and so, we feel, of all time.

Bridges, born 1844, and dying 1930, was a near contemporary of Hardy and Doughty, and like them wrote his best poetry in late life. At Oxford he was a friend of Gerard Manley Hopkins, and these two we may be sure discussed poetry and the possibility of new verse forms in which both were so much interested. Religion and prosody—these may often have been subjects of their conversation. Having studied classics and philosophy, and

given some attention to theology, Bridges curiously enough
elected to be a doctor and indeed for a short time actually followed
the profession of medicine. But he was not tied to it by the need
of earning a living. Music and poetry engaged his leisure, and he
continued to read Greek and Latin and make a serious study of
the French, German and Italian languages; and from 1882
onwards he lived for the most part in the country, enjoying a
life of learned leisure, and cultivating his own muse. He made a
close study of verse forms and especially the prosody of Milton,
and experimented with metre and rhythm with a view to attain-
ing more elasticity in verse. He studied Aristotle, copied Shelley
and made use of Milton, and by his Italian studies sought to
introduce into the English language some of the richness of vowel
sounds, attempting perhaps to achieve by study what Rossetti
had done by nature. In the work of his early and middle life, in
dramas, masks and shorter poems, he attained a consistently high
level of metrical excellence. Conventional critics discerned in him
all the virtues; he had vigour, sweetness and unfailing elegance;
his similes were apt, his versification faultless; his very simplicity
was that of a scholar; and his ingenuities were reasonable ingenuities. He could write serious poems on Greek themes with
classical aptitude; light lyrical poems which were musical and
pleasing; and could turn a triolet or a rondeau with grace, and
even made something by no means intolerable written, according
to rule, in Latin hexameters or pentameters. And he could be gay.

> Je donnerais pour revivre à vingt ans
> L'or de Rothschild, gloire de Voltaire,
> I like that: Béranger in his printems,
> Voltaire and Rothschild! But of old Voltaire,
> I'd ask what Béranger found so sublime
> In that man's glory to adorn his rhyme.
> Was it mere fame?

There was some surprise when he was made Poet Laureate in
1913. Yet there was a far greater surprise when in 1929 at the age
of eighty-five he produced a long poem, *The Testament of Beauty*,
which far surpassed anything he had done before, and indeed
belongs almost to a different order of poetry.

It is a didactic work in the same sense that the *Georgics* of
Virgil or the *De Rerum Naturæ* of Lucretius or Pope's *Essay on*

Man are didactic works; it has a persistent thread of argument about mind and matter, duty and pleasure, God and art; yet the texture is poetry; it advances by statements which spring to life through imagery; and the long similes in which it abounds often invest gravity with rare beauty. Here, we feel, are the conclusions to which all the experiences of a long life have led in a mind which still thrills responsively to outward beauty, and with even more intensity than in youth. The poem as a whole, full of poetic zest no less than wise reflection, gives point to the lines in the Introduction:

> 'Twas late in my long journey, when I had clomb to where
> the path was narrowing and the company few,
> a glow of childlike wonder enthral'd me, as if my sense
> had come to a new birth purified, my mind enrapt
> re-awakening to a fresh initiation of life.

He never loosens his hold of his argument, which in fact is his confession of faith, his account of man's excellences and failures, of the 'mystic rapture' which is the source of wisdom and beauty, and his justification of the claim that

> Verily by Beauty it is that we come at WISDOM,
> yet not by Reason at Beauty.

And in this recital we do not feel it to be an irrelevance that in speaking of the archæologist

> who yesteryear sat down in Mesopotamy
> to dig out Abram's birthplace in the lorn graveyard
> of Asian monarchies

he should linger in delight to describe the finds:

> Drinking vessels of beaten silver or of clean gold,
> vases of alabaster, obsidian chalices,
> cylinder seals of empire and delicat gems
> of personal adornment, ear-rings and finger-rings,
> Craftsmen's tools copper and golden, and for music a harp;
> withal in silver miniatur his six-oar'd skiff,
> a model in build and trim of such as ply today
> Euphrates' flowering marshes; all his earthly joys
> gather'd to him in his grave, that he might nothing lack
> in the unknown life beyond, but find ready to hand
> his jewel'd dice and gaming board and chamber-lamp,
> his toilet-box of paints and unguents. . . .

It is a diversion just such as that which again and again delights us in the *Iliad*, easing the burden of argument or narrative. The production of this poem in extreme old age comes near to being a major contribution to twentieth-century poetry.

The best known work of Alfred Edward Housman (1859–1936), *A Shropshire Lad*, belongs to 1896, but his *Last Poems*, published in 1922, and some of *More Poems* (1936) show undiminished power, and suggest that if he had been less occupied in the scholarly labour of editing Manilius, Propertius, Lucan and other Latin authors, and had been less convinced, in his creative moments, of the fatuity of human life, he might have held a much more important place among the poets of his time. With the severe views that he held it needed a period of 'continuous excitement', mysteriously alluded to by himself, to unloose his tongue in the simple, lyrical poems dealing with primitive themes in musical language, with a sweetness broken by irony and the tang of cruel disillusion. Music came to him under the stress of emotion, but controlled by his scholarly sense for metre, and saved from any possibility of prettiness by his sense of irony, his conviction of the transitoriness of beauty and of love, and his haunting awareness of the approach of death. Anticipating more famous lines written by Laurence Binyon he writes with envy of

> The lads that will die in their glory and never be old.

What could be more pessimistic than the late poem in which he recalls 'other summers':

> They came and were and are not
> And come no more anew;
> And all the years and seasons
> That ever can ensue
> Must now be worse and few.

Yet strangely enough even the cruellest pessimism which thrust itself into his most charming ballads is not depressing; for we are in the presence of a strong if obstinate character, who finds exultation in his pessimism and his power of turning beauty into pain, pain into contempt, and both into accomplished verse.

A word here about Gordon Bottomley (1874-1948) is, I think, appropriate, though he was a good deal younger than the four poets I have just discussed. If he had been an Irishman he might have become a great poet and something more than a distinguished writer of romantic poems and poetic dramas, work on which he was conscientiously engaged throughout an active literary life of fifty years. If he had been born in Ireland the inspiration which he undoubtedly drew from Yeats and the 'Celtic Twilight' would have had a real background in racial history and legend; lacking that, he fell back on the dream reality which he discovered through literature and the less substantial stuff of fancy. His earliest work (published 1897) shows distinct traces of the influence of D. G. Rossetti, but soon Yeats must have become the dominant influence, though his reverent reading of writers of the past helped to mould his style—Æschylus, Shakespeare, Milton, the Ibsen of *Peer Gynt,* old Scandinavian literature, and English and Scotch ballads. If we should attempt to place him in relation to the life and ideas of the time in which he lived we could only do so negatively; he is elusive because he so much withdrew himself from the life which we think of as real life, and chose to live in a world of his own peopled with figures of the past who, in his imagination, have become larger than real men and women, more tragic, if possible, more fantastic in some cases, more grotesque, creatures born of dreams fashioned with gem-like exactitude, symbolic persons who stand for aspects of humanity; he handles his tools with scrupulous care and loving attention to words and the sound of words. An escapist? In a sense, yes, the escape in his case being from common sense into uncommon sense, from the trite into the significant, the marvellous. The world in which he moved was a sort of transfiguration of reality, and what this is to him he seeks to render faithfully in fit language. Reading his poems we see him developing from within outwards, using as the raw material of his experience what has come to him from literature, legend, myth, and investing the life that he does see around him with the quality of legend and myth, showing man in the round, larger than life, more heroic or more villainous, more elemental. He absorbs this raw material into his imagination the more effectively because sense-perception plays an intensely active part in his mental make-up; he is remarkably responsive to the impact of the physical senses. Touch, visibility, sound, even odour provide him with strong images which keep his poems within reach of the ground. In *The End of the World* (1907) all the senses combined to give images of a dreadful world of snow and enfolding, desolating cold.

> The coldness seemed more nigh, the coldness deepened
> As a sound deepens into silences;
> It was of earth and came not by the air;
> The earth was cooling and drew down the sky.
> The air was crumbling. There was no more sky.

He deals in portents and magic and heroic happenings, and in human life rarefied and universalized. None the less there was a certain practicality in his make-up which enabled him to use his art effectively for the purposes of communication. The second half of his literary career was devoted mainly to poetic drama, and he succeeded where so few modern English writers have succeeded, in making poetic dramas which were really dramatic, and actable on the stage. He experimented successfully in the writing of short pieces in verse which lent themselves to intimate presentation, and choric plays with symbolic characters, where the effect of poetic speech could be enhanced by rhythmic movement, music, and simple but artistic scenery and costume. In the best of his longer plays, *King Lear's Wife* (1915), *Gruach* (1921) and *The Riding to Lithend* (1909) he shows heroes and heroines under the influence of a powerful passion, at a moment of critical action, and in a scene of romantic grandeur; by concentrating on the single action and the dominant passion he secures unity, speed and sustained interest. In these striking works, our incredulity suspended, we hear echoes from the Celtic Twilight resounding in remote and legendary places.

Chapter Eleven

'GEORGIAN' POETS

OF the five poets whom I have just been considering four
—Hardy, Doughty, Bridges, Housman—pursued rather
lonely paths. They did not belong to groups, could not easily be
assigned to a school, and stood somewhat apart from the stream
of contemporary literature. Bottomley, too, was for some time
a solitary figure in the world of letters, but a little later, drawn to
other poets by mutual sympathy or a common interest in poetic
drama, he was to some extent associated with the group which I
must now mention. Flourishing in the reign of George V, it
came to be known as the 'Georgian Group', though in fact some
of those who were thought of as belonging to it were unconscious of the association, and the qualities for which they were
distinguished are various. In so far as some of them thought of
themselves as the heralds of a new age, opening a new era in
poetry, they have come under the ridicule of their successors
who see them as imitators of the past, or ostriches with their
heads in the sand—original only in ignoring all that was most
representative of their time. Robert Graves, who at one time was
himself claimed as a member of the group, has written amusingly
about them in his book *The Common Asphodel* (1949): 'The
Georgians' general recommendations were the discarding of
archaistic diction such as "thee" and "thou" and "flower'd" and
"whene'er" and of poetical constructions such as "winter drear"
and "host on armed host" and of pomposities generally. . . .
In reaction to Victorianism their verse should avoid all formally
religious, philosophic or improving themes; and all sad, wicked,
café-table themes in reaction to the nineties. Georgian poets
were to be English but not aggressively imperialistic; pantheistic
rather than atheistic; and as simple as a child's reading book.'
Their subjects were to be 'Nature, love, leisure, old age, childhood, animals, sleep . . . unemotional subjects.'

Such is the rather severe account of Georgianism given by one
who has certainly grown out of it. The poets generally attributed
to this group are roughly those whose work is exemplified in five

volumes of *Georgian Poetry*, dated respectively 1911–12, 1913–15, 1916–17, 1918–19, and 1920–22, edited by 'E. M.'. 'E. M.' is Sir Edward Marsh who died in 1953. The poems given in each volume were drawn entirely from the publications of the two, or three, years shown in the title. In the Prefatory Note to the first it was stated that 'this volume is issued in the belief that English poetry is now once again putting on a new strength and beauty'. It was hoped that it would 'help the lovers of poetry to realize that we are at the beginning of another "Georgian period"'.

The poets whose work was represented in the first number were: Lascelles Abercrombie, Gordon Bottomley, Rupert Brooke, G. K. Chesterton, William H. Davies, Walter De la Mare, John Drinkwater, James Elroy Flecker, Wilfrid Wilson Gibson, D. H. Lawrence, John Masefield, Harold Monro, T. Sturge Moore, Ronald Ross, Edmund Beale Sargant, James Stephens and Robert Calverley Trevelyan. Most of these names reappeared in the second volume, but to them were added Ralph Hodgson and Francis Ledwidge. In the 1916–17 volume we find for the first time W. J. Turner, J. C. Squire, Siegfried Sassoon, J. Rosenberg, Robert Nichols, Robert Graves, John Freeman, Maurice Baring and Herbert Asquith. The 1918–19 volume added Francis Brett Young, Thomas Moult, J. D. C. Pellow, Edward Shanks and Fredegard Shove. In 1920–22 we meet also Martin Armstrong, Edmund Blunden, Frank Prewett, Peter Quennell, V. Sackville-West, Richard Hughes and William Kerr.

In the last volume of the series the editor stated that he had 'tried to choose no verse but such as, in Wordsworth's phrase:

> The high and tender Muses shall accept
> With gracious smile, deliberately pleased.'

That expresses well enough the Georgianism of the most Georgian of these poets—the 'gracious smile' they evoke, their acceptability to the tenderest of Muses. In reading this list of representative poets we must conclude that if the quantity of poets engaged is in any way equalled by their quality the period must indeed have been one of great poetic 'strength and beauty'.

But the first thing one is compelled to notice—and it is to the credit of the editor and the period—is that several of the poets included might well have been disengaged from the group,

so little do they essentially belong to it. What on earth, we may
well ask, is G. K. Chesterton doing here? His rollicking, cheerful,
contemporaneous verse, so spirited, so unliterary, has nothing
whatever to do with the 'Georgian' spirit. And D. H. Lawrence,
so impassioned, so lawless, so assertive—what has he to do with
these rarefied ones, these poetry-minded reincarnations of the
poets? And Robert Graves, again, with his restless, idiosyncratic
mind—can he be placed among all these writers of such estimable
verse? And James Stephens, does he not belong more properly
to the world of Irish romanticism?

And there are one or two, we feel, who cannot easily be
allotted to any group, who were poets before genius began in
1911, and remained poets when it stopped in 1922. Among these
the one who seems to me to be surest of a lasting place in English
literature is Walter De la Mare (born 1873). When we first
come to his poetry we are delighted by the deftness and variety
of the versification, the simplicity and purity of the language,
and its elfin fancy. We read on, and find the triumphs repeated
again and again. Here is genuine lyrical quality, with a strange
enchantment, that of a haunted place—one is reminded of
Coleridge, of Edgar Allan Poe, but it is different; there is a
graciousness which comes from delight in the sights and sounds
of the country, in the coming of sunlight and darkness, in children
and old people, but it is mingled with a kind of apprehension as
of another world existing side by side with the world of everyday. What he describes he sees very clearly and expresses in the
simplest of words, yet as if it had its being in a dream which was
the higher reality. In his introduction to *Behold, This Dreamer!* he
says: 'All lyrical poetry beats with the heart, tells not of things
coldly and calmly considered, but of things seen and felt in a
sudden clearness of the senses, and with a flame in the thought';
and adds: 'Every imaginative poem . . . resembles in its onset
and in its effect the experience of dreaming'. The dreamland
which gives the atmosphere of so much of his poetry has in it a
kind of magic which is sometimes eerie, sometimes elfish, sometimes quaintly humorous with the topsy-turvy-dom of children's
fairyland. His faculty for bridging the border between waking
and dreaming, between reality and fantasy, and with a most
admirable invention, is as apparent in his prose as in his poetry—
for instance, in that perfect book for grown-up children, *The*

9

Three Mulla-Mulgars (1910), peopled with characters whose very names make poetry:

> Thumb, Thimble; Thimble, Thumb,
> Leave your sticks and hurry home:

or

> Tough old Dubbildideery.

And none could have been so well fitted to write about Lewis Carroll, author of *Alice in Wonderland*, as he did so charmingly in 1932. His poetry is always Wonderland brought to earth, or the earth transfigured by Wonderland, and with such skill in the management of metre, as in the famous *The Listeners* (1912).

> 'Is there anybody there?' said the Traveller,
> Knocking on the moonlit door;
> And his horse in the silence champed the grasses
> Of the forest's ferny floor:

And few have ever so successfully welded the grotesque with the profoundly pathetic, to the enrichment of the emotion.

> Owl and Newt and Nightjar,
> Leveret, Bat and Mole
> Haunt and call in the twilight,
> Where she slept, poor soul.

Exquisite in his own domain, De la Mare is admittedly limited in his range; but he is certainly not limited by the boundaries of 'Georgian' poetry.

Nor is William Henry Davies (1871–1940). Davies is one of those natural singers in the English language who from time to time seem to have grown out of the soil since the days when 'Sumer is y-cumen in' was first recited or sung in the thirteenth century. There have been hundreds of Nature poets who went out to find Nature. But it was Nature that found Davies. His experience was authentic experience gained in the days when he wandered (for several years in America) as a 'tramp', sleeping in the open air, at home with beast and bird, hobnobbing with the roughest of companions, hungry, falling in love, but also finding delight in the reading of seventeenth-century poets. He has told the tale in his book *Autobiography of a Super-Tramp* (1908) which Shaw was responsible for commending to a publisher and the literary public; and soon it was discovered that he was a poet writing verses fresh and sweet with a spontaneity amazing in that self-conscious time, with a sort of childlike wonder at nature's recurrent marvels. Now they remind us of the melodies of Herrick, now of the *Songs of Innocence* of Blake, not, it is true, sustaining the perfection of the first, or reaching the unearthliness of the second, but with a direct response to simple beauty surpassed by neither of them. He was wholly unsophisticated, and remained so for many years in spite of association with other writers. His work was too effortless to be consistently good, for he had little critical apparatus by which to judge it, and only his intuitive liking for literature and his own sensibility to guide him. But there are some dozens of his lyrics so lively in music and feeling, so engaging to a sensitive ear, that their survival can hardly be in doubt.

Nor can Laurence Binyon (1869–1943) or Thomas Sturge Moore (1870–1944) properly be classed as 'Georgian' poets, both having made reputations in the Edwardian period and earlier, though both willingly associated themselves with younger men who were winning their spurs. Sturge Moore was a delicate, sensitive writer, much influenced by Keats; he wrote, more especially, on classical themes, with taste and feeling. Binyon to his contemporaries seemed to be a man of remarkable all-round culture, with sound judgment and refined taste; and in his earlier books these qualities might have seemed to indicate the limit of his poetic powers. Among the more notable of these was a dramatic poem, *Attila* (published 1907), a well-constructed play in which there is vehement blank verse and speed of action; but the passionate dialogue, for all its fitness of phrase and imagery, is so Shakespearean as to make us feel that it is a copy rather than an original. Yet the profound feelings which were stirred in Binyon during the first Great War led to some short pieces which were among the most moving poems produced by any of the writers of that time, and one of them at least is unforgettable, containing the stanza which begins:

They shall grow not old, as we that are left grow old.

In his last years he was saddened but not spiritually weakened by the coming of the second War. During that period we may think of him, retired from his active life at the British Museum, living in an ancient farm-house on a high down set in a garden well filled with flowers, a scholar, a poet, translating his Dante into English, remembering old pleasures and dreams and contrasting them with a grievous present, perplexed by this war as he had been by the last, writing poetry out of the fullness of his experience, as Yeats and Hardy did in their closing years, labouring up to the last to reflect the glow of fires still burning. *The Burning of the Leaves and Other Poems* (published posthumously in 1944) were written under the shadow of war, which seemed to penetrate all other life and twist awry the more normal pageant of birth and decay among natural things. They present various aspects of his experience—the sense of the transience of things which he gets from the burning of withered flowers and leaves, 'all the spices of June' gone, 'all the extravagant riches spent and mean', recalling other splendours of 'the world that was ours' and is 'ours no more'. Yet for him, as for Robert Browning, nothing that is past is ultimately gone. Even in the 'black ruins' of war and the mocking of old laughter he has still the heart to think of Man as 'the proudest ruin', and to rejoice

> because no furnace will consume
> What lives, still lives, impassioned to create.

He writes at this stage only when his perception is charged with deep feeling, but at the same time with scholarly fastidiousness. This student of Dante has a sense for the just word and its sound. At the end he touches greatness, coming nearer than before to those splendours he often sought in vain in the earlier days on whose brightness he looks back with regret. Perhaps that was because:

> A memory floating up from a dark water,
> Can be more beautiful than the thing remembered.

It looked at one time as if Lascelles Abercrombie (1881–1938), so far from being a typical Georgian, might be destined to bring into English poetry a certain hardness and virility, much needed at that time, to steady his feeling for beautiful words and give body to his intellectual reflections. In an early poem *Mary and the Bramble* we see him in his gentler mood; the philosophical conception of the mortal in human beings struggling to drag down the immortal is treated allegorically, with beautiful poetic imagery. We can if we like forget the allegory in this story of the virgin 'in her rapt girlhood' with 'eyes like the rain-shadowed sea':

> Feeling not the air that laid
> Honours of gentle dew upon her head.

But his next poem, *The Sale of St. Thomas*, is full of lines of Elizabethan energy. He tells

> Of monkeys, those lewd mammets of mankind

and of flies staring

> Out of their faces of gibbous eyes.

But in the long run the intellectual and critical side of Abercrombie's mind was destined to prevail over the poetically creative; and though he continued to write interesting verse his later years were devoted mainly to criticism which was both philosophical and imaginative.

John Masefield (born 1878), who has been Poet Laureate since 1930, has been an active figure in the literary life of England for forty years, though he has scarcely fulfilled the promise of his youth. In his teens, a shy and sensitive boy, he went to sea and endured a rough life in ships and foreign ports; the impressions he gained of tropical waters and luxuriant tropical coasts have enriched the many admirable stories he has written of the sea or tropical countries—of which *Captain Margaret* (1908), not uninfluenced by Conrad, is perhaps the best. In his early twenties he attracted attention with his *Salt Water Ballads* (1902). *Ballads* (1906) where, though his style was obviously influenced by Kipling, the experience and the sweetness were all his own; and a little later he produced the best of his plays, *The Tragedy of Nan* (1909). At the age of about thirty-two or thirty-three he seems to have felt it his duty to turn his back on the imaginative themes which had hitherto attracted him, and make poems on some of the graver, or more sordid, aspects of modern life treated in an up-to-date realistic form. In other words, he seems to have made up his mind that he too must not shrink from joining the company of the 'prophets', in the sense in which I have used the term. The result was a series of long narrative poems—*The Everlasting Mercy* (1911), *The Widow in the Bye-Street* (1912), *Dauber* (1913), *The Daffodil Fields* (1913)—each of which delighted the general public because it pleased them with a stirring story and gratified them with an excellent moral. In middle and later life Masefield did not frequently adopt this mode; but he had become a prophet, and that is a difficult role to abandon.

The Georgian poets, *qua* Georgian, seem to be vanishing under our hands. Which are they, where, as defined by Graves and suggested by E. M.? F. S. Flint, with his *In the Net of the Stars* (1909) and *Cadmus* (1915), perhaps yes. Also James Elroy Flecker (1884–1915), best known for his *The Golden Journey to Samarkand* (1913), and *Hassan*, published posthumously. Rupert Brooke (1887–1915), judged by his Rugby and Cambridge verse, fits as well as any into the Georgian pattern. But Brooke was no more than what seemed at the time a splendid possibility—his was precocious talent, brilliant facility, glittering youth, and an early reputation a hundred times enhanced by his death in the Mediterranean in April 1915—leaving these lines for his countrymen:

> If I should die, think only this of me:
> That there's some corner of a foreign field
> That is for ever England.

And the talented John Collings Squire (Sir John Squire, born 1884) would have fitted well into the picture if he had written only ostensibly serious verse, whereas in fact there was the spice of wit in his parodies and he wrote innumerable sensitive appreciations of contemporary writers who were congenial to him. For many years between the wars he wrote a literary causerie every week in the Sunday newspaper, the *Observer*. In 1919 he founded a literary magazine, the *London Mercury*, and continued to edit it till 1934. The poets whom he gathered into his genial circle—he liked the Georgian aroma—talked and wrote their verses and he printed them in his magazine. (In 1934 it was taken over by the present writer, but by that time poets of a different order were arriving, and it was these who made their contributions to the *London Mercury* during the five years before the second World War).

John Freeman (1880–1929) contributed many poems to Squire's journal, but earlier under the impact of the first Great War he had written a few more memorable, of which *The Stars in their Courses* (first published in 1914 in the short-lived *New Weekly*) has a certain splendour of form and feeling. What Charles Hamilton Sorley (1895–1915) might have become we cannot tell. His poetry (*Marlborough and Other Poems*, published posthumously) is that of a boy writing with sensibility and fineness and a touching confidence in his nation's cause—he died in action before he had time to develop an original style. Julian Henry Grenfell (1888–1915) writing before the full sordidness of war was known, voiced the gallant spirit of the young who went into battle longing to live or die for country:—

> And he is dead who will not fight,
> And who dies fighting has increase.

He was killed in action. So was Wilfrid Owen (1893–1918); but he was to experience uglier phases of the war; yet of all the young who died in action he best expressed the splendour and pity of the sacrifice. Another poet, not quite so young, Siegfried Sassoon (born 1886), was moved by the horror and gruesomeness of the slaughter to strike away from the gentler conventions and denounce the senselessness of war in ironical, embittered verse. But his poetic temperament, reacting rebelliously against the cruelty, found its most ample expression in the prose works written later, *Memoirs of a Fox-hunting Man* (1928) and *Memoirs of an Infantry Officer* (1930). Similarly with Edmund Blunden (born 1896), his poetry for the most part scarcely rises above the gentle Georgian, but in his book *Undertones of War* (1928) he was one of the first Englishmen to describe in prose, well modulated and eloquent, the terror and ugliness of war's realities and its effect on sensitive, courageous and finally disillusioned youth. More tempestuous, more bitter, more original both in his poetry and in his prose was Robert Graves (born 1895), in whose early verse we already begin to observe the new impatience with stale traditional images, while his prose account of the war, in *Goodbye to All That* (1929) was a piece of vehement writing which strips from that war any shreds of glamour that might be left.

And finally, there was Edward Thomas (1878–1917), an older man who was killed in the war, who had lived the irksome life of a gifted and inadequately rewarded littérateur, and surprised the reading public after his death by leaving a volume of poems whose passion and eloquence lifted them much above the accomplished work by which he had formerly been known.

And so we leave these so-called Georgians, most of whom defy the classification, and pass into a world of a very different complexion.

Chapter Twelve

INTERIOR VISION

D. H. Lawrence—James Joyce—Dorothy Richardson—Virginia Woolf

THE revolutions that have been turning the world upside down in the last fifty years are all one revolution—a moment only in the history of mankind, though it seems long-drawn-out for us who are living in it and already able to distinguish the earlier phases from the latest. We have seen how the Butlers, the Shaws, the Wells's, the Galsworthys and others had been teaching their countrymen to throw over the obsolete ideas and dogmas of the nineteenth century, and imbibe new conceptions of freedom and self-assertion; and we saw with what eagerness and naïve optimism intellectuals and social reformers set out to build a brave new world believing that they could adapt all the wonderful changes that science, invention and economic knowledge were introducing into our midst to the needs of a quickly progressing society, marching under their guidance towards the millennium. The earlier years of the century seemed wonderful years of achievement and hope. In breaking with tradition it seemed that society was throwing off its chains. There was movement at a tremendous pace. But could the mind of humanity stand the strain? Could its mental and spiritual make-up adapt itself to these colossal changes in the outer form of the world?

Even before the first Great War there were signs that perhaps it could not. Those who can remember the two or three years that preceded 1914 agree about the restlessness of those days—the excitement aroused by a Post-Impressionist exhibition was not very different in kind from the excitement which led militant suffragettes to march on Whitehall. The Italian Marinetti, denouncing *Passé-isme* and proclaiming *Futurisme*, was rivalled by the English artist Wyndham Lewis, with his Vorticism and 'Rebel Art Centre'; and round the corner, in the sphere of poetry, were writers like Ezra Pound and Richard Aldington, turning from *passé-isme*, and announcing their ambition

To smash the false idealities of the last age.

It was a moment when men and women resorted readily to violence In the industrial field there were strikes and threats of strikes. In politics the promise of Home Rule to Ireland threatened to lead to civil war in Ulster. And then came real war to turn all the energies of the nation in another direction.

I am only concerned with the literary manifestations of this restlessness which raised the temperature in England as I think it did in other countries of Europe. We see it in literature as a sense of maladjustment leading to efforts at readjustment. Up to this point the literature of the new age had been concerned in the work of clearing the ground of dead matter, exploring failures in the organization of society, laying bare what was obsolete in moral standards, ridiculing hypocrisy, and sometimes preaching the religion of a generous, instinctive humanism. Along these lines it had gone as far as it could go in handling externals; it had proceeded in broad daylight in dissecting the visible, tangible world of behaviour; even when the method had been psychological it was with a psychology which explained the outward show of action. It had been straightforward and easily intelligible. It had exhibited the chemistry of social revolution, and individual reaction to change. But it had not yet carried the revolution into the mind itself. That was soon to come. In the next phase the conflict was to take place inside the individual mind; the revolution was to be staged in the mysterious recesses of the soul; the hidden parts of the conscious or even the unconscious were to be dragged into the open, and the readjustment, if any were possible, was to be made within the privacies of the percipient or suffering mind. Literature had revealed a restlessness writ large in the life of society, and the young men and women who had absorbed it had not far to go in discovering the same restlessness writ small in the soul. It needed no Freud to teach them this, Freud himself being only one manifestation of the consciousness of his time.

David Herbert Lawrence (1885–1930) should be put at the very centre of the dark current of feeling and perception which seemed for a time likely to overwhelm English literature and profoundly alter its character. Not that we should think of him as an explorer like James Joyce, deliberately adopting a new technique in order to express something hitherto unexpressed, still less as a pioneer, like T. S. Eliot, bent on finding a new idiom with which to re-interpret life. If ever there was a man for whom writing was 'spontaneous utterance' that man was D. H. Lawrence. It almost seems as if the only fully consciously directed effort he made was in the initial act of releasing himself from the inhibitions which restrain ordinary men, so that what he wrote came like an instinctive cry wrung from him by the joy, the anguish, the fear or the doubt which his spirit experienced under the varying impact of life. As artist he yielded himself completely to his own sensitive temperament, and the current carried him along. He belongs to the same order of beings as Emily Brontë, a wild creature obeying instincts, fierce and gentle, passionate and submissive, tempestuous and placid by turns. He was a romanticist whom circumstances compelled to behave like a realist. He was a Christian, driven into the camp of anti-Christians; a moralist, doomed to have his books condemned for immorality; an ordinary man who got trapped in a corner as a rebel and was forced to sustain the character. Never a very original thinker he stumbled upon certain ideas which were becoming current and clung to them tenaciously. An idea coldly expressed is a new thing when it turns into a conviction passionately lived. With a few such ideas he became possessed and poured them forth in the torrent of his novels, poems and letters. The words in which he clothed them derive their character from his sensitiveness to beauty and his immense emotional vitality.

The son of a coalminer, born in an unlovely mining village in Nottinghamshire, he was saved from the worst harshness of circumstance by the devotion of a mother, whose memory was a warming influence throughout his life. Delicate in health and in danger of consumption he was unable to follow his father's vocation; won a scholarship at Nottingham High School; and after an interval as a clerk spent two years at Nottingham University College studying to become a teacher. He passed first in all England and Wales in the Uncertificated Teachers' Examination. From 1905 to 1911 he was an elementary school teacher at Croydon. From what we know of his mother and early associates we may be sure that his youth was not starved of books and ideas. Yet we must not forget the proletarian setting. Lawrence was a man who grew up with a working-class consciousness, seeing life from the worker's point of view, not without some prejudice against what is thought of as privilege, and prepared to resent 'superiority' whether it was intellectual or social. Something of this resentment remained with him throughout his life, and partly accounts for that challenging, provocative attitude which led him to exaggerate every view he entertained.

His duties as a school-teacher did not prevent him from writing poems and stories. Ford Madox Ford had the perspicacity to see his merit, and published stories of his in the *English Review*. His first book, *The White Peacock*, appeared in 1911; *The Trespasser* in 1912; and his best-known book, *Sons and Lovers*, in 1913. In this powerful novel there are many crudities, yet it succeeds because he is handling a theme wholly within his competence. He knew the mining village which he describes, and brings it to life. He had felt its ugliness and the beauty of the near-by country in which he had so often walked. He tells the story of his own life and two women who deeply influenced him; one, his mother; the other, the girl Miriam, refined, spiritual, nunlike whose love could give and demand the utmost for the mind but grant nothing to the flesh—here already we have the conflict between body and spirit which was to be the major obsession of his whole life and of his books. The problem which is henceforward to afflict him is already stated, crudely but clearly, in the letter which Paul, exasperated and desperate, writes to the too ethereal Miriam:

> May I speak of our old, worn love, this last time. It, too, is changing, is it not; Say? has not the body of that love died, and left you its invulnerable soul? You see, I can give you a spirit love, I have given it this long, long time, but not embodied passion. See, you are a nun. I have given you what I would give a holy nun—as a mystic monk to a mystic nun. Surely you esteem it best. Yet you regret—no, have regretted—the other. In all our relations no body enters. I do not talk to you through the senses—rather through the spirit. That is why we cannot love in the common sense. Ours is not an everyday affection. As yet we are mortal, and to live side by side with one another would be dreadful, for somehow with you I cannot long be trivial, and, you know, to be always beyond the mortal state would be to lose it. If people marry, they must live together as affectionate humans, who may be commonplace with each other without feeling awkward—not as two souls.[1]

[1] *Sons and Lovers,* Chapter IX.

There already we have the idea which later he was to re-express again and again in more exaggerated terms, as in that strange book, *The Man Who Died* (published in 1929), where he speaks of what he imagines to be the Christian ideal of loving bodylessly, 'with the corpse of love', contrasting it with 'the reality of the soft warm love which is in touch, and which is full of delight'.

At about the time when he was writing *Sons and Lovers,* or just after, he came much under the influence of Edward Garnett, who accepted him as a 'genius' and urged him to fulfil his mission and write of the life that he knew, and especially the passionate life, with candour and fearlessness. Under this influence and many others which were in the air in 1913-14, the young Lawrence, son of a miner, just escaped from school-teaching, began to think of himself as a priest ordained to deliver his message to the world, and if need be to say the forbidden things without reserve. In a letter to Catherine Carswell[1] written a year or two later he said: 'the essence of poetry with us in this age of stark and unlovely actualities is a stark directness, without the shadow of a lie, or a shadow of deflection any where.' That spirit of determined candour was to bring him trouble, which only made him the more determined to avoid a 'shadow of a lie'. His book *The Rainbow* was banned for indecency in 1915, as was *Lady Chatterley's Lover* thirteen years later. With the naïveté of a provincial, his head a little turned by sophisticated praise, he had responded impetuously to that mood of the time which favoured gestures of freedom from inhibitions and the assertion of the excellence of the passionate life. But some of the same leaders of literary opinion who had showered praises on him at the start deserted him when he went a little further in exploiting the qualities they had praised. But by this time he was converted to a complete belief in himself. He had a 'demon' which was leading him on. With simple self-assurance he pursued the same or similar themes in *The Lost Girl* (1920), *Women in Love* (1921), *Aaron's Rod* (1922), *Kangaroo* (1923) and in that more interesting attempt at reconstruction, *The Plumed Serpent* (1926). Many circumstances of his life combined to make him feel frustrated and rebellious. During the war he was

---

[1] Author of *The Savage Pilgrimage: A Narrative of D. H. Lawrence* (1932), an appreciative and sensible corrective to much of the gush that has been written on Lawrence.

twice rejected for military service on grounds of health, and he could have been under no suspicion as a 'conscientious objector'; but he was embittered by his ejection from a prohibited area which was due to his marriage to a German wife and his known views about war. The banning of *The Rainbow* deprived him of royalties and markets for his work, and he was constantly in straits for money. In 1919 he left England for Italy, and spent most of the remainder of his life in Italy and New Mexico, visiting Australia in 1922. But his disappointments and frustration never destroyed his confidence in the 'demon'; those who have represented him as a 'tortured soul' living in anguish are challenged by Catherine Carswell, who insists that 'he had far too magnificent a talent for enjoyment, far too fine a capacity for work, to be miserable in the true sense of misery, which is dreariness, regret, sterility and doubt'.

In a book on Swinburne the French critic Georges Lafourcade, who wrote so excellently about English literature, pointed out that in 'the simple, straightforward manner' in which Swinburne treats the deepest sexual impulses he was a forerunner of Lawrence. That, I think, is true in the sense that the excellence of both lies in their power to extract exaltation out of the life of the physical senses—*all* the physical senses, and not merely those connected with sex. When Lawrence in one of his poems writes:

Oh but the water loves me and folds me,
Plays with me, sways me, lifts me and sinks me, murmurs:
 Oh marvellous stuff!
No longer shadow!—and it holds me
Close, and it rolls me, unfolds me, touches me, as if it never could
 touch me enough,

we notice the likeness to Swinburne, except that Swinburne would never have fallen to 'Oh marvellous stuff!'

In Swinburne's essay on Blake there occurs a relevant passage, not I think mentioned by Lafourcade: 'Let no reader now or ever forget that while others will admit nothing beyond the body, the mystic will admit nothing outside the soul.' But Blake denied the reality of the distinction between body and soul; the physical thing for him was not a symbol; it was already completely spiritual. For him, demanding the union of body and soul, there was no need to mortify the flesh to gain access to the spirit.

What mortified the flesh must also mortify the spirit; the joy of the one was the joy of the other. Lawrence never perceived this essential unity, and was conscious only of opposition. He might, it is true, appear to be using the language of Blake when he wrote:

There is only one evil, to deny life

words which might be taken to mean that when the flesh is mortified, as Miriam had asked Paul to mortify it, there is a maladjustment of life; and that is a denial of it. But he really goes much further than that; he differs fundamentally from Blake in that he emphasizes the dualism of body and spirit; there is always a conflict between the two. He sees modern civilization ranged on the side of a spiritual which has become 'respectable', 'superior', 'gentlemanly' against healthy bodily instincts imprisoned and stifled. That way, the way of sensual abnegation, meant, in his view, impotence, not sexually only but of the whole man. The main concern of his novel *Women in Love* is to show disaster consequent on the abnegation of the flesh under the tyranny of an apparently spiritual ideal.

Lawrence, championing the cause of the frustrated, finds himself cast for the role of a rebel. At every point contemporary civilization presents the arch-enemy to be resisted. Thus in *Pansies* (1929):

Why have money?
why have a financial system to strangle us all in its octopus arms?
why have industry?
why have the industrial system?
why have machines, that we only have to serve?

and again:

The young today are born prisoners,
poor things, and they know it.
Born in a universal workhouse,
and they feel it.
Inheriting a sort of confinement,
work, and prisoners' routine
And prisoners' flat, ineffectual pastime.

He is constantly girding at the 'superior persons'. He gives a series of 'Don'ts'.

Don't be a good little, good little boy
being as good as you can.

How angry he can be! How querulous and crude in his complaints! Yet with what sensitiveness he responds to the stimulus of beauty, with what gusto he abandons himself alike to the description of joy or the equally energetic description of pain. For all his ill-health he was intensely alive. No doubt there was restlessness, even fever, in his impassioned activity. However unbalanced his views, he usually escaped morbidity because he was buoyed up by his sense of a mission—to stand up against the condemnation of the elemental instincts, to assert the splendour of the physical life when it was sanely enjoyed; and it may be that he was reassured also by that more reconstructive element in his faith which, according to Dilys Powell, was the 'pivot of his work'—'the idea of renewal and resurrection'. 'Lawrence sees civilization dying round him; very well, then, it must die, but it shall be reborn, and so with each man and woman.'[1] Lawrence loved his theorizing; it was necessary for his mental well-being to round off the picture of the mission to which his life was dedicated. In the mystical he swims in seas of words, but all the time, with the words, it is the senses that he touches rather than the mind. There is only one doctrine that he fully masters and illustrates—the doctrine of the essential purity of the body for the pure, and the impurity of those who would deny it—the beauty that comes through the medium of what can be touched and seen, the conflict that comes from its denial. All this was one-sided, unbalanced, because he was a rebel against the opposite extreme, and also because he was no thinker. But by dint of his vitality, his acute sensibility and the 'demon' which gave him eloquence his prose and his verse vibrate to his vision of the secret places, showing life distorted, perhaps, but still alive. His work is not great literature, but it has importance beyond its intrinsic merit in expressing some essential characteristics of his age. English literature had to produce at that time at least one D. H. Lawrence.

But there were other, and bigger fish to come out of that turgid sea. James Joyce (1882-1941) was Irish, not English, but Ireland in his young manhood shared the literature of England and many of her problems; and Joyce, for all his intensely Irish subject-matter, stands in the main stream of literature as it was

[1] *Descent from Parnassus* (1934), by Dilys Powell.

running at that time in Britain and Ireland. And he stands there consciously. He knows what he is about. Lawrence drifted with the stream, and as if by accident found himself near the centre. But Joyce, abundantly equipped with knowledge, fought his way through to the conclusions by winning his experience, arguing all the way, and then by deliberate plan. He set himself the task of building in a certain way, and left his work, the finished product of intuition and reason, for the world to contemplate. No accident here. This was a design, a planned revolution to by-pass a world lulled to sleep by a secretive morality and an outworn art.

His reputation rests upon two very long books, *Ulysses* (1922) and *Finnegans Wake* (1939). *Anna Livia Plurabelle* appeared in 1930, and *Haveth Childers Everywhere* in 1931. A book of simple poems was published as early as 1907, and his volume of short stories, *Dubliners,* received and deserved some attention in 1914. The long fragment of an autobiographical novel published after his death, *Stephen Hero,* tells the history of Joyce's undergraduate life at the National University in Dublin; he put that work aside and re-wrote the whole story in the brief, highly finished novel, *A Portrait of the Artist as a Young Man* (1916).

There is nothing revolutionary in this fascinating book except in the decision taken by the hero at the end. It is an account of the struggle in the mind of a youth sent to study at a Jesuit college with the prospect before him that he may become a priest, and of his subsequent career at the University. The style is swift and direct. There are scraps of realistic conversation which serve to bring the dreamer down to earth. The prose in a few passages becomes poetic and exalted. We are aware of the tension in the mind of young Stephen Dedalus, the crisis approaching, precipitated by the vision of a young girl on the sea-shore, which draws from him 'an outburst of profane joy'. 'To live, to err, to fall, to triumph, to recreate life out of life! A wild angel had appeared to him, the angel of mortal youth and beauty, an envoy from the fair courts of life, to throw open before him in an instant of ecstasy the gates of all the ways of error and glory. On and on and on and on.'

So far he may not seem to have gone further than D. H. Lawrence, except that his release is not from vague inhibitions, but from precise religious dogmas and a way of life which had been for him the subject of studious reflection. But it is only at the end of the book, when Stephen, a university student, has gone further on the road of experience and study, that he makes the decision of his life. He tells a fellow-student that he has 'lost the faith'.

Look here, Cranly, he said. You have asked me what I would do and what I would not do. I will tell you what I will do and what I will not do. I will not serve that in which I no longer believe, whether it call itself my home, my fatherland or my church: and I will try to express myself in some mode of life or art as freely as I can and as wholly as I can, using for my defence the only arms I allow myself to use, silence, exile and cunning. . . . And I am not afraid to make a mistake, even a great mistake, a lifelong mistake and perhaps as long as eternity too.

So he turned his back on Dublin and went to live in Paris that he might the better shake off the distraction of Dublin life and see it from afar. He must not be thought of as a man primarily in revolt against the accepted order of society—had he been just that the traditional techniques of literature might have been adequate. What he is concerned about is not to alter society but to *see* it in what he believes to be a truthful way—to get a clear impression in his own mind, as Benedetto Croce would have said, of the substance of life and then to render it in language which will translate the interior vision. To express his impressions, as Croce put it, that was his intention, as it was with Pirandello, though the result for the latter was a very different thing. But not merely was Joyce to present the spectacle of life through his interior vision; that vision, in his own mind, included the interior vision of each of his persons. The eight hundred pages of *Ulysses* (in the edition I have before me) deals with but a single period of twenty-four hours in the life of Dublin, where the hero, Stephen Dedalus, and Mr. Leopold Bloom (to whom we are first introduced with the information that he liked 'thick giblet soup, nutty gizzards, a stuffed roast heart, liver slices fried with crust-crumbs, fried hencod's roes') and a host of middle, lower-middle and working-class Dubliners are observed going through their day in streets, shops, offices, restaurants, bars and brothels; and we observe not so much what they do but what they see, think, feel and furtively surmise. To him all these people are as naked as the Emperor in the fairy-tale. The stream of impressions which passes through the mind of each person is dragged to the surface no matter how muddy it is, how profane, how obscene—that is what the man looked like walking through Dublin—that is what he was, God help him.

The spectacle is of all sorts. At one time we get the impression of youthful exaltation in excited and endless argument, as when Stephen unfolds his theory of Hamlet, and Russell insists that 'the supreme question about a work of art is out of how deep a life does it spring'. Sometimes there is full-blooded derision of sentimentalism (which to Joyce was the accursed thing)—'The sentimentalist is he who would enjoy without incurring the immense debtorship for a thing done.' Lord Tennyson is always Lawn Tennyson (the recent traditional poets were no more loved by Joyce than by W. H. Auden). But it cannot be denied that the spectacle of the exalted is far more rare than that of the profane, obscene and indeed the filthy. When Joyce looks into the mind and holds up his vision to the mirror he sees what Freud was disposed to find, the obscene sexual animal everywhere emerging from the depths. If this indeed is what the civilized world really is when its inner secrets are dragged into the daylight it is not surprising that censors asked that we should avert our eyes and hide the horrid truth. And then, of course, is it the truth?

It is only at first that the book makes really difficult reading. Ordinary grammatical English is not in Joyce's view fitted to express the flux of ideas that pass through the mind of Mr. Leopold Bloom or Buck Mulligan or Gerty MacDowell. We get a succession of images indicated by single words or half-formed sentences or twisted quotations—that is how the mind proceeds before the flux of ideas is reduced to order—and Joyce aims at presenting the whole of life, both external and as it gushes up from the depths of the unconscious, in all its wild disorder. There is no sparing of fastidious feelings, nothing held in reserve; the quality of the work lies in the fact that here at last a tract of life as seen by Joyce is brimful of a buoyant and boisterous life of its own; however much we may dislike it its vitality is beyond question. It is horrible, but it is masterly.

If *Ulysses* is comparatively easy to read, not so *Finnegans Wake*, published in 1939, on which he had worked hard for sixteen years. In the former we have already the beginnings of the Joycean language—the short-cuts, the unfinished sentences, the onomato-poeic words of the interior monologue. But in *Finnegans Wake* the language appears fully developed as a thing of his own invention, though no doubt for him the process of invention was gradual; strange words were needed to construe the strange images in his mind; in proportion as the images in his mind were distorted from the normal so the words which indicated them became distorted from the shape of ordinary words. This lively, boisterous, grotesque language of his invention was doubtless that in which he thought when he was composing and presenting the dream of an Irish day. The reader might well be excused if at first he thought he was reading gibberish written in joke, as Lewis Carroll wrote the poem of the Jabberwock. But a man of Joyce's calibre does not sit down for sixteen years to write several hundred thousand words of intentional gibberish. Foreseeing the difficulty he assured the anxious reader that there need be no doubt ('no idle dubiosity') about the book's 'genuine authorship and holus-bolus authoritativeness'. The best first approach to it is through the ears, not the eyes. To hear passages recited—the ideal reciter was Joyce himself—was to find words that had seemed terribly obscure springing to life and evoking vehement responses in the imagination. Without that assistance the reader, if he thinks it worth while, must prepare for hard work. He has not merely to tackle the vocabulary with its twisted and fantastic words, but also the lightning changes from narrative or description to reflection, from one time and place to another, from the view-point of one person to that of another or to that of the author himself.

The wake of Finnegan provides the peg for a theme which is to be coextensive with the whole of that life in which Joyce is interested. The subject-matter is manorwombanborn—a punning term which expresses humanity in the raw as seen by the author, mostly on the seamy or ridiculous side—men drunken, or sus-pected of crime, or in the dock, or lawyers, or judges or respect-able, self-righteous persons—women sentimental or desperately unsentimental, but in any case reduced to the lowest common denominator of their sex. 'I will try to express myself,' Stephen said in *A Portrait,* 'as wholly as I can.' 'To see life foully' is an expression used in *Finnegans Wake* in misquotation of Matthew Arnold. His shunning of the conventional language of literature corresponds to his attitude to that which it expressed, the conventional, surface valuations of life, and especially those of the moralist or sentimentalist, or, among writers, 'those crylove fables fans who are "keen" on the pretty-pretty commonface sort of thing you meet by hopeharrods'.

But if so many of the people guyed with so much gusto in this book are coarse, drunken, criminal, hypocritical, hypercritical, self-deceiving or ridiculous, the author himself, we feel, is psychologically disinterested; he is not in the least concerned about the goodness or badness, ugliness or beauty, of his remarkable world, but merely concerned to show that it is like that—you may take it or leave it. He is a scientist describing the objects revealed by his mind-searching microscope—his joy is in the fact that he is able to see them wriggle, not that they wriggle. And this is where he differs to an important degree from Swift, whom in some respects he so much resembles. Swift knew that he was presenting a caricature, that is to say, an exaggeration of the beastliness of the human race. Joyce, making humanity no less beastly, has not the least idea of exaggeration—that, for him, is exactly what men are like. He shows the caveman himself springing out of the depths of the civilized man, and all the worse because he is civilized.

Joyce could scarcely have shown his contempt for the human race more thoroughly than by devoting sixteen years of his life to writing a book in a language which no one can completely understand. But his sense of the comic was no doubt richly tickled by the knowledge that he was providing texts for industrious Joycean students to exercise their wits upon for years to come. The field of linguistic research is widened—offering, shall we say, in the choice of subjects, ancient Irish or modern Joyce? Those who choose the latter will find something gritty, really gritty, to get their teeth into. For he wrapped up his vision in a maze of words which his fantastic imagination had distorted from their familiar shapes. He heaped these words together in tangled skeins which can only be unravelled so far as we can follow the gambols of his darting mind. He set some pretty jigsaw puzzles for sophisticated people to talk about. But the book is 'holusbolus authoritative', which means that the industrious reader who can understand it will derive intellectual profit from it as well as credit. But there is one thing his imitators are apt to forget. Since his mode of self-expression was wholly (not necessarily 'foully') individual, to imitate him successfully it is necessary to do something utterly different.

Perhaps this chapter should have begun with Dorothy Richardson, who after all, in the English language, was first in time to pursue this new path of adventure. Joyce started on the same road a year or two later than she, and Lawrence, stumbling towards it, never quite got there. Dorothy Richardson at the start may not have seen the way ahead quite so clearly as Joyce did, but she knew what she did not want, and soon in the course of writing discovered what she did want. In a Foreword to that series of books which together make up *Pilgrimage* she speaks of the choice which faced her in 1911 when she was proposing to write a novel. Behind her lay Balzac and Bennett, 'realists by nature and unawares', who in their respective ways had represented 'the turning of the human spirit upon itself'. Then had come other realists, intent on 'explicit satire and protest'. Reviewing the scene, she decided to 'attempt to produce a feminine equivalent of the current masculine realism'. But the process of writing disillusioned her; she became aware of 'a stranger in the form of contemplated reality having for the first time in her experience its own say'. The images in her own mind, things seen, remembered, felt, began to speak for themselves. Reality, in so far as it could be focused in the text, began to reveal 'a hundred faces, any one of which, the moment it was entrapped within the close mesh of direct statement, summoned its fellows to disqualify it.'

Reality, for her, is not such as to admit of direct statements which will satisfy or remain valid. All that she cares to record is that of which alone she is certain, impression following impression in the 'stream of consciousness', in the language appropriate to something so logically inconsequent. She tells us that 'in 1913, the opening pages of the attempted chronicle became the first chapter of "Pilgrimage", written to the accompaniment of a sense of being upon a fresh pathway, an adventure so searching and, sometimes, so joyous as to produce a longing for participation.' Meantime, while pursuing what she thought to be a 'lonely track', 'news came from France of one Marcel Proust, said to be producing an unprecedentedly profound and opulent reconstruction of experience focused from within the mind of a single individual and since Proust's first volume had been published and several others written by 1913, the France of Balzac now appeared to have produced the earliest adventurer.'

Was she then really the second of these literary adventurers? She mentions another, Henry James, who certainly might have taught her one part of her technique, that of 'keeping the reader incessantly watching the conflict of human forces through the eye of a single observer'. And James himself had learnt much from Flaubert. But that is only one element in the distinctive technique she uses, the second being defined by that appreciative novelist, May Sinclair, in the concluding sentence in the following quotation:

> She [the narrator] must be Miriam Henderson [who is the heroine throughout the *Pilgrimage* novels]. She must not know or divine anything that Miriam does not know or divine. . . . Of the persons who move through Miriam's world you know nothing but what Miriam knows. . . . In identifying herself with this life, which is Miriam's stream of consciousness, Miss Richardson produces her effect of being the first, of getting closer to reality than any of our novelists who are trying so desperately to get close.

During the 1914–18 war—an incident among public affairs that had no noticeable effect upon the mind of the author— Miriam had dawned freshly upon the world like a being from another sphere, a sphere we had only recently acquired the faculties to be aware of. *Pointed Roofs*, the first volume of *Pilgrimage*, was published in 1915, two years after the first volume of *A la Recherche du Temps Perdu*. It was followed by *Backwater* (1916), *Honeycomb* (1917), *The Tunnel* and *Interim* (1919), *Deadlock* (1921), *Revolving Lights* (1923), *The Trap* (1925), *Oberland* (1927), *Dawn's Left Hand* (1931), *Clear Horizon* (1935) and *Dimple Hill* (1938). In *The Tunnel* Miriam had become her brightest, most irrefutable, transcendent self, transforming the dingy atmosphere of Mornington Road and the Wimpole Street surgery where she worked with the sparkling crystal of her moods. In *Interim* she was still illuminating a dull and rather purposeless world by her manner of expressing it. In *Deadlock*, in *Revolving Lights* and in subsequent books we find Miriam still living within herself— her environment shifting from point to point within her mind

—and finally, as the author's inspiration diminishes, we become aware that this method, deprived of the intensity of inspiration, is not enough to make the common round of Miriam's life continuously interesting to a reader. *Pilgrimage* is a river. Miriam's mind, perceiving persons so shrewdly, marking its memories of little things and of a few high ecstasies, was the river, passing this memorable point and that on the bank and, as it left each behind, moving on with the same rhythmic, rippling flow—towards no conceivable goal. Goals are among the things Dorothy Richardson would leave severely to 'men'.

But it is not enough to point out that a novelist has adopted a new technique. No technique justifies itself unless it produces results, and cannot confer high distinction unless, corresponding to the inner matter, that matter itself has high value. In the case of this writer, there *is* a quality, entirely her own, which constitutes her unique claim to distinction.

That quality lies in her femininity. She is perhaps the most complete incarnation that has ever existed of one of the warring elements in the eternal sex war. Hers appears to be the authentic voice of essential woman using the distinctively feminine faculties to express the world. No doubt it was not by chance that she was first trying her hand at writing at the moment when the militant suffragette movement was at its height. Not that the suffragette way was her way. It was not by attempting to do what men do, or by 'assimilating masculine culture' that women (according to Miriam) acted in their own true part. Miriam's part was to act, think, feel and experience life with the sentience that belongs to the feminine side of human nature and to do so in the full consciousness of what she was doing. Jane Austen in her way was just as feminine as Dorothy Richardson, but she had no consciousness of opposition—she merely failed to make men real whenever she liked them. Charlotte Brontë was just as feminine, but, protesting, she succumbed to femininity. Virginia Woolf has immense power of presenting the feminine point of view, but she can get outside it, as Dorothy Richardson cannot. The latter not merely presents the feminine point of view; she is it. She is conscious of the part, glories in it, and wages (through Miriam) relentless war on the amusing monstrosity of the male intelligence.

This is evident in nearly all her books. It is a governing element from first to last. 'Men' generalize, make statements, argue and evade life by rationalizing it. We hear of the 'clever superficially true things men said'. Miriam in *The Tunnel* found that it was only by pretending to be interested in 'statements' (which were not *things*) and taking sides about them that she could have conversation with men. To cultivate the trick of thinking in such terms might be a fine talent in women; but it would mean 'hiding so much, letting so much go; all the real things. The things men never seemed to know about at all.' In *Revolving Lights* Miriam rejected Michael because to marry would be 'to go into complete solitude, marked for life as a segregated female whose whole range of activities was known; in the only way men have of knowing them.' And similarly in *Clear Horizon*, Hypo is introduced mainly to be guyed as a nice clever man using his 'clumsy masculine machinery of observation', meeting realities with formulæ; he is enclosed and enmeshed in opinions and in the masculine illusion of freedom.

Yet Dorothy Richardson is not primarily destructive. On the contrary, she is all the time constructively exhibiting the feminine mind in operation, with all its virtue. It resides in the actuality of experience, the individual experience that is knowable only here and now, in this moment of perception, and in the next moment, and the next, and such fusion of all the moments as you may get in the rarer acts of divination. Even Miriam with all her feminine power is often conscious of being defeated. In listening to music at a concert she was aware of 'passing along the surface of its moments as one by one they were measured off in sound that no longer held for her any time-expanding depth', tormented by knowing that her 'authentic being' was far away in her consciousness, till suddenly 'a single flute-phrase, emerging unaccompanied, . . . spread coolness within her, refreshing as sipped water from a spring.' Paths of new adventure in the search for personality open before us.

In the later books of the *Pilgrimage* cycle, beginning with *Clear Horizon*, the author's art has undergone some change. Miriam has now been re-surveyed, re-experienced. She is still in essence the same; not very much older, if one can judge of age at all in such a history; still existing in a time when motor-cars and aeroplanes were only just beginning to be familiar; and, what is more important, so far as mere happenings have any importance for the spiritual life, in a time when the militant suffragette movement was going on, and providing a suitable opportunity for the exit of Amabel, incomparable Amabel, from Miriam's life. But the author, in the interval that has elapsed, has changed more than Miriam, not, indeed, in what is essential to her point of view, but in her art. She has become, strangely enough, a literary person such as before we could never think of her being —in the sense, say, that Virginia Woolf was a literary person —*composing* her sentences with much elaboration, arranging her pattern, advancing with less appearance of spontaneity but more certainty to her end. The thoughts and impressions that used to fly over the pages in short exclamatory sentences now move slowly, analysed minutely and guardedly, almost in the manner of Henry James. In summing up all the impressions that have gone to the making of Miriam as she is now, in minutely exposing the mature subtleties of apprehension with which she takes in each situation her record has acquired an intellectual character; Miriam is no longer merely perceiving; she is seen severely reflecting upon perception. At this stage her mind is filled with memories; and memories, for her, evoke criticism of past thought. In this book the synthetic method of the male mind is not wholly lacking.

The distinctive excellence for which Dorothy Richardson stands in her more characteristic books required that she should have just such a vehicle as she chose; her technique exactly serves her purpose. One should not omit to add that it does also lend itself to artistic laziness—to following the line of least resistance in recording the unordered flow of impressions as they pass through the mind. This unselectiveness will tend to estrange readers who are not willing to submit themselves wholly to the moods and fancies of a Miriam which may turn out to be moods and fancies not easy to recapture for another generation. Of this kind of laziness the author cannot altogether be acquitted, and it is scarcely a consolation to know that she came near to conquering it when inspiration diminished. But does not this mean that she depends on inspiration, and that she had it? The defects of her method almost become virtues since with them she has made that half of human nature whose capacities transcend articulation as nearly articulate as possible. In that respect her work is unique.

An elegant lady writing reviews for *The Times Literary Supplement*. That is how anyone might have thought of Virginia Woolf (1882–1941) knowing her work only before she was thirty-nine years of age. The daughter of that active philosopher and littérateur, Sir Leslie Stephen, she was brought up in an atmosphere of high thinking and refined leisure, never to lack either worldly means or opportunities for cultural nutrition. When her father died in 1904 she lived with a sister, who was a painter, and two brothers, reading, reviewing books, travelling and guarding, as was necessary, her delicate health. In 1912 she married Leonard Woolf, whose intellectual interests were complementary to her own. Human as well as material circumstances were favourable to the development of her powers. It is easy in the light of her later work to read into her first two novels traits indicative of her genius (*The Voyage Out*, 1915 and *Night and Day*, 1919) but the truth is they were written before she discovered her real bent. In the first the story of Ridley and Helen Ambrose and Rachel Vinrace, ending with the death of Rachel, is clever, delicately written, subtle, describing external events in the traditional manner. It was well received by reviewers, as many other meritorious books of the time were received. The second novel, *Night and Day*, was less deserving. It is a comedy of love affairs which go astray and come right, told at great length, with a wearisome over-elaboration of tea-parties and visits and conversations in polite, sophisticated Chelsea circles—all well written, refined and uninspired. These two books are part of her history, but not what we think of as Virginia Woolf.

If it had been possible for her to go on like that—and, of course, it was not—she might have been remembered for a little while as an elegant blue-stocking interested in Greek philosophy and the Elizabethans, with a taste for music and pictures, with correct judgment and exacting standards, and a slightly snobbish distaste for the common herd—an accomplished littérateur. She is aware of the super-refined in herself, and is not in the least ashamed of it. 'How little one is ashamed of being . . . an unmitigated snob', she wrote in one of her articles. Yet she would scarcely have said that if she had not also been aware of something very different— a temperament almost painfully alive to the feeling of life—the excitement aroused in her by the process of living and the perception of objects, her intensity of response to the stimuli of sights and sounds and the spectacle of persons living their humdrum busy lives, full of little thoughts as if there were no universe around them and no death at the end. The world of her percep- tions was so crowded, so filled with impressions crying out for expression that the strain of it on her receptive temperament would surely have been unbearable had she not found some form of artistic release. (It was necessary for her from time to time to rest her over-burdened mind in a nursing home). But what form of release? She looked around at the foremost novelists of the day —the Wells's, the Bennetts, the Galsworthys—and found that they had nothing to give. In the long run, in her view, they were 'materialists' (how shocked Galsworthy would have been to be so described!) with nothing to offer for the spirit. Their method for her was too coarse, too regardless of the fine and the rare, too unperceptive. But there were others. There was Proust, so delicately aware of a number of things, so perceptive of the myriad impressions that make up the passage of time. And there was Joyce, unfolding life in a succession of images just as life does in fact unfold itself, with a frankness that might be imitated; but surely without the coarseness, which was alien to her. Still nearer to the mark was Dorothy Richardson, whose book *The Tunnel* she had just been reading. Here was a woman sensitive like herself, alive to the little significant realities of passing moments, who got behind the skin to the most intimate processes of perception—but how formless! The raw material of life as she wanted it, but without shape, without theme, without the concentration and selection which are necessary for a work of art. Supposing she took this method and used it, subduing the whole to the classic demands of a literary composition. Along this road lay the means of expression which she needed if her talent was to bear fruit.

We get the first tentative efforts in her new way of writing in the sketches in *Monday or Tuesday* (1921), followed triumphantly by *Jacob's Room* (1922) and *Mrs. Dalloway* (1925). In *Jacob's Room* we still have continuous narrative, but it is presented through a series of pictures, and the movement is mainly that which goes on in the minds of the characters.

Simeon said nothing. Jacob remained standing. But intimacy— the room was full of it, still, deep, like a pool. Without need of movement or speech it rose softly and washed over everything, mollifying, kindling, and coating the mind with the lustre of pearl, so that if you talk of a light, of Cambridge burning, it's not language only. It's Julian the Apostate.

And here is a picture which suggests the still potent influence of Joyce:

The street market in Soho is fierce with light. Raw meat, china mugs, and silk stockings blaze in it. Raw voices wrap themselves round the flaring gas-jets. Arms akimbo, they stand on the pavement bawling—Messrs. Kettle and Wilkinson; their wives sit in the shop, furs wrapped round their necks, arms folded, eyes contemptuous. Such faces as one sees. The little man fingering the meat must have squatted before the fire in innumerable lodging houses, and heard and seen and known so much that it seems to utter itself even volubly from dark eyes, loose lips, as he fingers the meat silently, his face sad as a poet's, and never a song sung. . . . Every face, every shop, bedroom window, public house, and dark square is a picture feverishly turned—in search of what? It is the same with books. What do we seek through millions of pages? Still hopefully turning the pages—oh, here is Jacob's room.

In kaleidoscopic vision the pageant of human beings proceeds down the years towards the end—the death of Jacob in the war is foreseen by the reader and, when it happens, taken for granted. Moments succeed moments; Virginia Woolf never lets us forget their remorseless succession—nor the death which for each individual obliterates them.

The quintessence of her art is in four books: *Mrs. Dalloway* (1925), *To The Lighthouse* (1927), *The Waves* (1931) and *Between the Acts*, published posthumously, without final revision, in 1941. The nature of her aim is indicated in a passage in her book of literary essays, *The Common Reader*, published in 1932:

The thirty-two chapters of a novel . . . are an attempt to make something as formed and controlled as a building: but words are more impalpable than bricks; reading is a longer and more complicated process than seeing. Perhaps the quickest way to understand the elements of what a novelist is doing is not to read, but to write. . . . Recall, then, some event that has left a distinct impression on you—how at the corner of the street, perhaps, you passed two people talking. A tree shook; an electric light danced; the tone of the talk was comic, but also tragic; a whole vision, an entire conception, seemed contained in that moment.

This may recall Turgenev's account of the origin of the fictive picture. In Virginia Woolf's novels we shall not look for a plot in the ordinary sense of the term but clearly something that is her firm substitute for a plot—a situation in which life is crystallized, a situation involving a number of persons, and a succession of moments in their involved lives as represented by the ideas or images which pass through their minds—image following image in correspondence with the remorseless beat of time. It is her art to arrange life in the pattern revealed to her in the instant of intuition; the pattern is the form under which the situation is unfolded—it may be Mrs. Dalloway about to give and giving a party, and we have Mrs. Dalloway being what she is and feeling what she feels, with all the vivid life of London going on around her, each Londoner responding to that life with his or her own thoughts and feelings—Mrs. Dalloway, reacting to commonplace life and, at one moment, to the awareness of death, yet pursuing her dutiful aim, to give a successful party. *Mrs. Dalloway* is a complete tract of luminous life—life in a single day lightly and a little cruelly shown as a sample of eternity. At the outset Mrs. Dalloway, walking from Hyde Park and looking at the omnibuses in Piccadilly, has the feeling that 'it was very very dangerous to live even one day'. And later, musing about life:

> Oh, it was very queer. Here was So-and-so in South Kensington; someone up in Bayswater; and somebody else, say, in Mayfair. And she felt quite continuously a sense of their existence; and she felt what a waste; and she felt what a pity; and she felt if only they could be brought together; so she did it. And it was an offering; to combine, to create; but to whom?

So the party was her gift.

> All the same, that one day should follow another; Wednesday, Thursday, Friday, Saturday; that one should wake up in the morning; see the sky; walk in the park; meet Hugh Whithead; then suddenly in came Peter; then these roses; it was enough. After that, how unbelievable death was!—that it must end; and no one in the whole world would know how she had loved it all; how every instant . . .

Each of these four books, *Mrs. Dalloway, To the Lighthouse, The Waves, Between the Acts,* having its clearly definable theme, is composed like a piece of music, proceeding note by note, phrase by phrase, with crescendo and diminuendo, the beat of time being actually marked by the voice of Big Ben, or an alarum clock, or the regular crash of the waves—the *noise* of the waves is also seen as *light*—vision and sound interact in darting images which make you see and hear. Serious as the author is, she is not solemn—there is gaiety and insidious irony in the picture of human fatuity—but there is tenderness too. The portrait of Mrs. Ramsay in *To the Lighthouse* is her finest piece of characterization —the Mrs. Ramsay who is so alive even death cannot end her— but also, in showing all the life-destroying qualities of her dogmatic husband, she evokes from him too something that is admirable and all-too-human. Her last novel, *Between the Acts*, (though in some passages suffering from lack of revision) is perhaps the most amazing of her books. It is a creation of the most fantastic Midsummer Night's Dream out of the slightest material. A country-house party is collected in a distinguished house to see a local pageant which is to take place in the grounds. The pageant takes place. And that is all. Yet the atmosphere evoked by this collection of ill-assorted people and players, none of whom departs from his or her proper character, becomes tense, charged with electricity, with a kind of fatuous excitement that verges upon hysteria, yet at the end, though we have been up with the witches to a Brocken Festival, we know that nothing much out of the ordinary has happened on that quite ordinary Saturday afternoon. There are no heroes or heroines, though the centre of the stage is occupied now by Isa, her mind talking second-rate poetry to itself, or Mrs. Swithin, her thoughts far back in the past, hearing the waves on a still night, or Miss La Trobe ambitiously set on winning triumph from her pageant—but they are no more heroes than the performers in the pageant are heroes; they come and go in a pattern of separate thoughts and feelings combined as in an elaborate musical composition—excited music at times verging on the hysterical. It is a tract of life at a chosen moment going on with feverish intensity below the surface—another sample of eternal but repetitive time.

The Years, published in 1937, is not one of Virginia Woolf's best novels, yet it is important as a kind of summing up of her philosophy, of her account of the world which it had been her function to reveal in fiction. Her subject here explicitly is Time and events and persons repeating themselves in time—or if not repeating themselves, then—to what are they tending? In the spring of 1880 the weather was perpetually changing, and 'sent clouds of blue and purple flying over the land'. In 1891 the autumn wind blew over England and 'twitched the leaves of the trees'. In 1908 it was March and 'the wind was blowing. . . . It was scraping, scourging.' And only the other day—the present day— on a summer evening 'the sun was setting; the sky was blue still, but tinged with gold, as if a thin veil of gauze hung over it.' During the whole period the seasons have not failed to reassert themselves with their variations and episodes. And the clocks, too, arranged by human agency, have gone on striking regularly and, at dramatic moments, noticeably—'the sound of the hour filled the room; softly, tumultuously, as if it were a flurry of soft sighs hurrying one on top of another, yet concealing something hard. Lady Pargiter counted. It was late.' And it has been late, the reader remembers, twenty thousand times since the story opened.

Is this another version of what Bennett attempted in *The Old Wives' Tale*, or Galsworthy in *The Forsyte Saga*? Or of *A la Recherche du Temps Perdu*? In any broad account of our time-conscious society its time-consciousness sooner or later is bound to come in. But Virginia Woolf is not concerned to discover in the changing externals of life an explanation of changes in habits and thought. The outer changes are noted only lightly and in passing —Eleanor gets into a taxi now instead of a hansom when she goes to a party—but these are only concomitant facts, part of the setting, like the March wind or the autumn leaves, and less significant than those too persistent chimes of bells. Impressions come into the mind of this and that person; they are transient and repetitive; and the change which makes its most melancholy mark may be that of a house, long occupied, now 'to let', the sort of transition which is due simply to the recurrence of death and the dissolution of families and the way of all flesh at all times. In these fifty-odd years the Pargiters and the rest of the human race have been going on, repeating themselves, talking and talking, going to parties, having such slender little adventures, perpetually filling the vacuum with activities soon to be translated into memories—always memories.

Into this Heracleitean flux the author does introduce certain fixities—individual characters, pertinacious in going on being themselves. This is for her the one sure immovable point—the character of a person which can be identified only in terms of itself and not of its period. Of such a character, in this book, are Rose, Kitty, North and, far the most vital, Sara, a fay-like person in whose excitable talk images chase one another in delirious fancy—or occasionally someone just caught sight of, 'a lovely face', for example, 'like a page on which nothing has been written but youth'.

But where is it all going to, what is it about? Why, thinks Martin, when he goes to Lady Lasswade's dinner party, why had he gone? 'What is the tip for this particular situation?' the practical Peggy asks herself at Delia's party. 'Round and round they go in a circle.' Eleanor, hearing Nicholas say what he had said years before, thinks: 'Does everything, then, come over again a little differently? If so, is there a pattern; a theme, recurring, like music; half remembered, half foreseen? . . . A gigantic pattern, momentarily perceptible?' And Peggy, opening a book while others talk, reads: 'La médiocrité de l'univers m'étonne et me révolte . . . la petitesse de toutes choses m'emplit de dégoût.'

One may feel that the author has chosen for her world those whom she needs for just that world, excluding too much to make it representative. In *The Years* Sara is the only person whose portrait gives any impression of capacity for passion, and even she is as much elf as woman. Most of the people are not doing any-thing—they have no work; they are taking houses, or visiting their stockbrokers, or going to parties, dining, talking, marrying punctiliously—they have no projects; they move round and round idly in a circle. Virginia Woolf here, as in all her books, has packed her house. The world she knows is a severely limited one. But within its limits she has made it complete; of a section of society she has given an ordered impression, fine in detail and in texture, made luminous by the flickering flames which she discovers burning, faintly or brightly, in each individual. Also she is as often gay as melancholy. What a spirited and lively conception was that of *Orlando* (1928) which can be read as an allegory of the double sex of the poet, and his one-ness with all his spiritual ancestors, but, more especially in the first half, can stand as pure narrative with brilliant satire and gay description. It is a *tour de force* unlike any other of her works. Small as her social world is, there are many sides to her genius, and a back-ground of knowledge informing it.

Just as Proust introduced something new into French fiction, so Lawrence, Joyce, Dorothy Richardson and Virginia Woolf into English. Lawrence struck out into the wild jungles of emotion in his effort for release, but he was raw, moody, uncertain of himself or his art, an untamed thing at the mercy of unreasoning instinct. Joyce was more certain of the road over which he meant to travel, and invented a new technique; but the very power he thus acquired to handle the more savage emotions led to exultant exaggeration of the savagery, and therefore an unsatisfying travesty of human nature. In the long run over-confidence in his own method led him to stretch it beyond its capacity, with the result, in *Finnegans Wake,* that he is only fully intelligible to himself (which, in a work of art, objectively expressed, is absurd). Dorothy Richardson provided a perfect example of the stream of consciousness running on, pure and undefiled, through winding valleys of the spirit. But there was no unity of theme—scarcely a theme at all—and her art suffered from this lack. It was left for Virginia Woolf to bring all these elements together, to arrange human beings in characteristic attitudes, and to weave tenuous strands of thought and feeling into a firm, recognizable poetic pattern. All is of gossamer, but it is woven with deft, delicate hands into a strong fabric. Behind this tremulousness, this apprehensive response to nature, there is a mind at work, scornful of pedants, but believing in truth. After her, in her own country, the serious novel could never again be just what it had been before.

Chapter Thirteen

T. S. ELIOT

IF it is true that after Virginia Woolf, in her own country, the serious novel can never again be just what it was before, can it similarly be said that after Thomas Stearns Eliot (born 1888) serious poetry can never be what it was before? To Eliot himself this would seem a redundant question. No work of art, in his view, can leave art unmodified; indeed not only must it modify the present and the future, but even the past.

> The existing monuments form an ideal order among themselves, which is modified by the introduction of the new (the really new) work of art among them. The existing order is complete before the new work arrives; for order to persist after the supervention of novelty, the *whole* existing order must be, if ever so slightly, altered; and so the relations, proportions, values of each work of art toward the whole are readjusted; and this is conformity between the old and the new. Whoever has approved this idea of order, of the form of European, of English literature, will not find it preposterous that the past should be altered by the present as much as the present is altered by the past.[1]

These words were written at a time when T. S. Eliot in his poems appeared to be defying the whole existing order, throwing tradition into the dust-bin, requiring poetry to make a new start. Was it really the case that in his early work he professed traditionalism and practised the opposite? To clear up this point it is well to consider his criticism first. He is one of the few poets who have been perfectly clear in their own minds about the function of poetry before allowing themselves to write it—or at least publish it. He has thought himself into a consistent view about literature; as a critic, he brings carefully sharpened tools to each fresh task of literary judgment. As we read him we have the feeling that he knows just where he stands in relation to the ages, and is ready to explain, reasonably and urbanely, where anyone else stands. If all critics were of his kind they would be engaged

---

[1] From 'Tradition and the Individual Talent'. *The Sacred Wood* (1920).

together in 'a simple and orderly field of beneficent activity';[1] there would be no need for the gently ironic words in which he regrets the rarity of the critic who endeavours to 'compose his differences with as many of his fellows as possible, in the common pursuit of true judgment'.

We may observe that just at that time, in the early twenties, a number of his fellows had been together in acclaiming a classicist trend in certain contemporary literature. In that literature the classicism was of the surface; there was much in it that was artificial and finicky. With Georgian poetasters rippling round him Eliot set himself to establish principles of a sound classicism. He stands for 'order' in literature; and order implies authority— not that of Aristotle, or Boileau, or any other single law-giver, but not the less sure because it is distributed among the whole body of writers who have contributed to the great tradition of literature. By 'tradition' he does not mean the handing down of old ways of doing things, which we are to imitate. Rather, just as Benedetto Croce said that history is humanity's memory of its own past, so Eliot says, 'the conscious present is an awareness of the past'. We know more than the 'dead writers', but they are 'that which we know'.[2]

> The historical sense compels a man to write not merely with his own generation in his bones, but with a feeling that the whole of the literature of Europe from Homer, and within it the whole of the literature of his own country, has a simultaneous existence and composes a simultaneous order.

Literature is conceived as a continuous process in which the present contains the past; by fresh creation expressed not in terms of the old world but of the new changing world, it modifies the past and helps to complete it. The function of his critic is to relate literature to the whole current of conscious creative effort. It is in a spirit very different from that of the Neo-classicists that we find him insisting on the need, not of narrowly defined rules of writing, but of a sort of training, or *askesis*[3]—even, in some cases, a convention—so that the work of the artist will accord with and not defy the permanent spirit of tradition. Thus of Blake (to whom he is not very sympathetic) he says that what his genius

---

[1] 'The Function of Criticism.' *Selected Essays* (1923).
[2] 'Tradition and the Individual Talent.'
[3] 'Dialogue on Dramatic Poetry.' *Selected Essays* (1928).

required and lacked was 'a framework of accepted and traditional ideas'.[1] Or again, the Russian ballet, at its best, delighted us because it 'seemed to be everything that we wanted in drama, except the poetry. . . . It seemed to revive the more formal element in drama for which we craved.' It rested upon a tradition and severe discipline. It was a 'system of physical training, of traditional, symbolical, and highly skilled movement'.

And similarly in regard to the drama, he considers that the weakness of the Elizabethan plays, and also the weakness of the realistic plays which William Archer admired so much, lay in 'the lack of a convention'.[2] He asks us to conceive what the Elizabethan drama might have been if it had been 'formed within a conventional scheme—the convention of an individual drama-tist, or of a number of dramatists working in the same form at the same time'—presumably in the same sense that the Greek traged-ians or authors of morality plays of the type of *Everyman* worked within a certain form or, might I add, the Habima players when they produced their Hebrew plays with a formidable precision of technique? (Which indeed is to ask that the Elizabethans should have been something utterly different from what they were, gaining much—but at what loss? Yet Ben Jonson, writing of Shakespeare, agreed with Eliot.)

I cannot here pursue the arguments with which Eliot in essay after essay, discussing Elizabethan, or Caroline, or modern writers, endeavours to show what has been or might have been gained by precision, by formalism, by something akin to ritual, by that scrupulous absorption in the object which makes a work of art impersonal and universal. He is re-stating the claims of classicism in its demand for order, poise and 'right reason'.

What is surprising in one so detached in his sympathies is that he should so definitely take sides between classicism and roman-ticism, and that he should follow, though in a broader spirit, the old prejudice which made men feel that if the one was right the other was all wrong. One would rather have expected him to recognize—as did Pater, a critic to whom he has been less than fair—that there are here two opposite tendencies which from early times have asserted themselves in literature, each corresponding to distinctive merits and defects, and requiring correction the one

[1] 'William Blake.' *The Sacred Wood* (1920).
[2] 'Four Elizabethan Dramatists.' *Selected Essays* (1924).

by the other if in the long run a 'mean' is to be achieved. Æschylus combined the merits of both. But on the whole, since English writers have at no time since the eighteenth century been in danger of a deficiency in romanticism—rather the opposite—there is much to be gained in English-speaking countries by the cool sanity, the analytical judgment, the fastidiousness exemplified in Eliot's severely intellectual criticism.

It is to use the word 'tradition' equivocally to say that the Eliot of this severe intellectual outlook, a professed classicist, an uncompromising upholder of tradition, was also the man who led the attack on the writing of 'traditional' poetry, appearing as the foremost innovator of our time. For Eliot does not admit that this so-called 'traditional' poetry is within the tradition in its true sense. The literary language which he rejected was that which had served its purpose in the past but for modern use had become 'dead'. In his view the writer who is to carry on the tradition will not imitate the idiom of his predecessors, but will use a language 'which is struggling to digest and express new objects, new groups of objects, new feelings, new aspects'.[1] And this language for him had to be strikingly different from that of his predecessors precisely because both the external world and the world of ideas, when he was a young man, were strikingly different from anything that had been before. Just as Joyce in his way, and Dorothy Richardson and Virginia Woolf in their ways, had felt the necessity of a new mode of writing to express their inner sense of the passing show and the realities behind it, so with Eliot.

Possibly his awareness of the 'deadness' of much contemporary English verse-writing was sharpened by his early upbringing in the United States. He was born in St. Louis, and had his first university education at Harvard, though he went thence to the Sorbonne and to Merton College, Oxford, made England his literary home, and after a few years was naturalized as a British citizen. He began experimenting with poetry, as a few others were experimenting, and was interested in the novelties of another young writer, also of American origin, Ezra Pound (born 1885). Ezra Pound was a versatile, infinitely ingenious juggler with

[1] 'Swinburne as Poet.' *The Sacred Word* (1920).

words, who, having travelled and studied in Spain, Italy and Provence and delved industriously among early poets, especially Provençal, found subjects ready-made to his hand and unfamiliar metres in which to clothe them. He came much under the personal and literary influence of Ford Madox Hueffer, who was not only diversifying his prose with expressions drawn from common speech, but was writing highly original verse—'vers libres or rhymed vers libres'[1]—cultivating young poets whom he described as 'mes jeunes', including the talented Imagist poet, Richard Aldington (born 1892). Under this encouraging influence Pound went on with his experiments. The poet, Kathleen Raine, mentioning him in Britain Today (December, 1949) curiously enough alludes to him as a 'major poet', but proceeds most justly, I think, to sum him up:

> His verse is a magpie's nest full of the junk of dismantled civilizations, China and Provence, Greek gods, and all kinds of European cultural bric-à-brac, some of it almost new, bundled pell-mell overseas to adorn a brand-new American poetic tradition.

It is proper to add that Yeats was among those who were impressed by Pound; and it is not surprising that Eliot, experimenting himself, was struck by the enterprises of the clever versifier who, if he had done nothing else, had completely emancipated himself from the modes of the Georgians. But what these two poets in their youth had in common was superficial and accidental. Both appeared to have wide learning acquired in several languages, and Eliot had it. Both sought to extend the range of poetic language by introducing words used in intimate speech but commonly regarded as inappropriate in literature. Both were looking for more elastic metrical forms. But Eliot, modernist as he was, had behind him the majestic background of the literature of many ages, and had absorbed much of its spirit. He scorned out-worn images and clichés, though he could effectively borrow phrases from well-known poets, and in so doing, in the new context, create an astonishing new effect. He was to be precise not only in his use of words, but also in the exact, wonderful fitting of their sound to his meaning. There is often a kind of slow stillness in the speech as of a voice far away beyond

[1] See On Heaven and Poems Written on Active Service. Published in 1918, but read to friends earlier.

a mountain, utterly impersonal, interrupted sometimes by a colloquialism which brings the voice suddenly near, close to the earth, so that we have a startling contrast between two aspects of the thought—and thus a new imaginative synthesis.

He had his own generation 'in his bones' and the poets of the past in the background. In his earlier period we may feel that it is the poetry of disillusion, irony, disgust—the contemplation of a trivial, sordid, empty world. He strikes a characteristic note in the opening words of the first of his published poems, *The Love Song of J. Alfred Prufrock* (1917):

> Let us go then, you and I
> When the evening is spread out against the sky
> Like a patient etherised upon a table;
> Let us go, through certain half-deserted streets
> The muttering retreats
> Of restless nights in one-night cheap hotels
> And sawdust restaurants with oyster-shells:
> Streets that follow like a tedious argument
> Of insidious intent
> To lead you to an overwhelming question . . .
> Oh, do not ask, 'What is it?'
> Let us go and make our visit.
>
> In the room the women come and go
> Talking of Michelangelo.

There already in a few lines we have the beauty of nature, the sordidness of a city, the pretentiousness of snobs, the questioning of a philosopher. And soon we are to have the meaninglessness of time:

> evenings, morning, afternoons,
> I have measured out my life with coffee spoons.

life repeating itself dingily 'in a thousand furnished rooms' with

> the damp souls of housemaids
> Sprouting despondently at area gates

'Rhapsody on a Windy Night' turning into the reminiscence

> Of sunless dry geraniums
> And dust in crevices

or Aunt Helen, who 'lived in a small house near a fashionable square',

> Now when she died there was silence in heaven
> And silence at her end of the street

while for Mr. Apollinax, visiting the United States,

> His laughter tinkled among the teacups.

Nor are we in a much less desolate and desolating universe in the *Poems—1920*, where, in *Gerontion*, we read

> Here I am, an old man in a dry month,
> Being read to by a boy, waiting for rain.

So far we have had little but the vanity, the desiccation, the morbid futility of half-living things, but in *The Waste Land* (1922) his imagination takes a higher flight, surveying the desolate scene with searching gaze, relentlessly uncovering its baffling contrasts, looking in vain for a meaning where there is only

> A heap of broken images, where the sun beats,
> And the dead tree gives no shelter, the cricket no relief,
> And the dry stone no sound of water.

And we hear again the quiet voice from beyond the mountains chanting dreadfully the disenchantments:

> Here is no water but only rock
> Rock and no water and the sandy road
> The road winding above among the mountains
> Which are mountains of rock without water
> If there were water we should stop and drink
> Amongst the rock one cannot stop or think
> Sweat is dry and feet are in the sand
> If there were only water amongst the rock
> Dead mountain mouth of carious teeth that cannot spit
> Here one can neither stand nor lie nor sit
> There is not even silence in the mountains
> But dry sterile thunder without rain
> There is not even solitude in the mountains
> But red sullen faces sneer and snarl
> From doors of mudcracked houses.

And we still have ringing in our ears the publican's refrain 'HURRY UP PLEASE IT'S TIME.'

In an Appendix to a book of translations from Langland's *Vision of Piers Plowman* (1949) Nevill Coghill speaks of three planes of meaning in a mediæval allegory: (1) the simple meaning of the story, *sensus litteralis*, (2) the transferred meaning, its parable-sense, *sensus allegoricus*, (3) the moral meaning ('extracted by the poet and peppered through the poem'), *sensus moralis*. But, he goes on, 'religious allegory added a fourth plane of meaning . . . which adumbrated the spiritual world of being'. This was called *sensus anagogicus*.

The Waste Land (1922) is not in the strict sense of the term an allegory, for it does not tell a story. But the three senses can be detected in it and to some extent, with the help of the notes which Eliot himself has added, interpreted. But have we not also at least an 'adumbration' of that fourth world of being, the spiritual? If we had read only *The Waste Land* we might not be quite sure of that, but when we know the *Four Quartets*, written much later (published in 1943), where the *sensus anagogicus* becomes almost explicit (so far as that is possible), we may be quite sure towards what Eliot was already beginning to feel his way.

Later, in that masterly 'Aristophanic Melodrama', *Sweeney Agonistes* (1932), as also in that terrifying poem, *The Hollow Men* (1925)—

> We are the hollow men
> We are the stuffed men
> Leaning together
> Headpiece filled with straw—

he is already moving towards an interpretation of the Waste Land which he had depicted so lugubriously, though in both these poems his sinister and desolating irony remains.

From then onwards we are to find the philosopher (or theologian?) becoming predominant. This does not mean that he is to cease to be a poet. A poet, as a poet, is not one who deals in statements, arguments, proofs, teachings or persuasions; he shows or reveals. None the less the matter of thought may be his subject. Argument itself, when it is the best sort of argument, and not for the sake of winning, may produce a sort of fire, an illumination, from which truth emerges as a vision rather than an intellectual concept. It is thus in Plato; the argument proceeds as philosophy till suddenly, at some moment, the truth emerges as a vision perceived and hailed with delight, and actually the ending is a parable such as that of the cave—philosophy is transformed into poetry. Eliot, in philosophic mood, remains a poet, for it is his function, as a writer of verse, to turn what he holds to be true into something that can be perceived—that is, æsthetically apprehended. For the poet there is danger in such writing, and Eliot does not always succeed; but in the main the result has justified him.

He is a thinker endowed with the perceptions of a poet. He is thinking, thinking, all the time—and it would be impossible that his thought should not control his poetry, or, conversely, that his poetry should not control his thought. At first, looking round on the world of our time, he seemed content to affirm the Heracleitean flux—all things flow, and nothing abides. Vanity of vanities, all is vanity. Having studied with philosophic and æsthetic admiration the *Appearance and Reality* of Bradley, he was to interpret what he had experienced in the first and more destructive part of that book in the symbolic language of his earlier poetry. Later on it is as if the reconstructive part of the book lingered more constantly in his imagination, but his philosophic contemplation more and more became associated with revealed religion, and religion especially as conceived by Anglo-Catholics. He becomes preoccupied with the relation between literature and ethics and theology. In his essay 'Religion and Literature' included in *Essays Ancient and Modern* (1936) he says that 'the "greatness" of literature cannot be determined solely by literary standards', though he adds: 'we must remember that whether it is literature or not can be determined only by literary standards'. Whether that distinction comes to much in the last resort we may doubt, for he himself says a little later: 'Though we may read literature merely for pleasure, of "entertainment" or of "æsthetic enjoyment", this reading never affects simply a sort of special sense; it affects us as entire human beings; it affects our moral and religious existence.' He clearly implies that if the entire human being of the reader is affected by a poem, the entire being of the poet has gone to its making; and this is not far away from Coleridge's doctrine that the 'synthetic and magical power' of imagination 'brings the whole soul of man into activity'. It is a matter of concern, then, to the poet no less than to the moralist if it is true, as he suggests, that modern literature 'repudiates, or is wholly ignorant of, our most fundamental and important beliefs'. He affirms that 'the whole of modern literature is corrupted by what I call Secularism, that is simply unaware of, simply cannot understand the meaning of, the primacy of the supernatural over the natural life: of something which I assume to be our primary concern.'

T. S. Eliot's poetry is a force in modern literature which does something to redress the balance. We observe his concern with what is our 'primary concern' in his religious, ethical and mystical plays—*Murder in The Cathedral* (1935), *The Family Reunion* (1939) and *The Cocktail Party* (1949)—the last having some of the qualities of a sermon which militate against success as a play. His mystical faith is declared explicitly (so far as mysticism can be explicit) in the four poems published together in *Four Quartets*, consisting of *Burnt Norton* (1936), *East Coker* (1940), *The Dry Salvages* (1941) and *Little Gidding* (1942).

In these four poems we have reflective writing of a high order turned into vision by imagination. We find philosophic statements and poetic images so welded together that we cannot say which is the philosophy and which is the poetry, for the two become one. As always with this author the Time motive is dominant, but it is only to emphasize the self-contradiction which inheres in the very conception of time, and the reality to be sought that transcends it. The Heracleitean doctrine is reaffirmed as all that we know so long as we are still bound by the Time category. 'You cannot step twice into the same river' Heracleitus had said; and Eliot:

> You are not the same people who left that station
> Or who will arrive at any terminus
> While the narrowing rails slide together behind you.

Burnt Norton begins with the now familiar words

> Time present and time past
> Are both perhaps present in time future,
> And time future contained in time past.

He speaks of the illusion inherent in the 'knowledge derived from experience'.

> The knowledge imposes a pattern, and falsifies,
> For the pattern is new in every moment
> And every moment is a new and shocking
> Valuation of all we have been.

All 'go into the dark'—

> The vacant interstellar spaces, the vacant into the vacant,
> The captains, merchant bankers, eminent men of letters,
> The generous patrons of art, the statesmen and the rulers.
>
> And we know that the hills and the trees, the distant panorama
> And the bold imposing façade are all being rolled away.
>
> I said to my soul, be still, and wait without hope
> For hope would be hope for the wrong thing; wait without love
> For love would be love of the wrong thing; there is yet faith
> But the faith and the love and the hope are all in the waiting.

In *Little Gidding* we find some explanation of his own method of writing.

> For last year's words belong to last year's language
> And next year's words await another voice.
>
> The end is where we start from. And every phrase
> And sentence that is right (where every word is at home,
> Taking its place to support the others,
> The word neither diffident nor ostentatious,
> An easy commerce of the old and the new,
> The common word exact without vulgarity,
> The formal word precise but not pedantic,
> The complete consort dancing together)
> Every phrase and every sentence is one end and a beginning,
> Every poem an epitaph.

We are not wholly depressed by the remorseless decrees of the sombre verses which affirm the 'dessication of the world of sense', for we become aware that we are not invited to persist in lamentation, but rather to search for another end—a consciousness that is not itself in time, though 'only through time time is conquered'. Outside time, 'I cannot say where', there is 'the still point' without which 'there would be no dance'—'the still point of the turning world'. Behind the procession of appearances moving between birth and death he is aware of a spiritual reality which cannot be defined in terms of temporal life; and this consciousness imposes its morality—the 'right action' which is 'freedom from past and future':

> For most of us, this is the aim
> Never here to be realised;
> Who are only undefeated
> Because we have gone on trying.

The poet ends with a solution which is religious, 'with the drawing of this Love and the voice of this Calling', bidding us 'not cease from exploration'; a voice, 'not looked for'

> But heard, half-heard in the stillness
> Between two waves of the sea.

It is easy to say what there is not in T. S. Eliot. There is no joy, no exultation, not even pleasure except the pleasure which is shown as spurious. There is no portrayal of common emotions, except when they are depraved, or silly. All the things which common men think of as practical and desirable vanish into insignificance under his vision. The passionate experience that Lawrence clutched at is illusion. Life in time is so inconsequential, so valueless in itself, that we cannot on this plane hope to do more than 'arrive where we started'; the 'exploration' which he commends must be for goals not of this world though we are bound to seek it through the processes of this world. We can only *not* be left with a sense of sourness, barrenness, vacuity if we have— as most have not—the capacity and passion of the saint to live in a region which transcends experience. He excels by introducing us to our own generation, and appears to end by inviting us to turn our backs on it. It is as if the only excuse for living is that it is an opportunity for dying.

Yes, he did introduce his contemporaries to their own generation. So much was that 'in his bones' that he was able to give to the language of poetry a new idiom which is that of our time, employing images which are fresh and vigorous, and a metrical form which discards the banality of the over-familiar, the second-hand, the outworn. He has been so much alive to this generation as to drag to light some of the hidden things which were gnawing at its heart and sapping its spiritual vitality. He is not content merely to expose stupidity, hypocrisy, vanity, but in lifting the veil makes us aware of all mankind, all history behind and the horror of the human soul alone in the Waste Land unless it is redeemed by courage and faith. During the thirty years of continuous writing in which his work has shown developing power his influence has been primarily among intellectuals, and especially the younger of them. His mind, for all his imagination, is highly intellectualized. Thought comes first with him; and though ideas with him engender light and heat and, embodied in symbols, become the matter of exciting poetry, the resultant works have proved baffling to those who were not spiritually of his generation and not willing to face the difficulties and open their minds to his spell. The magic was not lacking. The younger poets came under the spell and found in Eliot the inspiration they could not find elsewhere. He brought into poetry something which in this generation was needed: a language spare, sinewy, modern; a fresh and springy metrical form; thought that was adult; and an imagination aware of what is bewildering and terrifying in modern life and in all life. He has done more than any other living English poet to make this age conscious of itself, and, in being conscious, apprehensive.

Chapter Fourteen

NOVELISTS—RECENT AND CONTEMPORARY

THE task of the literary historian would be simplified if there were no over-lapping between generations. But the generations move imperceptibly one into another. The last appears to be still flourishing when its successor is already confident of victory. At any moment the men and women who read and write are of many ages and belong to different climates of thought and feeling. Older writers may still be quarrying in the pit which first they dug and still have something pertinent to say; or they may be inspired by the new and produce a blend all their own. Shaw, Wells, Bennett, Galsworthy and Forster were still among the most conspicuous imaginative writers when Joyce, Virginia Woolf and T. S. Eliot had made their mark; in Yeats we have the case of a poet who formed a style in the last century, yet had so developed in mind and spirit that in 1939 the freshness of his poems thrilled the moderns.

This overlapping occurs in every age, but it is the more noticeable during the last thirty years because the changes that have occurred have been so decisive and abrupt. We must remember that the majority of readers do not readily welcome the pioneers, the advance-guard; they prefer to rest in the familiar. Moreover the pioneers will not all be of one kind; some will start from one point, some from another, and pursue divergent paths —and who can say which of them may turn out to be blind alleys? Among the writers who have the new generation 'in their bones', to use Eliot's phrase, are some who will look like innovators, and others who will produce their effect without any sensational deviation from the familiar.

As an example of the latter we might take Katherine Mansfield (1888–1923)—the pseudonym of Kathleen Beauchamp, who married George Bowden in 1909, and Middleton Murry, the critic and essayist, in 1918. This sensitive and exquisite writer belonged no less than Virginia Woolf or Dorothy Richardson to a period which demanded release from the outworn, whose nerves were delicately responsive to the disharmonies of our time; it asked for experience in terms of perception and intuition. Her *Journal* and her *Letters* (published posthumously in 1927 and 1928) remind me in many ways of the *Journal* of Marie Bashkirtseff, revealing frankly and intimately her feelings about life and people, her suffering from incurable illness, and her striving for artistic perfection. But there was this important difference between her and Marie Bashkirtseff: Katherine Mansfield lived long enough, as the other did not, to achieve success in her art, and to know that her efforts were not in vain. She owed much to French writers, but the most obvious influence in her writing is that of Tchekov. *In a German Pension,* a collection of short stories published in 1911, did not yet show how great her talent was to be. But in *Bliss,* a volume of short stories published in 1920, she proved her power, and the triumph was repeated in *The Garden Party* (1922) and in the posthumous collection *The Doves' Nest* (1923) and *Something Childish* (1924). It seemed that any significant fragment of life was enough for her. She observed it minutely, described it simply and objectively, and at the end the point had been made, without apparent effort, leaving the reader thrilled, disturbed or emotionally enlightened. Her early death deprived her country of a writer of short stories belonging to a kind which, in English literature, had never before been done with so much skill and subtlety of perception.

In the uneasy years after the first Great War there were many talented writers who deliberately and often ostentatiously turned against all that could be thought of as *Passé-iste.* New schools with provocative labels were thrust into a short-lived prominence, their adherents seeking to prove their excellence on the strength of theories of art which they had ingeniously invented or borrowed. Futurism, Vorticism, Imagism and Expressionism all had their vogue, just as Existentialism (more especially in France) has to-day. The principles of Imagism were not far removed from those which Joyce practised but did not preach, though it tended to be more concerned with the surface of experience than the depths. Richard Aldington (born 1892) was the ablest of the exponents of Imagism, a school of poets and novelists who aimed at presenting the content of consciousness in the most direct and truthful way through the vivid images of which it consists. A theory of art is only worth anything to an artist when it conforms to his mode of perception, and is not, as is often the case, artificially imposed on him by his reasoning. Richard Aldington had enough real talent to avoid the dangers of preconceived theory, and in later years, devoting himself more to prose than poetry, has produced many deservedly successful novels and some highly intelligent criticism.

Wyndham Lewis (born 1884), artist, novelist, poet and pamphleteer, has a place all by himself. In 1914, provoked by the Futurist proclamations of the Italian artist Marinetti, whose motto was 'Automobilisme', he founded the 'Rebel Art Centre' whose motto was 'Vorticism', and in the fiery pages of his illustrated periodical *Blast* announced allegiance to principles of energy, conflict and abstract geometric conceptions. In the next few years the war switched him away from painting and writing to service as a gunner in France; and he came back to civil life to spend the next twenty years firing continuous literary broadsides on the 'enemy' whom he discovered on all sides insidiously threatening society and the artist. Although painting occupied part of his time, satirical novels, poems and books of social analysis poured from his vigorous pen in quick succession.[1]

His writing had many of the qualities of his paintings, which were steely abstractions of line and colour—shapes, sometimes terrific and grotesque, commentaries, in a certain sense, on normal life, but sometimes so exaggerated as to pass the bounds of satire. His books, like his pictures, were thought-products which he went on stamping out with inexhaustible robot force. *A priori* conceptions determined his artistic expression, but because he was genuinely an artist these abstract ideas were absorbed into his imagination and objectified in his vision. He was from the start, and remained, a rebel, his mind and whole personality in an attitude of perpetual defiance to the view which commonly prevails—the customary, the obtusely accepted. He is armed against catch-words (except his own), proof against seductive sentiment, quick to see (and exaggerate) the flaw in

[1] They included *Tarr* (1918), *The Art of Being Ruled* (1926), *The Childermass* (1928), *The Apes of God* (1930), *Hitler* (1931)—a singularly prophetic work—*One Way Song* (1933), *The Mysterious Mr. Bull* (1938), and *Rude Assignment* (1951).

authority to which indolence submits. Essentially he has been against automatism—that of the organism which lives only in response to familiar and recurrent *stimuli*—and since the greater part of social life is automatic there has been material enough for his satire. The critic H. G. Porteus has aptly pointed out that in his novels there are no *personnages sympathiques*. There is mocking laughter; there is terror; but seldom a trace of any resolving element of compassion.

Many people, looking back on the years between the wars, recall the feeling they then had that in literature as in life men were 'marking time', aware that one age had passed and that another was coming. In the twenties this feeling produced that sense of fatuity and mock-frivolity which was exposed by T. S. Eliot. There were novelists who seemed to be content to reflect the prevailing disillusion in their pictures of a reckless, excitable, pleasure-seeking society. Aldous Huxley was among them. William Alexander Gerhardi (born 1895) was another. His first novel was entitled *Futility: a Novel on Russian Themes* (1922), and in a series of clever novels he seemed to move lightly from theme to theme with the sole apparent object of showing that nothing matters except the fact that nothing matters. Yet another, in the field of drama, was Noel Coward (born 1899), the clever playwright, actor and producer who delighted by his nonchalant discoveries of social absurdity. Evelyn Waugh (born 1903), with the same awareness of the froth and foolishness so evident in the social life of the twenties and early thirties, has more importance, for behind his satire we are conscious of an understanding which is justly critical. His manner was agreeably light and detached; the dialogue and narrative in his earlier novels *Decline and Fall* (1928), *Vile Bodies* (1930) and *Labels* (1930) were deliciously funny. Later, when he became more serious in his manner, readers found his grave reflections an inadequate compensation for the loss of his light bantering and witty inconsequence—powers in which his peculiar excellence lay. His excursions into high ethical problems and Abyssinian politics were well enough but they were not the Waugh they had known. In *Scoop* (1938) he made a happy return to his earlier vein. His later satirical work *The Loved One* (1948) shows him embittered, sardonic and laboured in his irony. But so clever and versatile a writer may well prove capable of producing other books deserving attention.

In that period the output of well-written fiction was enormous. One was inclined to feel that there were too many clever authors who had learned the technique of writing a novel with a well-constructed plot, conforming to all the rules so competently laid down in Percy Lubbock's book *The Craft of Fiction* (1921) and worthy of being selected by the Book Society as a 'Book of the Month'. A few stand out conspicuously from the rank and file of the distinguished by some rarely individual quality. Robert Graves, whom I have already mentioned, was one of these. Somewhat embittered by his war experience, described with force in *Goodbye to All That* (1929), he pursued his course in strange by-ways, producing among other books several novels, of which perhaps *I, Claudius* (1934) was the most remarkable. A writer of a very different type whose work lay off the beaten track was Edward Garnett's son, David Garnett (born 1892). He made his name in 1923 with a brilliant little masterpiece, *Lady into Fox*, a fantasy written in choice, elegant language. It was followed by *A Man in the Zoo* (1924), *Go She Must* (1927), *The Grasshoppers Came* (1931) and *Pocahontas* (1933). Equally subtle in fantasy, and light in touch, but more tender in its humanity, is *Lolly Willowes* (1926), the work of Sylvia Townsend Warner (born 1893), novelist, short-story writer and poet. She has produced many fine studies, more especially of feminine character, sensitively written, her latest book, *The Corner That Held Them* (1948), being an imaginative reconstruction of life in a fourteenth-century Benedictine convent. A Northern Irish writer, Forrest Reid (1876–1947), wrote his last book, *Young Tom*, in 1944, one of many books the excellence of which lay in the truthful and sympathetic presentation of the thought and spirit of boys. Very fine work about ships and sailors, written with sensibility, has been done by a self-taught writer, James Hanley (born 1901).

Then, of course, there are authors who, writers of many clever books, have the happy inspiration which results in a *tour de force*; an example being *A High Wind in Jamaica* (1929) by Richard Hughes (born 1900); and another, *Tobit Transplanted* (1931), by Stella Benson (1892–1933), in which highly ingenious use was made of the Apocryphal story in a Korean setting. Stella

Benson was a brilliant descriptive writer skilled in evoking Far-Eastern scenes.

But, as I say, the contemporary reviewer was confounded by the number of clever novelists who called so often for superlatives from his pen. There was, and is, Rose Macaulay, who, having made a name with *Dangerous Ages* (1921), has gone on producing novels, books of criticism, essays and travel books, distinguished by a sharp perception, austere judgment and caustic humour. Throughout the last thirty years Rebecca West (born 1892), armed with a quick and pungent wit, has been a forceful personality in the literary world, whose books, clever as they are, have never been quite equal to her personality or her reputation; but there are thought and powerful writing in her novels *The Return of the Soldier* (1918), *The Judge* (1922), *The Thinking Reed* (1936); and during the war she produced a massive and provocative work on her researches in Jugoslavia *Black Lamb and Grey Falcon* (1942). Among the clever and deservedly noticed novelists of this period were many women—Sheila Kaye-Smith, Storm Jameson, E. M. Delafield (died 1943), Romer Wilson, Emily Hilda Young (died 1949), Winifred Holtby (1898–1935) and Clemence Dane (Winifred Ashton) who has not only written many skilfully devised novels, the best of which was *Legend* (1919), but also several plays, the most successful of which was *A Bill of Divorcement* (1921). A high place among these women novelists is held by Ivy Compton-Burnett.[1] Her method is to present groups of upper-class persons talking with preternatural cleverness or stupidity about everyday things, and let their talk betray their characters till sinister truth emerges, sometimes suddenly and violently. She is a subtle and mordant writer who provokes intense admiration in some intellectuals and irritation in others.

Among the men who held their own against the women novelists was Hugh Walpole (1884–1941: knighted in 1937). He wrote at least one good book, *The Dark Forest* (1916), under the inspiration of war experience, and built up a wide reputation through facility, persistence and adroitness. Frank Swinnerton

---

[1] Author of *Dolores* (1913), *Pastors and Masters* (1925), *Brothers and Sisters* (1929), *Men and Wives* (1931), *More Women Than Men* (1933), *A House and its Head* (1935), *Daughters and Sons* (1937), *A Family and a Fortune* (1939), *Parents and Children* (1941), *Elders and Betters* (1944) and *Two Worlds and their Ways* (1949).

(born 1884) is a more genuine writer, most of whose novels are peopled with London characters faithfully observed and wittily represented. Francis Brett Young (born 1884)[1] has presented delicate character-studies and describes the rural midlands with feeling. Two other novelists must be mentioned here—R. H. Mottram (born 1883), author of *The Spanish Farm* (1924) and many other novels, and Richard Church (born 1893) who, with novels, poems, books of criticism and essays is one of the most versatile and prolific writers of the period.

Of popular novelists foremost among best-sellers in the last thirty years there are two who might be taken seriously by literary critics. No two writers could be more unlike each other than Charles Langbridge Morgan and John Boynton Priestley, both of whom first saw the light (in the literal sense) in 1894. The first is inevitably thought of as an æsthete, his style refined, sensuous, artificial, but mobile enough to convey the action and emotion which have so often taken his readers by storm. *Portrait in a Mirror* (1929) was his first notable success. *The Fountain* (1932) and *Sparkenbroke* (1936) captivated the middle classes in Britain, America and Europe. In France his serious reputation stands higher than in Britain.

There is no such æstheticism about Priestley. He is blunt, downright, honest-to-God British in style and sentiment. Before he became a popular idol he was a lively essayist making spirited contributions to the *Saturday Review* and the *Weekend Review* and wrote an admirable nightmarish story *Benighted* (1927) which is perhaps the best of his books. Then he set himself with great determination to write a picaresque novel which everyone was to read; and they did. In *The Good Companions* (1929), as in all his subsequent novels, he identifies himself with the man-in-the-street, writing about this not wholly mythical person from the average point of view of that person himself—cheerful, optimistic, sententious, eating and drinking, loving stories, eschewing dishonest subtlety. He stands for robust good health, sound morals, simple, anti-morbid reflection. He has, with his customary thoroughness, mastered the technique of the stage, and

[1] Author of *The Young Physician* (1919), *Portrait of Clare* (1927), and *Cotswold Honey* (1940) and other novels.

the popular intellectual or moral problems posed in his plays gratify the self-esteem of his audiences; for it is never difficult to understand him. He is a successful broadcaster and a formidable public speaker—a valuable patriot. His *Festival at Farbridge* (1951) became one of the events in the Festival of Britain.

We now approach, not without fear and trembling, a number of authors who, differing as they do in every other way, have this in common, that they are intensely preoccupied with the problem of Good and Evil, and the conflict between them in the modern world; and in all cases the problem owes its importance to the fact that they are humanists, who find it hard to reconcile human frailty and human suffering with omnipotent Goodness. There is a good deal in common between two men, who were friends, Charles Walter Stansby Williams (1886–1945) and C. S. Lewis (born 1898), a Fellow and Tutor of Magdalen College, Oxford. In reading their more recent books I instinctively thought of another writer, older than Williams, and much older than Lewis —John Cowper Powys (born 1872)—who had, like them, a catholic interest in literature, and something of the same spiritual aloofness, but none the less, as essayist, novelist and man, approached the world from exactly the opposite theoretical point of view. Powys was content to embrace life without accepting the validity of theological premises. But such premises are implicit in everything written by Williams and Lewis. Williams was a very versatile yet very thorough writer. He produced poems, plays, criticism, novels, and stories with mystical themes, the best of his books being, I think, his last, *All Hallows Eve* (1945).

This book is a kind of sublimated 'thriller'. It is packed with fantastic adventure. There are moments of suspense which will make the reader hold his breath. It is sensational, but with a significance which belongs to an exalted order of experience, and could hardly have been written by anyone who did not know his Dante and Milton well, and had not peered into strange by-ways of theology and psychology. One may compare the book with the ghost-stories of M. R. James, who had similar skill in making us sense the tangible evil of the Devil, and smell the horrible odour left by his presence. But Williams did not set out to make our hair stand on end, but to tell a straight story, plausible enough granted the hypotheses, of persons dead and living who have influence on one another at points where their realms touch. It is not all allegory, but without its spiritual meaning it could not exist. In the story we watch a sort of wrestling match between the powers of good and evil, between selfishness and pure selflessness—or love. On the one side a dead girl Lester and a living girl Betty, on the other, another girl, the petty-minded Evelyn and the 'sorcerer'—a sinister, formidable personality of unique will power and devouring ambition who has set himself to be a sort of spiritual Hitler, using his psychic powers to induce the civilized and uncivilized world to accept him as a prophet. The book is sensational in the last degree, with gangster-dom transferred to the world of spirits. But is it more sensational than *Paradise Lost* or the sixth book of the *Æneid*? Lester returns to the world of the living as simply as Æneas went to the shades of Avernus. Williams, succeeding in carrying us along with him in suspension of disbelief, was justified in choosing a subject so strange and full of miracles.

C. S. Lewis is equally strange; equally devoted to the fantastic. He is a scholar who wrote a very brilliant and illuminating book on mediæval allegory, entitled *The Allegory of Love* (1936). But he has chosen in recent years to cast his ideas about good and evil, and especially about the moral crisis through which the world is now passing, in the form of fiction. The most remarkable of his novels, and the most beautiful, is the allegorical *Perelandra* (1943), which describes the journey of a certain Dr. Ransom to the planet Perelandra, where he was the spectator of the unsuccessful tempting of a new Eve by the Devil. This book is an amazing *tour de force*. It is not often that a story-teller can make the idyllically beautiful seem beautiful, but it is a delight to re-member Lewis's lovely islands in his lovely planet and to savour them like the most delicious of spring mornings. But the most brilliant thing in the book is the encounter between Dr. Ransom and the scientist turned Devil, and the girl, an exquisitely naïve and ingenuous Eve; and the plausible conversation in which they argue with her to seduce her or save her soul.

We meet Dr. Ransom again in *That Hideous Strength* (1945) where, having saved Perelandra, he is engaged in the more difficult work of trying to save our own less fortunate world. There are some very ugly things of modern life which he presents for our inspection. He must have written the book shortly before the first appearance of the atom bomb, anticipating something as bad or worse.

> The physical sciences, good and innocent in themselves, had already, even in Ransom's time [that is, our time], begun to be warped, had been subtly manœuvred [by powers of evil], in a certain direction. Despair of objective truth had been increasingly insinuated into the scientists; indifference to it, and a concentration upon mere power, had been the result. Babble about *élan vital* and flirtations with parapsychism were bidding fair to restore the *anima mundi* of the magicians. Dreams of the far future destiny of man were dragging up from its shallow and unquiet grave the old dream of man as God.

He asks us to suppose that a critical moment in the history of the world has just arrived when the old Druid, Merlin, incarnating the dark powers of magic, could be awakened from slumber, and his forces united with those of omnipotent science; fallen man would shake off the limitation of his powers; Nature would be enslaved by the irresistible cunning of science and magic; and 'hell would be at last incarnate'. The story is set in the middle of the twentieth century when the Devil is making his last terrific bid for mastery. The gentle Dr. Ransom is fighting for the good powers; the evil powers are seen entrenched at Belbury, the stronghold of a gang of scientists with totalitarian ambitions. How plausibly, ingeniously and humanly these devils talk in this University of fiends! The author's good folk are not so interesting as the demons. In the celestial sphere of Perelandra he is at home among the angels, but on earth he is at his best among the devils.

Aldous Huxley (born 1894), too, has become preoccupied with the problem of good and evil; and in his case, perhaps, it is a pity. He is undoubtedly among the cleverest of living English writers. That is both his good and his bad fortune. Without this cleverness we should have been deprived of the exquisite bantering of his earlier novels with their cynicism so lightly worn as to leave no sting, with mellifluous sentences which were not so studied as to be tiresome. And in the twenties, when he shone in this vein, in such books as *Chrome Yellow* (1921), *Antic Hay* (1923) and *Point Counter Point* (1928), the gentle mockery of life which had become the vogue was still fresh enough to have the charm of novelty. He was easily first in this kind. He charmed, he amused, he stimulated the critical faculty. To-day, when he has become so serious, so disgusted with the world, so intent upon the pursuit of eternal verities, his cleverness is still with him, but it is like a thing of the flesh impeding his progress along the mystic way, on which, as preacher, he would lead us, but from which, as artist, he wilfully strays.

As early as 1932 his light satire is already beginning to be transformed into bitterness and denunciation. The novel which appeared in that year, *Brave New World,* was concerned with a society in which the reproduction of the human species is arranged by biochemists in the laboratory. The result, of course, is not nice, and Mr. Huxley lets us know that he prefers a world where love is not regarded as a relic of savagery. In 1941, when he produced *Grey Eminence,* he seems to have settled down to the theme which has since been his principal preoccupation, that of the world, the flesh and the devil in opposition to eternity. In this biography of Father Joseph he rather strained historic facts to present the conflict between the religious mystic and the man of the world. We have the same theme in his novel *Time Must Have a Stop* (1945), where Huxley, though he appears to be espousing the cause of God and Eternity, evidently takes more delight in the Devil and his fleeting allurements—the *fascinatio nugacitatis,* the 'magic of triviality'—the 'being spellbound by mere footling'. In this book the uncle of the hero, Eustace, is one who might have been the subject of a *Marius the Epicurean,* but in Huxley's hands turns into a very naughty kind of Marius who, on principle, and in sheer protest against the evil of being good, pursues wine and women and the 'cult of decorous behaviour', and justifies himself wittily in argument and charmingly in action by being sympathetic and good-natured to everyone. After the death of this voluptuary we watch his disembodied spirit valiantly seeking to defend his temporality against the assaults of eternity. The saint, Bruno Rontini, 'loving God selflessly every moment of every day', is an artistic anti-climax. The artist and the mystic are at war within Aldous Huxley. In this book the artist generally gets the upper hand, but in doing so is constrained to make wry faces at the serious matters which are his theme. It is disconcerting to observe him, obsessed by the Rabelaisian absurdity of the human race, unable to express himself without ribaldry and constant resort to schoolboyish naughty talk, and the next moment asking us to survey the scene with the mystical serenity of the saint.

If in this book we are convinced that Huxley esteems the saint but loves the devil, not so in his latest work, *Ape and Essence* (1949), written in the form of a film-script. Here his abomination of the human species in the form which he thinks it is now assuming has reached such a pitch that he can find no terms too hideous in which to describe the sub-human monsters who survive an atomic war. It is difficult to see what purpose is served by this fantasy of unrelieved ugliness. Is it intended as an awful warning? If so, it is not convincing. We may hope it is only a lapse in the career of this very brilliant writer.

Arthur Koestler is a Jew who was born in Hungary, has farmed in Palestine, has travelled all over Europe, and some years before the war became a Communist. He has recently explained what there was in Communism which irresistibly attracted him, and the mental and moral struggle he underwent in renouncing it. He joined the British Army in 1940 and since the war has pursued his literary life in Wales.

Long ago George Meredith pleaded the case for more brain-stuff in fiction, and endeavoured to set an example himself. Arthur Koestler, in a very different way, has made a similar attempt, and succeeded. It is in ideas that he is primarily interested, hard, comprehensive ideas about modern society, about history, and humanity, backed by facts and logical argument, but when he is writing fiction these ideas are always presented as forces operative in the lives of individual persons. No novel was ever more full of 'brain-stuff' than *Darkness at Noon*, where he dissected with the skill of an anatomist the tortuous logical proceedings that go on in the mind of an orthodox Communist and the reflections of the just-less-than-orthodox Communist who was in prison. This book gives probably the best account that has ever been written of what goes on within the prison walls in a Communist country when an accused is under examination.

Koestler has behind him the experience to give a truthful and realistic account of the terrible technique by which the Communists set out deliberately to subdue the minds of their victims. He has also the artistry to reconstruct the reflections and emotions of the victim and to turn the sequence of words into an ordered tragic drama. He proceeds objectively. The author does not obtrude himself. This, he has been saying, is what happened; this is how these persons thought; there is the picture—take it or leave it.

Thieves in the Night (1946) is another novel whose interest lies in thoughts, the thoughts being the subject-matter of the author's imagination. The scene is set in Palestine just before the second World War, but already there were all the makings of the conflict between Jews and Arabs which was to come, with the Jewish settlers active, purposeful, intent on making the country their own, the Arabs resentful of the intruders and fearful of being dominated by them, and British officials burdened with the thankless task of keeping the peace between them. Koestler introduces us to a small pioneer settlement of Hebrew immigrants where a number of sophisticated young Jews are making an experiment in Communism, not that of Moscow, but of the original Essenes who founded communities in the desert based on the sharing of labour and its fruits.

How skilfully he describes the daily life of these energetic, nervous people, addicts of Marx, devotees of Beethoven, talking glibly in terms of Freud and Jung, while digging the soil, shouldering a rifle, and producing quiversful of children; and something also of the lives of the less enterprising Arabs in the neighbouring village whose Mukhtar remarks: 'We have no propaganda offices in the capitals of Europe and no gold to buy newspapers and influential friends. We are a poor, simple and hardworking people who only ask that the earth which belonged to our fathers and fathers' fathers should not be taken away from us.'

The hero is a man who threw in his lot with the Jews from intellectual conviction. He looks upon them as the 'exposed nerve' of the human species. Jewry he conceives to be a 'sick race', suffering from the disease of homelessness. 'I became a socialist' he exclaims, 'because I hated the poor; and I became a Hebrew because I hated the Yid.' The burden of the book is to show how it comes that this race of people, suffering from centuries of homelessness and from persecution in Europe, have become intent upon finding a home at any cost; how it has happened that, for all their imagination and humanity, they closed their eyes to the claims of the Arab, passionately pursuing their own ends even if it led them, as it did, to violence and terrorism.

Arthur Koestler is an artist. He tries not to take sides. He shows the good and the bad, the wise and the foolish, the beautiful and the ugly, in Jews and Arabs and British. If the balance is weighted just a little in favour of those who interest him most, that does not prevent the book from being a searching study in psychology, objective in method, humane in spirit and brilliant as a picture of human beings. This author is breaking new ground in fiction. He is writing novels which illuminate the major problems of the contemporary world without deviating from the way of the imagination.[1]

'To-day our world seems peculiarly susceptible to brutality. There is a touch of nostalgia in the pleasure we take in gangster novels, in characters who have so agreeably simplified their emotions that they have begun living again at a level below the cerebral.'

'There seemed to be a seediness about the place you couldn't get to the same extent elsewhere, and seediness has a very deep appeal: even the seediness of civilization, of the sky-signs in Leicester Square, the "tarts" in Bond Street, the smell of cooking greens off Tottenham Court Road, the motor salesmen in Great Portland Street.'

'When one sees to what unhappiness, to what peril of extinction centuries of cerebration have brought us, one sometimes has a curiosity to discover if one can from what we have come, to recall at which point we went astray.'

These passages are taken from a comparatively early book by Graham Greene (born 1904)—*Journey Without Maps* (1936), an account of his travels in the savage, unsavoury hinterland of the Republic of Liberia. They are indicative of his approach to life, which is the same as his approach to literature. He is aware of all the funny things which made Gerhardi think life so

[1] The *Age of Longing* (1951), its scene in Paris, is a somewhat pessimistic diagnosis of the mental unrest caused by the ideological war.

amusingly tiresome; of all the extremely horrible things which seem to have driven Aldous Huxley to detest the human race; of the war between principles of good and evil which set Williams and C. S. Lewis speculating fancifully about the intervention of superterrestrial forces in our mundane affairs. But his approach to these sinister things is different. His greatest admirers cannot but marvel at the manner in which, unflinchingly, he so often seeks out what is repulsive and putrescent, though one notes that in these adventures there was always the chance of finding— what?—'*King Solomon's Mines*, the "heart of darkness", or . . .?' Graham Greene would never commit himself to saying 'romance', though he was willing to be 'aware of Proteus rising from the sea'.

In his more important books one can never forget that he is a convert to Roman Catholicism, but his religion leads him not to turn his back on the wicked world, but to embrace it, and to wrestle with it and plumb its depths, not in any hatred even of its foulness, since even there, in creatures bestial and unredeemed, he recognizes the image of God. No doubt the motives in his personal and literary adventures are mixed; no doubt he is moved by love of life, desire for amusement, curiosity, even the want of literary 'copy' and much beside the desire to probe the realities of ugliness and sin and all that challenges beauty and holiness. I do not think he went to Liberia as a crusader or a missionary; but I am sure it was more than the search for copy which sent him there and to other 'dark' parts of the world, or made him spend his nights in squalid bomb shelters during the bombardment of London and get himself sent to pestilential West Africa on a war mission.

In asserting that Graham Greene is a writer worth taking very seriously one should be careful not to treat him only seriously, as if he himself were one of our social problems. He is a man with tastes as well as convictions. His preoccupation with the painful does not preclude pleasure. His wit is not all savage satire. He can be harsh and he can be gentle—he is not, like some of his contemporaries, ashamed of gentleness. He enjoys excitement, and his novels seldom fail to create excitement in his readers. Some of his books have been written simply to entertain, and have been described by him as 'entertainments'. Among the best of these is *The Ministry of Fear* (1943), a sort of sublimated thriller in which the author takes the reader breathless through dark plots and leaves him bewildered and enchanted. Even his much more serious book, *Brighton Rock* (1938), is so admirably constructed as a book of adventure and crime, so quick in its pace and compelling in its horror, that we are not wholly absorbed by the moral problem and the precocious criminality of its young hero. In the book which at this moment is the latest of his novels, *The Heart of the Matter* (1948), the moral and spiritual issue is dominant. The devil is in the world with a vengeance, and the spirit wrestling with it in a world of black horror; but in this case—what is rare with Greene—the theme has overburdened the novelist, with the result that we are not wholly convinced, nor is our interest necessarily held.

Certainly there may be differences of opinion about *The Heart of the Matter*, but at least one book of Greene's stands beyond question. *The Power and the Glory* (1940) will rank among the major novels of this century. The scene is laid in a Communist State in Mexico. It is a book which deals almost exclusively with the painful and the squalid; people degenerate, or hopeless, or hypocritically complacent, or deeply sunk in poverty and vice, living among rats and beetles and dirt, in a society in which we meet only one straight-living man—the Communist Lieutenant conscientiously engaged in hunting and shooting offenders—and only one saint, and he is a drunkard and the father of an illegitimate child. Yet out of this material Greene has made his masterpiece. The story unfolds itself in a series of sharply drawn scenes. These realistic snapshots of a horribly human hell present a sustained and exciting plot. Only the Communist Lieutenant, purposeful, buoyed up with his ideological faith, knows exactly what he is about. The 'Whiskey Priest' is a fugitive from justice. The rest drift dreadfully in meanness, or poverty, or fear—fear of this world and the next. 'I would rather die,' says one of the least obviously unfortunate of the persons. 'Of course,' says her husband; 'that goes without saying. But we have to go on living.' 'I am not afraid of other people's ideas,' says the Communist Lieutenant, after he has been listening all night in the forest hut to the story of Calvary. In the filthy crowded cell where a score of prisoners are cooped up for the night a woman offers the priest a drink. He had been saying: 'God so loved the world. . . . My children, you must never think the holy martyrs are like me. You have a name for it. . . . I am a whiskey priest. I am in here now because they found a bottle of brandy in my pocket.' 'One of the Fathers has told me that joy always depends on pain. Pain is part of joy,' says the priest, when he has been saying Mass to the villagers who have sheltered him for a night. 'There was a smell of hot wax from where a candle drooped in the immense nocturnal heat. . . . The smell of unwashed human beings warred with the wax. He cried out stubbornly in a voice of authority. "That is why I tell you that heaven is here: this is a part of heaven just as pain is a part of pleasure." '

He said 'Pray that you will suffer more and more and more. Never get tired of suffering. The police watching you, the soldiers gathering taxes, the beating you always get from the jefe because you are too poor to pay, smallpox and fever, hunger . . . that is all part of heaven—the preparation. Perhaps without them, who can tell, you wouldn't enjoy heaven so much. Heaven would not be complete. And heaven. What is heaven?'[1] Literary phrases from what now seemed to be another life altogether—the strict quiet life of the seminary—became confused on his tongue: the names of precious stones. Jerusalem the Golden. But these people had never seen gold.

This passage makes explicit what is elsewhere implicit in Greene's work, where he takes us into hideous depths of the human hell in order to touch the heights of redemption and beauty—redemption through suffering—beauty through ugliness. 'I'm a bad priest . . . I know—from experience—how much beauty Satan carried down with him when he fell. Nobody ever said the fallen angels were the ugly ones.' The character of this unwashed, all-too-human priest, living 'in mortal sin' is one of the most disconcerting and moving things in fiction. The author has painted a stark picture of human pitifulness with the sinner-saint discovering the angel within the maimed human soul. 'Hate was just a failure of the imagination.' 'When you saw the lines at the corners of the eyes, the shape of the mouth, how the hair grew, it was impossible to hate.' But Graham Greene does not preach. He is ruthless, aloof; in his detached rearrangement of life at its worst he evokes pity and the extremity of terror, and dares to re-interpret Scripture in terms of its original charity.

[1] A comparable glorification of suffering in contemporary literature may be found in the (much less compassionate) satisfaction of Reilly on hearing of Celia's crucifixion over a tropical ant-heap in T. S. Eliot's *The Cocktail Party* (1949).

I do not think there is any living English novelist whose work, at its best, and within its limits, so nearly reaches artistic perfection as Rosamond Lehmann's. I say 'within its limits', for with all her cleverness she is not a considerable thinker, like Graham Greene; she takes little interest in public affairs; she does not appear to be concerned about the world's religion or the world's morals. She presents the inner lives of certain human beings—mainly of the middle and upper classes, though she can be quite sympathetic to people of a humbler class—their feelings, their perceptions, their crises, their experiences within the scope of an arranged situation. People come first with her, especially young people, indeed children. 'Novelists must be able to love men and women,' she wrote in an essay on *The Future of the Novel*.[1] 'Their greatness depends on this. Appreciation, compassion for humanity is what the great nineteenth century novelists felt. . . . They criticized human beings, they laughed at them, they condemned their wicked ways, but they loved and believed in them enough to endow their heroes and heroines with a moral stature which time cannot affect.'

In the same essay she makes another demand which her own writing admirably satisfies. 'The novelist,' she says, 'must care tremendously about words, about every word in every phrase, every sentence, every paragraph; about the rhythms of prose, which can be as subtle as those of poetry, and although less concentrated, should give almost if not quite as much trouble in the making.' And in another paragraph she perhaps gives the explanation for the fewness of her books. 'There is a "still centre" for the novelist as for any other artist.' It is as true for the novel as for a poem that 'Its genesis is the image, or isolated images which have become embedded in the mass of accumulated material in the author's "centre".' Rosamond Lehmann only sets herself to write when something is pressing to emerge from her creative consciousness. When it does, it is something of a fine spiritual texture, delicately spun, beautifully wrought, shining with a gemlike purity.

As a very young woman she made her reputation with *Dusty Answer* (1927), a novel in the first half of which she gave an extraordinarily spirited, one might almost say spiritual, picture of the life of a group of children; the atmosphere of the riverside

[1] Published in *Britain Today* (June 1946).

home and its inmates was exhilarating and magical. The author had not so thoroughly thought herself into the life described in the second part of the book, in which the main character was becoming adult; the cleverness, the good writing, remained, the seriousness increased, but the magic disappeared. She never, I think, repeated that mistake. Her second book, *A Note in Music* (1930) was all of one piece. We notice here the influence of Virginia Woolf, as indeed we do in the two books that follow, *Invitation to the Waltz* (1932) and *The Weather in the Streets* (1936). *Invitation to the Waltz* is a little masterpiece. It is very slight. It records the reactions of a young and diffident girl to a social occasion; the occasion assumes its own importance for the young participant; every page trembles with delicate sensibility as we watch the incidents through the eyes of the girl. Slight as it is this book is perfect within its narrow limits.

For some time admirers of Rosamond Lehmann felt that she would always be at her best in making gracious, delicate vignettes of children or adolescents, seen through the eyes of one who refused to be more than just a little older than they. But in a later long novel, *The Ballad and the Source* (1945), she proved that she had it in her to do much more. In this book the technique of Henry James, as used in *The Aspern Papers,* is more evident than that of Virginia Woolf, but the style has become her own. This time she has ventured upon a daring theme, embracing a group of people in three generations cast for the tragic life—the disaster originating in a fault or error tragic in the Aristotelian sense, whose consequences cast their shadow on all concerned in the affair. Her skill in delineating the mind of a child justifies her use of the device employed by Henry James in *What Maisie Knew*; she tells the whole story as it became known to a girl who is only ten years, and later, fourteen years old. That such a story can be told through such a medium is strange indeed—it is one of passion, maternal love, paternal cruelty, incest, insanity, artistic fulfilment and many other amazing ingredients—yet the whole thing is achieved with delicacy and without any strain on the credulity.

It is the little girl, Rebecca, who tells us the grim story, who at different points in the narrative listens, rapt, as others tell her what they know of the affair, she egging them on to tell more and more, they responding to her eagerness. She gives it mostly as it is told to her, first in the random talk of an old needle-woman

13

who has known all the persons concerned for generations; next through the eyes of an elderly lady who confides to her with a scarcely believable frankness the troublous tale as she remembers it. The last, and bloodcurdling, details emerge from what a girl, aged sixteen, tells to Rebecca, aged fourteen, in a heart-to-heart schoolgirl talk.

The skill of the telling lies in the manner in which the past is recreated and brought into the present. Perhaps it could never have happened—that so much could have been told to a child, or so much understood. But the author has made it seem possible. And in spite of all, beyond a child's ken, that this little girl has been appointed to convey to us, she remains a child, and her relations with other children are robustly real. The pace of the story is slow and deliberate. We sometimes feel an almost too careful choosing of words. But the percipience which distinguished her earlier books is not dimmed, and responds to these wider tracts of life. Her admirers will be amazed by the touch of the sensational and even the monstrous towards the end of the book, but even more by the fact that so delicate a style can stand up against such violent matter. It has required a *tour de force* to avoid literary disaster; she has just avoided it, though the book would have been more satisfying if at the end we had not been plunged into such deep waters. It is a sign of the author's remarkable skill that she has dared to run so many artistic risks and has emerged triumphantly. With this book she advanced a reputation which already stood high. She has now reached the time of life when a novelist should be at his or her best.

Elizabeth Bowen competes with Rosamond Lehmann for first place among the women novelists now writing in England. (She was born in Ireland.) Those who prefer that passion should be deeply embedded in romance will give the palm to the former. Elizabeth Bowen in some earlier age might have been a lyrical poet or, if she had been writing prose a hundred years ago, it might have been in the manner of Emily Brontë. But to write in that unguarded way would have been quite impossible for one brought up as she had been, a student of modern literary technique—in the schools of Flaubert, Tchekov, James and Virginia Woolf. Passion with her would have to be modified by rarefication, feelings by subtle analysis; impulse to frankness would be subdued under the restraints of art. But for all that the poetry of passion would never be far away, and the expression or remembrance of young passion would not be absent because encompassed by a delicate net of interesting circumstance. Since she has so much of the lyrical poet in her it is not surprising that she is at her best in short stories. 'The short storyist,' she has said herself,[1] 'shares— or should share—to an extent the faculties of the poet: he can render the great significance of the small event. He can register the emotional colour of a moment. He gains rather than loses by being close up to what is immediately happening. He can take, for the theme of his story, a face glimpsed in the street, an unexplained incident, a snatch of talk overheard in a bus or train.' In early 1945 she felt that 'war-time London—blitzed, cosmopolitan, electric with expectation—now teems, I feel, with untold but tellable stories; glitters with scenes that cry aloud for the pen.'

And so we have some of the best of her work in such books of stories as *Encounters* (1923), *Ann Lees* (1926), *Joining Charles* (1929), *The Cat Jumps* (1934), *Look at all Those Roses* (1941) and *The Demon Lover* (1945). In many cases she strikes the note she wants us to hear in the first sentence, and it is that which we hear till the end. 'The mysterious thing was that the wood was full of people,' she will begin, introducing an ill-assorted couple who for a moment in autumn are to pass before the eyes of the people in the wood. I doubt if any other living writer of English has her power of evoking in a few pages 'the emotional colour of a moment', a mood which, evanescent as it is, lingers in the memory.

In her novels she excels above all in portraying women young, or recently young, of excessive sensibility suffering under the impact of passion. By her skill in describing a scene she can add atmosphere to the mood of the persons whose behaviour she shows. She has no lack of humour, and with it she deftly relieves the tension when it might have become oppressive. But we are always brought near to tragedy in the exhibition of temperament, torturing itself, in the young girls in *Friends and Relations* (1931), *To the North* (1932), *The House in Paris* (1938) or rather older women in *The Death of the Heart* (1938) or *The Heat of the Day* (1949).

[1] In an essay contributed to *Britain Today* (May 1945).

She conveys feeling with a sure as well as a sensitive hand. In *The Heat of the Day* the feeling she has to convey may be that awakened by a London park when the sun is setting, or the sounds and silences of London heard in a flat in war-time, or the sight of strangers at a funeral, or a house in Ireland haunted by memories and revisited after long absence, or two Cockney girls discussing life in a sordid bedroom, or lover meeting lover under the shadow of approaching disaster. In the description of slight things—minute, detailed description—there is a sense almost always of apprehension, of something beyond happening or about to happen, though the expectation as likely as not will never be satisfied by anything tangible or propoundable. In all her books we are taken through a world felt by the author in a certain way—in *The Heat of the Day* it is for the most part the world of London in war-time. In the background there is the war itself, on a grand scale in the distance or nearer at hand, more intimately perceived—bombings and blackout and people habituated to the war-time way of life.

In the centre of the story is Stella Rodney, who had married and divorced a husband twenty years ago, and now divides her attention between Robert, her lover, and the nineteen-year-old Roderick, her son. Has she come to be accepted by her son, she wonders, as a woman *capable de tout*? And there is another man, Harrison, whom the author does not consent to turn into the villain of the piece, as she might have done. 'In tragic life . . . no villain need be.' In this *milieu* we watch the behaviour of the subtle, the refined, the adult under the influence of emotion; and from these we turn to the *milieu* of the vulgar little Cockneys, Lorrie and Connie, and their reaction to experiences not fundamentally different. What is the difference that refinement makes?

The thread of plot on which the story is hung is sensational—which is as strange as the sensational conclusion noted in Rosamond Lehmann's novel; both authors can do so much without that violence. It transpires that Stella's lover is a traitor and is giving information to the enemy, and that the other man, Harrison, is playing upon her fears by telling her the truth and holding over her the threat of exposure. This is not convincing, nor is it easy to understand why Robert's hand should be turned against his country— there is nothing in his character to make this probable. Yet the author's procedure is never melodramatic. With a situation that will scarcely bear examination she has none the less pursued her own quiet way, evoking atmosphere in her own distinctive style, conveying her percipience of place and the people oddly assembled. At times the novel gets out of hand; the long plot bothers her, and she occasionally spends her power on situations and people for the sake of describing them when they have little to add to the theme. Though all is beautifully written, part is irrelevant and unproductive. But we move on to more essential passages which reveal all her skill and linger in the mind— the funeral scene, the visit to the empty house in Ireland, the talk between Roderick and his mad cousin Nettie, and a passionate love scene between Stella and Robert. 'I don't understand fine feelings' says Harrison to Stella. 'Fine feelings, you've got to have time to have: I haven't.'

There are fine feelings in every page of this and all her books; Elizabeth Bowen has time for them. Perhaps sometimes one wishes she were busier elsewhere—a little more Martha at the expense of Mary. But her humour comes to the rescue with delicious touches of comedy. With her, judgment is in control. She can go far into the upper air, but knows when it would be dangerous to go further.

The story of contemporary fiction is not exhausted when we have mentioned a few outstanding writers. At the moment it would not be true to say that any one definable 'movement' is uppermost, or that the more important writers can be interpreted as examples of a school. The greater writers who have been discussed in these pages have had their influence on the younger, but the parentage is not always obvious. V. S. Pritchett (born 1900) was producing promising work twenty years ago, and has now an assured place among established writers of novels and short stories. He is at home with almost Dickensian humour among working-class types, but there is a subtlety and a poetic background to his work, economy and precision in his style, and a detachment in approach to his subjects which are the reverse of Dickensian. It should be added that he is a very good critic. The versatile William Plomer (born 1903), who has written fiction, biographies, poems and critiques of books, is perhaps at his best in short stories, apparently not uninfluenced by

Kipling, and in narrative poems rich in movement and of a subtle, highly original piquancy. Joyce Cary (born 1888) started writing twenty years ago. The variety of his early personal experiences is reflected in the variety of the subjects he has treated, which are drawn from Africa, from artistic circles, from the working classes and upper-middle classes. He can be humorous and poignantly serious. A versatile, unpredictable, but always interesting writer.

Henry Green (born 1905) has a style and atmosphere which he has made his own. He wrote his first book, *Blindness* (1926), when he was still in his teens; attracted attention with *Living* (1929) and has since produced *Party Going* (1939), *Pack My Bag* (1940), *Caught* (1943), *Loving* (1945) and *Concluding* (1948). He shines as a writer of realistic dialogue, but is in essence a poet, with singular skill in leaving us with a sense of the symbolic significance of the life he has described.

H. E. Bates (born 1905) charmed before the war with his realistic stories of country life and the delicacy of his style, and has since done powerful work, part of it based on his war experience. William Sansom (born 1912) is a younger writer who had won admiration by his masterful presentation of the mechanism of contemporary life. Alun Lewis, a Welshman, poet and story-writer who showed promise of producing imaginative work of high distinction, was a casualty in the war. Another Welshman, Rhys Davies, is a poet in temperament but in practice a writer of novels and short stories, beautiful in conception and executed with rare delicacy and charm. He is generally at his best in writing on Welsh themes.

During the war Nigel Balchin (born 1908) wrote two remarkable books, *Darkness Falls From the Air* (1942) and *The Small Back Room* (1943), the latter being a masterly exposition of intrigue and heroism hidden behind the red tape of a war-time State department. George Orwell (died 1950) was a talented and versatile littérateur who, having won a deserved reputation with *Animal Farm* (1945), wrote a book *1984* which has been read all over the world, not because it was a very good novel—it was not—but because it exposed the more sinister realities of totalitarian government. A word must be said about the artist Mervyn Peake, who with *Titus Groane* (1946) and its sequel, *Gormenghast* (1951) succeeded in making a strange success in the sphere of the grotesque out of the most fantastic and unpromising material. And it has been interesting to find that a novelist, Stevie Smith, who made a success before the war with *Novel on Yellow Paper* (1936)—seriously gay, grimly comic, exquisitely inconsequent—has gone on since the war to achieve a greater (literary) success with *The Holiday* (1949). It is less effervescent in comicality but still has a light-heartedness which carries with it a terrifying burden of serious import, of apprehension, of awareness of the tragic problem of the individual and the corresponding problem of the human race in its present perplexities. A book amusing, serious and at moments profound.

Then there is another Green among the novelists—F. L. Green, who has combined fantastic romance with powerful realism in his presentation of character and exciting action, in *On the Night of the Fire* (1939) and *Odd Man Out* (1945), the latter being turned into one of the most notable films of recent years. Alex Comfort (born 1920) in his *This Side Nothing* (1948) has reminded some readers of Gorki, while P. H. Newby's (born 1918) procedure harks back almost to that of the middle-Victorians in the treatment of modern themes. Finally, a word must be said about a book of singular promise published in 1950—*One Omen* by C. M. Woodhouse (born 1917). Among the imaginative books produced by young writers since the war none has impressed me more or given me more pleasure. His earlier book, *Apple of Discord* (1948) was an excellent account of the intricacies of Greek politics which he studied when he was wandering in Greek mountains with the tough men of the Resistance from 1942 to 1944, and afterwards when he held official posts in Athens. This second book, presented in the form of twelve 'stories', shows that he has studied the technique of Russian writers. Here, giving rein to his imagination, he reveals a literary talent which should serve him in good stead as an imaginative writer on any theme that may attract him. He did fine work as a soldier. He is now doing fine work, intellectual and imaginative, as a writer.

Chapter Fifteen

SOME PROSE WRITERS

T. E. Lawrence—G. L. Steer—Lytton Strachey—Lloyd George—Winston Churchill

THE average annual production of new books in Great Britain, excluding reprints, new editions and translations, exceeds ten thousand, and tends to increase year by year. Between them they cover almost all subjects of human, or less than human interest, from aeronautics to religion, from archæology to veterinary science. The greater part of this literature is not literature at all in the æsthetic sense of the term, and does not concern us in this survey. Some of it deals with subjects which may be treated didactically, primarily with a view to giving information, as in historical or sociological text-books; such books may be elevated into literature by the vision of the writer. There are some imaginative works which may have artistic value in one medium, but lack it in another. There are plays, for instance, which have had deserved success on the stage, but when printed in books cannot hold their own as literature. Others succeed in both media. Priestley and Noel Coward are highly skilled in stage-craft; their plays are also readable in book form. That admirable study of the awakened love and idealism of a schoolboy by John Van Druten (born 1901) *Young Woodley,* (successfully produced as a play in 1928), reveals its subtlety in the written word. *Journey's End,* a realistic drama of life in the trenches by R. C. Sherriff (born 1896), produced in the same year, loses much when deprived of the theatre, but remains a notable piece of writing. Clifford Bax (born 1886), author of *The Rose Without a Thorn* (1932) and many historical plays, is an accomplished writer whose dramas may be read with pleasure; and Laurence Housman (born 1865) has written very many short plays on religious and historical subjects. Published often in book form before they were acted they won favour with amateur dramatic societies. His *Victoria Regina* (1937) had a big success on the London stage.

Of those who were continuously writing plays during the last
twenty years the most interesting personality was the Scotsman,
James Bridie (1888-1951. His real name was Osborne Henry
Mavor). There is a rich vitality in all the work of this quick-
minded, humorous, robust commentator on life and character. As
an observer he is interested in history, religion, myth, magic and
love, and romps through the ages discovering historical parallels
for modern situations. His *Tobias and the Angel* (1931) was the
first of his considerable successes in the theatre. He was prolific in
output and varied in theme. Two of his most successful plays
appeared during the war, *The Dragon and the Dove* (1942), and
Mr. Bolfrey (1943), a piece in which the devil is most ingeniously
introduced into modern Scotland. With Bridie's plays it was by no
means always certain that they would succeed on the stage, but the
least actable of them is always stimulating to read.

Of writers who have been making a reputation in the theatre
since the war one is Peter Ustinov (born 1921), author of *The
Banbury Nose* (1944) and the *Indifferent Shepherd* (1948). In a book
containing his plays, published in 1950, he gives an interesting
account of his technique. He is one of the more promising of the
serious younger playwrights. The second, older in age, but not in
reputation, is Christopher Fry; but his characteristic work is in
verse, of which I shall write in the following chapter. It is in poetic
drama, too, that Ronald Duncan (born 1914) has made his mark
with the highly successful *This Way to the Tomb* (1945), which
was followed, less successfully, by *Stratton* (1950).

No language is richer than the English in the literature of
travel, and its reputation has been well sustained in the last thirty
years. The Arab countries of the Middle East have especially cast
a spell over British travellers; the magic of it seems to have
increased for those who have had long familiarity with the Arab
people. The desert scene, the Arab temperament, the enduring
monuments of ancient civilizations, the survival of patriarchal
habits which seem familiar to all versed in the Old Testament,
something of all of these have appealed to certain types of Englishman in whom the love of practical adventure is allied to the
romantic and the mystical. Some quality in the Arab way of life,
not to be found elsewhere, has fascinated these Englishmen,

among whom a few have been superbly gifted with the power of literary expression. During the last century the travellers in the Middle East who have produced famous books have included Burton, with his *Pilgrimage to Mecca*, Doughty, with *Arabia Deserta*, Gertrude Lowthian Bell, with *The Desert and the Sown*, Colonel T. E. Lawrence, with *The Seven Pillars of Wisdom*, and Freya Stark and Bertram Sidney Thomas, with several notable books recording their experiences.

If Doughty is pre-eminent among them as a man of letters, T. E. Lawrence (1888–1935) is first as one who combined great literary talent with important practical achievements. His massive book, *The Seven Pillars of Wisdom*, was first issued in a small privately printed edition in 1926; an abridged version, *Revolt in the Desert*, appeared in 1927; and the whole work was published for general circulation, after his death, in 1935. After the Great War he enlisted under the name of Shaw as an aircraftsman and subsequently lived in carefully guarded retirement. He became a legend, a man of mystery, with whose name rumour was ever busy. To some it seemed that the mind of the public had been as subtly prepared for the posthumous publication as Lawrence himself prepared the minds of the Arabs for revolt against the Turks. But in neither case was the result disappointing. For *The Seven Pillars of Wisdom* is unique in literature. Lawrence was not merely a rare combination of man of action and man of letters. The distinctive qualities which fitted him for literature were qualities without which he could not have succeeded in Arabia; and his literary ability needed, or appeared to need, important events shaped by himself for subject matter. He had an epic theme to handle; there would not have been this epic theme if he had not forced events to take that shape; and he produced the epic. His book is as full of heroes as the *Iliad*, and its Achilles is the author himself. What amazing egotism, one may be tempted to say, what colossal arrogance. Egotistic in some ways he was; he was vain about many little things, with the kind of vanity which made him refuse to correct his spelling or to dress carefully in military circles or pursue orthodox methods of publishing. But he was far too interested in the realities of his work to be capable of wilfully falsifying the facts about it or exaggerating the part he took. In his contacts with universal ideas he was modest in the extreme; and he always felt himself in contact with such ideas

when he was guiding and pushing the Arabs and sharing their
manual labours.

> I had had one craving all my life [he writes]—for the power of
> self-expression in some imaginative form—but had been too
> diffuse ever to acquire a technique. At last accident, with perverted
> humour, in casting me as a man of action had given me place in
> the Arab Revolt, a theme ready and epic to a direct eye and hand,
> thus offering me an outlet in literature, the technique-less art.

That word *technique-less* comes strangely from one who owed
so much to the close study of Doughty and polished and re-
polished his own writing. Lawrence was primarily an artist in
this respect, that the life he would choose to live would have to
be an imaginative life, or one in which his perceptive temper had
free play. He could get on with the Arabs because among them
he could obey his intuition and follow his own code—which
required him to respect their code when asking them to work
with him. He had no patience with the conventional British
military mind, but none the less felt himself to be intensely
British; he contrasted the highly logical Frenchman with the
'imaginative British' who, as practical individuals, see their way
'through the half-closed eye, mistily, by things' essential radiance.'
He simply disobeyed or fooled headquarters when he thought it
inept, but admired those thoroughly British officers who would
do the sensible thing at a moment's notice in defiance of the rules.
He himself was called upon to do the 'sensible' thing all the time
among the Arabs with swiftness and finesse. In hard journeys on
camel-back in the desert he had to forgo even the leisure to 'see
the spiritual loveliness which sometimes came upon us by the
way'. 'In my notes the cruel rather than the beautiful found play.
. . . Pray God that men reading the story will not, for love of
the glamour of strangeness, go out to prostitute themselves and
their talents in serving another race.'
It was a gruelling life of incessant toil, often with illness and
pain—a life of action, but governed throughout by ideas. The
Arabs were discontented, hated the Turks, and wished their
overthrow, and when he joined them were already in ineffectual
revolt in the Hejaz. It would be difficult to bring them to concerted
action and impossible if they thought the British or the French
were playing for their own hands; they would be suspicious of

organized forces landed on the Red Sea, but they would be grateful for supplies, money and technical advisers. It was no use rallying them in the name of religion, for the Turks, too, were Moslems, and the Allies were Christian. But nationality, race—yes—they could be inspired with the ideal of 'vindicating the general rights of all Arabs to national existence'; they could be lured towards the northern goal of an autonomous Damascus or Baghdad. And only by such appeals could the quarrels between tribe and tribe and the blood-feuds be put aside. They must be heartened by successes, flattered, wooed and inspired with an idea which would grow till it became a crusade. When he heard old Auda ibn Zuweid declaring, 'It is not an army, it is a world which is moving on Wejh', he rejoiced, for it revealed a state of mind, the indispensable mass impulse.

Lawrence debated with himself all the theories of war he had ever studied. They were useless for his purpose. The destruction of the enemy—the Arabs could not destroy them. They would not even endure the sorrow of casualties. But they could destroy material; they could make lines of communication untenable. They could never prevail against the Turks as an army. 'But suppose we were an influence, an idea, a thing intangible, invulnerable, without front or back, drifting about like a gas? . . . As we wanted nothing material to live on, so we might offer nothing material to the killing.' It was to be guerrilla warfare, warfare depending on the minds of all the individuals waging it.

The scene is conveyed in muscular, thrifty language. There is drama and splendour in the portraits of the chiefs—Feisal, that conscientious artist among leaders; Auda, a Diomede of the Arabs; Abdulla, like sand—drawn as they make their entrances and exits. The story has the distances of heroic legend, yet the closeness of autobiography; it marches, like the army, by devious ways, but always towards a goal, which was to be accomplished—towards Damascus.

The Doughty-Lawrence tradition has gone on. Other British men and women have followed them, as administrators, exploring travellers, curious seekers after knowledge and experience, friends of the Arabs, drawn to the desert in spite of the toils it imposes. Several of them have claims to be remembered as writers but first among them, I think, Bertram Sidney Thomas (born 1892) and Freya Stark, now Mrs. Stewart Perowne.

Thomas fought in Mesopotamia from 1916 to 1918, and afterwards served as Assistant Political Officer in Mesopotamia and Assistant British Representative in Transjordan. But in 1925 his intimate relations with the Arabs enabled him to take up work in Muscat and Oman, and between 1926 and 1931 he made a number of journeys on camel-back mapping unknown areas of South Arabia. His books *Alarms and Excursions in Arabia* (1931), *Arabia Felix* (1932), *The Arabs* (1938) and *Four Strange Tongues from South Arabia* (1939) reveal his independent spirit and intuitive habit of mind and extraordinary range of knowledge. Freya Stark, equally bold and eager to seek the arduous adventure, is more essentially literary. Her books, so full of life and colour and witty observation, and understanding, are a delight to read even for those who do not know the fascination of the East. She, too, like her predecessors, has experienced the hardships of travel. She has visited remote regions in the Sultanate of Muscat and Oman and on the western borders of the Yemen, and has penetrated the little known Hadhramaut; and, on one long journey, falling sick, recovered only through the skilled attention of an Arab chemist. The tale is told in *The Southern Gates of Arabia* (1936), a book which had been preceded by *The Valleys of the Assassins* (1934), and was followed by *Seen in the Hadhramaut* (1938) and *A Winter in Arabia* (1940). During the late war she put her services at the disposal of the British Government, and some of her experiences during that period are recorded in *East is West* (1945).

It was not till some eight or nine years after the first Great War that the best books of personal experiences began to appear—books such as those by Edmund Blunden, Robert Graves and Siegfried Sassoon, already mentioned. In the same way it is probable that the best literature on the last war has yet to be written; the writers and the public have not come to the frame of mind when they can look back on it with detachment. During the period of operations many books of personal experience were written by fighting men and correspondents and were read by a public eager to know what soldiers, seamen and airmen were experiencing on near and distant battlefields. Among these were that moving book *The Last Enemy* (1942), by the fighter-pilot

Richard Hillary; *Sealed and Delivered* and *When We Build Again* (1942), by George Steer; *The End in Africa* (1943) and *African Trilogy* (1944), by the gifted war-correspondent, Alan Moorehead; *They Died with their Boots on*, by Gerald Kirsch; George Millar's lively record of adventure in *Maquis* (1945); and Eric Williams's story of escape from a German prison in *The Wooden Horse* (1949).

I would not like to pass over what was left, little as it was, by a young man of singular promise, Frank Thompson, who was born in 1920 and died in 1944. (He was the son of Edward Thompson, himself an author of no mean distinction, who wrote with knowledge and imagination about India.) He served for three years in the Middle East with the 'Phantom' Regiment, took part in the Sicilian landing, was parachuted into South Serbia in January, 1944, joined the Bulgarian partisans, and was finally, with his comrades, captured and shot. 'I give you the salute of Freedom,' he called out to the sobbing people as he was marched off to execution. Of his writings we have only his letters written to his family from 1941 to 1944, his diaries, and a number of poems. They are published in a memoir, *There is a Spirit in Europe* (1947). They reveal a man who must have been remarkable at any time, whose mind appears to have developed to an extraordinary maturity, perhaps owing to the testing experiences of war. His background was that of his family life, school at Winchester, and a shortened course at Oxford University. For the rest, he was a soldier, throwing himself vigorously into the life of the officers and men who were with him, learning languages, studying and making friends of the inhabitants of any country he visited, recalling the ancient associations of towns and buildings, always perceptive of the normal beauties which persist in spite of war.

Again and again in reading his letters and diaries one is struck by his intense awareness of the fact that he was living in a critical moment of the world's history, and that it was his function to take the fullest possible part in all that was happening, actively as a soldier, reflectively as a citizen, and zestfully as an individual capable of enjoying life. Admiring the achievements of the Russians he was attracted by the professions of Communism; but was a practising democrat in the sense that he could enter into the spirit of the rank and file of men, of British or any other nationality. 'Tommy Atkins . . . is a sociable follow and gets on like hot cakes with Greeks, Frenchmen, Palestinians.' He was not a fanatic, nor a pedant, and least of all a *poseur*. For all his youth and the Winchester, Horace, Lytton Strachey element in his 'blood stream', he was not at all afraid of showing himself an enthusiast. 'This nineteen hundred and forty-third year of grace,' he exclaims, 'is going to be a great year to live or die in.' To him it seemed that the greatest crisis of the ages had come, not only because the united nations were moving on the road to victory, but because he was thinking 'what a splendid Europe we shall build . . . when all the vitality and talent of its indomitable peoples can be set free for cooperation and creation.' 'How wonderful it would be to call Europe one's fatherland, and think of Krakow, Munich, Rome, Oslo, Madrid as one's own cities!'

His writings are the eloquent self-expression of a youth who not merely fought and died gallantly—many have done that—but who throughout persisted in seeing, and defining, the aim which he believed directed his and his fellows' efforts. If he could have foreseen what was to come after, would he have altered his view? It is enough to reply that if in all countries there had been many men like him the results would have been different.

Perhaps the best of all the comparatively recent books devoted to descriptions of war by an observer or participant, after *Seven Pillars of Wisdom*, is George L. Steer's *The Tree of Gernika* (1937). This record belongs not to the Great War nor to the World War, but to that episode in the Spanish War in which the newly created Basque Republic sought to maintain its independence against ground forces of General Mola's Spanish army, supported by German and Italian ground forces and powerful squadrons of German aeroplanes. George Steer (1909–1944) was among the most brilliant of the young men who left Oxford in the thirties. His gay, ardent, restless temperament sent him from country to country seeking adventure, if possible always at the point where exciting events had significance for the troubled contemporary world. Questing for work and amusement, his instinct for both led him to Abyssinia just before the Abyssinian war. There indeed he found work, but not exactly amusement. Having spent the whole period of the war in that country as a *Times* correspondent and witnessed its spoliation, he wrote his first book, *Cæsar in Abyssinia* (1936).

Wherever trouble was brewing, there George Steer was sure

to be found. So he went to Spain to observe the civil war, some-times in the service of *The Times*, sometimes independently. He was first in the Franco area, afterwards on the other side, in the Basque region around Bilbao. He went with a perfectly open mind, even with some pretence of cynicism about both the parties, and had a good deal to say which was not unfavourable to the Franco organization. The book which he planned to write, and had partly written, on his earlier Spanish experiences never appeared. He preferred to concentrate on a single episode in the tragedy of Spain, the struggle against hopeless odds of the little Basque Republic, which gained its autonomy only after the outbreak of war, and lost it. He told the story in *The Tree of Gernika* (1937).

The procedure by which the Basque Republic was destroyed had its own tragic import; but in addition it was of interest to the whole world because the Germans chose that little war as an opportunity to rehearse the bombing strategy which they were to use in the World War. Steer enjoyed the intimate confidence of the Basque leaders, but he was a correspondent, not a com-batant; and he described what he saw as an onlooker. He observed that what actually broke the heroic resistance of the Basques was not the Spanish troops, nor the insurgent warships attacking from the sea, nor the blockade—though these together must ultimately have prevailed—but the German bombers. He describes the '*mystique* of aviation' as deployed in the field, on lines of communication, and on open cities. Air bombardment, he concluded, does not effectively destroy the bodies of the infantry at the front, or its entrenchments, or even its dumps, which it generally misses; but it does tend to undermine its morale. But when it goes further, and creates despair among the population behind, that despair communicates itself to the infantry, and its will to resist is finally broken. Two years before the World War began Steer notes the method of war which was deliberately adopted by the Germans; it involved not merely attacking the front line, and bringing road traffic to a standstill, and bombing base-line headquarters, but also inspiring terror in civilians. By that policy they conquered the Basques. 'Yet, I wonder,' he reflects, 'whether atrocity pays as a weapon of war.' Consider its international repercussions. Consider 'the evil conscience of the people who had planned it?' Consider the popular feeling of people far away in Great Britain, whose imagination moves to conceive 'the blotting out of Hull, for instance . . . or the end of Portsmouth.' Does it pay—in the long run?

The Tree of Gernika outclasses anything that I have read of recent war literature. There were few books on the first Great War which equal it for exactness of narrative, for force, for imaginative communication, for variety of impressions conveyed, and sustained interest. While the imagination that made these things vivid for him is at work all the time, he is none the less severely exact in recording a multitude of relevant details. He is never loose or vague. He gives the facts with precision. He never attempts to throw a false glamour over people or places. There is a kind of mocking gaiety in his bitterness. He delights in the contrasts between the hideous and the lovely, as when darkness blots out the sight of blood and dirt and reveals only the 'level spurts of fairy flame. It is ethereal, war by night.' His adventurous spirit, his resource, his mischievous humour, his quick sympathy, his clear persuasive reasoning find expression in strong, nervous writing.

His subsequent books, excellent as they were, were not equal to *The Tree of Gernika*, not because his power was diminishing, but because the life of action gave him no leisure. He went to Abyssinia again with the conquering British Army. He was flown into Burma, and joined Wingate behind the enemy lines; and like Wingate, died there. Among the young men of promise who lost their lives in the war none had a brighter genius or a more generous spirit.

In the period between the two wars the art of writing biography took a new turn—some would say began[1] so far as English literature was concerned—under the influence of one man—Giles Lytton Strachey (1880–1932). How introduce him better than by quoting the words of an older writer, Sir Max Beerbohm, who thus opened his Rede Lecture delivered in 1943:

One day in the springtime of 1912 . . . I was lunching at the Savile Club. I had been living for two years in Italy; and there

[1] Perhaps we might regard the portraits of two fathers, the one by Samuel Butler in his novel *The Way of All Flesh*, the other by Edmund Gosse in *Father and Son*, as spiritual predecessors.

14

were some faces new to me. There was one that interested me very much; an emaciated face of ivory whiteness above a long square-cut auburn beard, and below a head of very long sleek dark brown hair. The nose was nothing if not aquiline, and Nature had chiselled it with great delicacy. The eyes, behind a pair of gold-rimmed spectacles, eyes of an inquirer and a cogitator, were large and brown and luminous. The man to whom they belonged must, I judged, though he sat stooping low down over his table, be extremely tall. He wore a jacket of brown velveteen, a soft shirt, and a dark red tie. I greatly wondered who he was. He looked rather like one of the Twelve Apostles, and I decided that he resembled especially the doubting one, Thomas, who was also called Didymus. I learned from a friend who came in and joined me at my table that he was one of the Stracheys; Lytton Strachey; a Cambridge man; rather an authority on French literature; had written a book on French literature in some series or other; book said to be very good.

There we have an attractively revealing picture of Lytton Strachey when he was just beginning to be known but was not yet famous. It suggests much that is characteristic of the man and the writer—the emaciated face, the delicately chiselled nose, the luminous eyes—the inquirer, the cogitator—the unconventional dress—the doubting Thomas—the clever student. And the very manner of Beerbohm's writing is somewhat like Strachey's, but gentler—with more fun and less irony. We see that he had already written a book on French literature—*Landmarks in French Literature* (1912)—and he was to write more about the French as well as about his favourite Englishmen in *Books and Characters, French and English* (1922) and in *Portraits in Miniature* (1931); and he left behind him some finely finished critical studies which were posthumously published in *Characters and Commentaries* (1933). We find him, then, at the time when Beerbohm first saw him, steeped in French and English literature, especially that of the congenial eighteenth century, and, so far as France was concerned, that of the late seventeenth century. The 'Age of Prose and Reason' was the age that pleased him most, and the poetry that went with it—that of Racine and Pope—which he was to justify so sanely. And we may surmise that the prose which tickled him most would have been that of Voltaire, and a much later writer, Anatole France.

Yet he was to do his most distinctive work, that by which he first became famous and by which he will chiefly be remembered, about the nineteenth century. It is found in two books of biography, *Eminent Victorians* (1918) and *Queen Victoria* (1921). In his later work, *Elizabeth and Essex* (1928), ingenious as it is, he has not the same success in getting close to his subjects. But it is not surprising that he should have so successfully chosen the century that he liked least. Lytton Strachey loved to praise, to appreciate, what he admired; but he loved still more to analyse that which was compounded of virtues and vices and to expose the human realities—or what he took to be realities—that lay behind the popular idol—especially the traditional 'Great Man' of the Victorian age: Gladstone, the Grand Old Man, or Dr. Arnold, the perfect Headmaster of a great public school. And having himself been born in the nineteenth century he could remember enough of it to know it with some intimacy, to clothe it with flesh and blood, and the appropriate sentiments and moral ideas. He was near enough to it to dislike it, and to return to it with the pleasure of chastising it, while not, of course, consciously understating its virtues. Moreover, was not the nineteenth century more than any other the period, or the subject, of massive 'official' biographies?

> Those two fat volumes, with which it is our custom to commemorate the dead—who does not know them, with their ill-digested masses of material, their slipshod style, their tone of tedious panegyric, their lamentable lack of selection, of detachment, of design? They are as familiar as the cortège of the undertaker, and wear the same air of slow, funereal barbarism. One is tempted to suppose, of some of them, that they were composed by that functionary, as the final item of his job.

Did not the nineteenth century offer awful warnings of what to avoid, and the ideal opportunity for Lytton Strachey to show how the thing might be done, artistically? These formidable works did indeed provide him with much 'indispensable information'— how could he have managed without them, unless he had been prepared to undertake much uncongenial research? Also they afforded an example to be avoided. 'How many lessons are to be learnt from them! But it is hardly necessary to particularize. To preserve, for instance, a becoming brevity—a brevity which excludes everything that is redundant and nothing that is significant—that, surely, is the first duty of the biographer. The second, no less surely, is to maintain his own freedom of spirit. It is not his business to be complimentary; it is his business to lay bare the facts of the case, as he understands them.'

'As he understands them'—that is of the essence of the matter in a Stracheyan biography. It is to convey what Pater calls the artist's 'sense of fact'. The artist biographer, having soaked himself in his material so much as he may think necessary for his artistic purpose, will then go on to express his impression—and state the facts 'as he understands them'. He will write his book much as the good historical novelist might do, though he will invent nothing unless it seems to bring out the truth 'as he understands it'. 'He will attack his subject in unexpected places; he will fall upon the flank, or the rear; he will shoot a sudden, revealing searchlight into obscure recesses, hitherto undivined.' This is what Strachey does; and he does it with subtlety, imagination and glittering ironic analysis, and in beautifully constructed, simple prose. *Queen Victoria* has the qualities of a novel; the four short biographies in *Eminent Victorians* might be short stories. They have the same imaginative treatment, and they are also commentaries on historic fact. The characters are conceived, and subtly; we see them unfold themselves in action; and history, thus peopled, begins to present new perspectives. Queen Victoria becomes less formidable, and actually more likeable. Mr. Gladstone ceases to be the 'Grand Old Man'; the feet of clay are exposed, and the idol becomes as alive as Quilp. But Quilp, it will be said, was a monstrosity, and a blatant one. Strachey's Gladstone also was a monstrosity, not blatant, but conceived by a highly subtle and sensitive intellectual. When he chooses his subjects—'certain fragments of the truth which took my fancy and lay to my hand' —he is proceeding in the manner of the artistic novelist, a Conrad or Henry James. A character in a certain setting—it may be a Gordon going into battle with a cane, 'a frenzied enthusiast'— gives him his starting-point; he elaborates it with so many of the available historic facts as will illuminate the character he has conceived; and interpretatively, in analysis sauced with irony or subtle mockery, unfolds his charming story. The result is always amusing; it may be illuminating; but it may be dangerous in that it is apt to distort history by too much avoidance of dull research.

For instance, supposing we compare his biography of Gordon, admittedly a short one, with a long book, *Gordon and the Sudan,*

produced by Bernard M. Allen in 1931—a biography of a very
different kind from Strachey's, based upon exhaustive research,
yet written with sympathetic imagination and literary skill.
Strachey suggests that it was the publicity given by Stead,
editor of the *Pall Mall Gazette*, to Gordon, then 'unrecognized and
almost unemployed', which turned him suddenly into 'the
favourite of the nation', a man whose 'name was on every tongue',
so that he was acclaimed as 'the one man living capable of coping
with the perils' arising from the Mahdi's triumphant insurrection
in Egypt.

The suggestion that he was dragged from obscurity by a
journalistic stunt is a travesty of the truth. Gordon's early service
in China had made him a national figure before he ever went to
the Sudan. Between 1874 and 1879 he achieved miracles in the
service of the Khedive of Egypt first in the Equatorial Provinces
and then in a region of about a million square miles which
included the Sudan and Darfur, suppressing the slave trade and
improving means of communication. So great was the reputation
he acquired for handling difficult African peoples that King
Leopold of Belgium overcame his distaste for anti-slavery enthusi-
asts and was at this moment desirous of employing Gordon as
executive chief in the Congo. All this Strachey brushes aside in
the interests of the picturesque. He had to depict him as dragged
out of obscurity by an enterprising journalist. Moreover if he
had examined telegrams of the period in the Public Record
Office, as Bernard Allen did, he would have discovered that the
Government's telegram to Sir Evelyn Baring in Egypt offering
Gordon's services to *inquire and report alone* crossed a telegram
from Baring asking for a qualified British officer to carry out the
executive work of evacuating the garrisons and the civilian population of the Sudan. All the controversies in which the character of
Gordon has been a shuttlecock largely turn upon this single fatal
incident—the crossing of two telegrams—but Strachey never
went to the Record Office and never learnt about the telegrams.

But it is only fair to him to say that though each of his biographies is coloured throughout by his personal likings and dislikes, he endeavours to state the essential facts so far as they were
easily available to him. In the first paragraph of *Florence Nightingale*
he lets us know that he dislikes her. 'A Demon possessed her.
Now demons, whatever else they may be, are full of interest.

And so it happens that in the real Miss Nightingale there was more that was interesting than in the legendary one; there was also less that was agreeable.' Yet for all his sneers the narrative does not conceal the fact that she did in fact against great opposition achieve the major reforms at which she aimed. The first page of Dr. Arnold reveals the future headmaster of Rugby as a pious and pompous prig, but it does become clear that it was Arnold who altered the character of the English public school and made it, for better or worse, what it is. Mainly, in Strachey's opinion, for the worse, for he is no more in love with the public school system than with Dr. Arnold himself. His mocking opening allusions to General Gordon, tripping about with a book, the Holy Bible, throws light on the biographer as well as his subject; yet Gordon's achievements are not intentionally minimized in spite of the picture of his preposterous simplicity. Strachey disliked these simplicities, except as objects for ridicule. 'Mr. Gladstone,' he remarks—'it was one of his old-fashioned simplicities— believed in liberty.'

Strachey, with his delightful malice, set a new fashion in biography. Is it not revealing that since his time this word *malice*, hitherto used to indicate a vice, has been constantly employed to indicate a merit? He belonged to the age of gay, frivolous malice; but he had the ability to give it dignity in brilliant prose. Max Beerbohm goes further in eulogy and says that the 'paramount quality' of his prose is, 'in one word, Beauty.'

Strachey, for English literature, had turned the writing of biography into a creative art. Among his successors were some who imitated and exaggerated his defects as well as his virtues, and others who developed his methods in interesting ways of their own. Philip Guedalla (1889–1944) was among the former. Indeed, he often chose figures from that same Victorian period— *Palmerston* (1926), *Gladstone and Palmerston* (1928), *The Queen and Mr. Gladstone* (1933)—and turned upon his victims the arrows of a pungent but undiscriminating wit. Among the latter are some who have developed the psychological approach to their subject and used it for the re-creation of an historical character. Thus Lord David Cecil (born 1902) in *The Stricken Deer* (1929), a Life of Cowper, and Catherine Maclean, in her *Dorothy Words-*

worth: *the Early Years* (1932) and Peter Quennell (born 1905) in *Byron in Italy* (1941). But we need not attribute to Strachey's influence all the intelligent efforts that have been made to estimate an historical character in terms of psychology. The subjects chosen by Harold Nicolson (born 1886) in his *Byron: the Last Journey* (1924) and *Curzon: the Last Phase* (1934) lent themselves to such a method. It is used by Veronica Wedgwood (born 1910) in her *Strafford* (1935) and *William the Silent* (1944); and is not absent in the vigorous biographical writings of G. M. Young. In auto-biography the more intimate personal manner is to be expected and had been employed long before Strachey was heard of; though seldom has it been written with such subtle portraiture, with so much skill in describing the physical and social setting, and with so much sense of design as in the series of books by Sir Osbert Sitwell (born 1892) which opened with *Left Hand, Right Hand!* (1945). If it were only for the portrait of the eccentric Baronet, his father, this autobiography would be likely to survive; but in addition it gives a characteristic picture of the social and artistic *milieu* in which the author and his brother Sacheverell and his sister Edith lived, and records their æsthetic pleasures when they travelled abroad or withdrew into the country. The Sitwells can hardly be thought of one without the other. The trio have moved graciously through the literary life of the twenties and thirties, decorating whatever they have touched; and they are as active as ever to-day. Through the better part of three decades Osbert has gone on, continuously evoking a subtle atmosphere in which to place his rarefied characters, producing essays, poems, books of travel, books on whatever touches his fancy in his euphuistic life, escaping the reproach of dilettantism through conscientious persistence in his art.

Elders and youngers have been working side by side in the spheres of history, sociology and literary criticism during the last thirty years. Some of the former have already been mentioned in this survey. Sir Herbert Grierson (born 1866) is still actively at work on books in which the humane critic is seldom submerged beneath the scholar. Sir Desmond MacCarthy (born 1878) who distinguished himself as dramatic critic of the *New Statesman and Nation,* and editor of the literary monthly, *Life and Letters,* succeeded Edmund Gosse in 1928 as writer of a weekly literary causerie in the *Sunday Times*, and has maintained there a high standard of criticism from that time to this. Middleton Murry (born 1889) at one time friend and critic of D. H. Lawrence, has an original if eccentric poetic temperament, and has written with fervour and esoteric conviction about Keats, Shakespeare, Blake, Pacificism and God. Ivor Armstrong Richards (born 1893) for many years between the wars had great influence at Cambridge University through his inspiring lectures on English literature and his attempts to explain artistic processes in scientific terms. His book *Principles of Literary Criticism* (1924) was a brilliant essay in the pathology of the æsthetic experience. I found that between his book and mine—*The Making of Literature: Some Principles of Criticism Examined in the Light of Ancient and Modern Theory*, (1928)—there was no common ground whatever. It is interesting that a critic whose scientific psychology would have horrified Coleridge showed in his book *Coleridge on Imagination* no mean capacity for appreciating his poetry and his conception of poetry.

Among critics who have been producing books and contributing to literary periodicals during the last twenty years one could not overlook that very human critic, with urbane and catholic taste, Professor Bonamy Dobrée (born 1891); Lord David Cecil (born 1902), a quiet and discriminating judge of literature; Raymond Mortimer (born 1895), lively, witty, versatile biographer and critic; C. M. Bowra (born 1898), a classical scholar who is equally at home with the ancient Greeks and modern European poets; V. S. Pritchett, as subtle and lively in his criticism as in his novels; and Cyril Connolly (born 1903), editor of *Horizon* during the war and until 1949, and, under the pseudonym of 'Palinurus', author of *The Unquiet Grave* (1944).

It would be outside the scope of this book to dwell on the distinguished work which has been done in the spheres of sociology, history and economics. The books of that great economist, John Maynard Keynes, afterwards Lord Keynes (1883–1946), were of a lucidity and brilliance which lifted them into literature. Sir William Henry Beveridge, afterwards Lord Beveridge (born 1879), for forty years known as an expert on social insurance and unemployment, produced during the war what was probably the most cogent and persuasive official report ever presented to a British Government—the historic book on

Social Insurance generally known as *The Beveridge Report*. Professor D. W. Brogan (born 1900), a student both of American and French life and politics, is the author of shrewd, forthright books on these subjects—*The Development of Modern France* (1940) and *The American Problem* (1944). Of the younger historians the most promising is A. L. Rowse (born 1903). His book *The Spirit of English History* (1943) reveals that rare gift of imagination which is necessary if history is to be an art. His comprehensive study of the Elizabethan age (the first volume of which, highly original and provocative, appeared in 1950) will owe as much to his personal examination of local relics and records as to printed material.

During the whole period under review one remarkable writer of prose has been producing books at not infrequent intervals—Winston Leonard Spencer Churchill (born 1874). It will be known to the reader that he had other occupations, including that of being Prime Minister from 1940 to 1945. But he was a writer before he was a politician. He wrote five books during the last century: *The Story of the Malakand Field Force* (1898), *The River War* (1899), *Savrola* (1900), *London to Ladysmith via Pretoria* (1900) and *Ian Hamilton's March* (1900). Shortly before he first became a Minister of the Crown he had written a life of his brilliant father, *Lord Randolph Churchill* (published in 1906); and among many books written during the next thirty years were his four-volume work *The World Crisis* (1923–29) and his masterly study of a great military strategist, *Marlborough* (three volumes, 1933–1936). But the greatest and most important of his writings are to be found in his war memoirs, *The Second World War*, the first volume of which appeared in October, 1948, the second ('Their Finest Hour') in 1949, and the third ('The Grand Alliance') in 1950. Others are on their way.

There is a sense in which, for the British at least, this book, written by a man in his seventies, will be the book of the century. For it is the authentic and inspired record of a short period in British history when Britain, under great leadership, was called on to achieve what the rest of the world deemed impossible. It is unique in the association of so important an author with so important a subject. There have been few occasions when the prime mover in historic events has also been their chronicler. Cæsar's *De Bello Gallico* is a great book, but its bare, laconic narrative does not deal with the most critical period of his time. His *De Bello Civili* does. Lloyd George's (1863–1945) *Memoirs* are powerful, but were written by a man who, courageous and brilliant as he was, could not speak for all elements in the nation at war in quite the same way as Churchill could in 1940. Within a few weeks after the latter's accession to the Premiership the Conservatives had forgotten their earlier grievances against him and Labour members were his ardent supporters. He was Minister of Defence in perfect harmony with his Service chiefs. The people in every class drew confidence from his words and responded with sacrificial zeal to his demands.

Lloyd George's *War Memoirs* (six volumes, 1933–36) is the only book which is really comparable with Churchill's *The Second World War*, giving as full an account of events under his own leadership in the Great War as Churchill gives of events when he was in control. But Lloyd George, unlike Churchill, was a speaker first, a writer only in his later years. Shortly after his fall from power in 1922, turning for the first time at the age of fifty-nine to the writing of books, Lloyd George was concerned to know whether his literary style too much betrayed the practice of the orator. 'Tell me frankly,' he said to the present writer, who had been invited to read the proofs of his book, 'Is this too rhetorical, too verbose? Are there signs of the tricks of the speaker?'

At that stage (1923) the speaker was very evident in Lloyd George's writings, but just as he always adapted his style in some degree to the character of the audience he was addressing, so, by the time he came to the writing of his *War Memoirs*, he had found an appropriate style, swift, forceful, loaded with emphatic but telling adjectives, still very Lloyd-Georgian, but effective for the purpose of this work. Incisive direct narrative or argument is interspersed with occasional flamboyant metaphors. The style as a whole is expressive of the man who so amazingly combined brains, practical intuition, unbounded vitality, and the naïve sentiments of a Welsh bard. The book is lucid and well-documented. The man of genius is apparent in the writing.

Also in Winston Churchill's; but the manner is different. He had been a writer before he was well known as a speaker. He had been a reader, as Lloyd George also was, but a more discriminating one. L. G.'s mind was drenched in the language of the Bible; it was the basis of his style; but throughout his life he devoured printed words of all sorts—biographies, histories of war, thrillers, newspapers. Churchill also is well versed in the Bible, and is fond of Biblical allusions, but it has left fewer traces on his style. He has read history consistently, and more especially eighteenth-century history. In his more solemn, pondered passages his language is reminiscent of Burke, though he has a wonderful way of turning suddenly and brilliantly to the modern vernacular, even slang. In narrative he is content with simple direct statements, leaving the weight of his matter to tell its own tale, so that his conclusions are all the more vivid by contrast with the straight evidence which has led to it. The man of letters is apparent in Churchill's speeches, though they have always been prepared with a view to the spoken word. In *The Second World War* the orator is not absent, but it is a book to be read. The man-of-letters is uppermost. It would be absurd to acquit either Lloyd George or Churchill of partiality; both of them believed in their unfailing rightness. Both—principal architects of victory—were supremely and audaciously self-confident, and thought their opponents invariably wrong. But whereas Lloyd George was partisan and appeared to be so, Churchill has an amazing appearance of detachment, of lofty aloofness; in the battle, he appears none the less above it; his is the voice of Fate, pronouncing decrees of doom, or offering resplendent hope. Each event appears to be witnessed under the perspective of universal history as he, inspired by his theme, unfolds the panorama, scene following relentlessly upon scene.

The first volume is devoted to the period between the two wars, during most of which he was not in office. 'It is my purpose,' he writes, 'as one who lived and acted in these days, first to show how easily the tragedy of the Second World War could have been prevented; how the malice of the wicked was reinforced by the weakness of the virtuous; how the structure and habits of democratic States, unless they are welded into larger organisms, lack those elements of persistence and conviction which can alone give security to humble masses.'

All the words and actions for which I am accountable between the wars had as their object only the prevention of a second World

War. . . . There can hardly ever have been a war more easy to prevent than this second Armageddon. I have always been ready to use force in order to defy tyranny or ward off ruin. But had our British, American and Allied affairs been conducted with the ordinary consistency and common sense usual in decent households, there was no need for Force to march unaccompanied by Law; and Strength, moreover, could have been used in righteous causes with little risk of bloodshed. In their loss of purpose, in their abandonment even of the themes they most sincerely espoused, Britain, France, and most of all, because of their immense power and impartiality, the United States, allowed conditions to be built up which led to the very climax they dreaded most. They have only to repeat the same well-meaning, short-sighted behaviour towards the new problems which in singular resemblance confront us today to bring about a third convulsion from which none may live to tell the tale.

From any other man such a statement would be arrogant in the extreme. But Churchill's record entitles him to speak thus. In speech after speech delivered during the seven years before the war this statesman, not in office, was as consistent as Demosthenes in his Philippics; as the Greek orator exposed the perils arising from the Macedonian dictator, so Churchill denounced the inadequacy of the measures taken to meet the growing menace of Germany.

At all times in this book we see the man animating the statesman. There is an element of simplicity in Churchill, a capacity for strong personal emotion, which endears him to the public as well as to his personal friends, and is evident in many passages—as, for example, when he tells of the dark waters of despair that overwhelmed him when Anthony Eden, who had been fighting so valiantly within the Government before the war, felt compelled to resign.

From midnight till dawn I lay in my bed consumed by emotions of sorrow and fear. There seemed one strong young figure standing up against long, dismal, drawling tides of drift and surrender, of wrong measurements and feeble impulses. . . . He seemed to me at this moment to embody the life-hope of the British nation. . . . Now he was gone.

Just as one felt in the war the strong but supremely human personality of Churchill controlling the course of events, so in this book his thoughtful, powerful, yet simple personality pervades the reasoning and narrative, influencing the heart as well as the head. His power is compelling, his courage, his earnestness are persuasive, his occasional weaknesses endearing. Even when we may think him wrong he makes us desire to find him right. Some, for example, may wish that he had taken a different line about India. But that defect belongs to the character, and we find it difficult to wish him to be other than what he is, the amalgam of so many Churchillian qualities. Whatever he is doing, or saying, or writing, he is palpably sincere and himself.

This sincerity of his, this explicable arrogance, this old-fashioned pride and humility, coupled with his high authority and his genius for describing contemporary events in the light of universal history, give to his book a character through which it deserves the world-wide attention it has received and will receive. It is a history which, if men can learn from history, should help to make history.

Chapter Sixteen

MODERN POETS

W. H. Auden—William Empson—Stephen Spender—Edith Sitwell—
Edwin Muir—Ruth Pitter—Christopher Fry

UNDER this heading I have to deal with two kinds of poet
—the so-called 'modern poets' of the 1930's who had special
characteristics, and those who are simply modern in the sense
that they are still writing, or have been recently. The former
consisted of a group of young men who stormed the fortresses of
the literary world in the ten years before the war and came to be
known as the 'modern poets'. They are still writing, though some
of them are modifying their modernism, and they are not receiving the same whole-hearted allegiance from the very young
which they could be sure of ten years ago. As they were when
they first developed their technique they are just far enough away
to be seen objectively, under an historical perspective; we can
now be sure that they constitute a class of writers as distinctive
in their way as were the metaphysical poets in the seventeenth
century. They were all inspired or at least profoundly influenced
by T. S. Eliot; the state of society which produced certain reactions
in him produced similar reactions in them, and his consciousness
of the age helped to clarify their own consciousness of it. Those
who clearly belonged to their charmed circle can be definitely
named, but there were some on the edge of it who were half in,
half out; and there were some who had wholly different origins
but developed distinct traces of their influence. There were
others, like Edwin Muir, who were fully sympathetic and understanding, but stood on ground of their own. Nor was it the case
that the 'modern poets' came into being under the exclusive influence of Eliot. They read Eliot; they read Pound and the Imagists;
they read D. H. Lawrence and Joyce; admired the later work of
Yeats; and had been moved, before they had studied to discard the
more obvious emotions, by the stark imagery of Wilfrid Owen's
pitiful war poetry. They had read Donne and Blake and Rimbaud.
But it was Eliot who gave them peculiarly what satisfied them.

He gave imaginative expression to the sense of disillusion which afflicted them. He exposed the hollowness of a society which seemed to them to have outlived any sense of direction or purpose. They paid more attention to his poetic example of a breach with tradition than to his precepts which enjoined the continuity of tradition. He had used the language of contemporary speech for his poetic purpose. Modern science, modern industry, modern use-and-wont provided him with images not before familiar in the language of poetry, and he had mingled them in an original way with images associated with quite other tracts of experience. He had shown them that the imagination can be enriched by skilful sequences of images indicating ideas not commonly synthesized. He had been economical in words, contemptuous of the trite, eschewing well-worn expressions destructive to the fine edge of meaning, exposing sentimentality with the objectiveness of a disinterested god. They followed him and went further along the road of poetic eclecticism. They exceeded him in the bitterness of their disgust with contemporary society. But when they, despairingly, sought for some way out of a world of futility they found it for the most part not, as he did, in religion, but in communism—a communism woven out of their persistent, though in some cases disguised, idealism.

Their poetry began to make itself distinctively felt midway between the wars. The members of the group were all very young then. The oldest of them (I exclude that interesting poet, William Plomer, who does not seem to me properly to belong here) was Michael Roberts (1902–1948). Roberts in his poetry does not really exemplify the characteristics of the group, but he cannot be left out since he did more than anyone else to organize it, bring the members together, and introduce them to the wider public. (See his two anthologies, the first of which was in the nature of a manifesto—*New Country*, 1933, and *The Faber Book of Modern Verse*, 1936). Cecil Day Lewis was born in 1904; William Empson in 1905; John Lehmann in 1907; Louis MacNeice in 1907; W. H. Auden in 1907; Stephen Spender in 1909; Charles Madge in 1912; George Barker (on the outer fringe of the circle) in 1913; Dylan Thomas (a variation of the species), in 1914.

The protagonists were upper- or middle-class intellectuals. They were educated at good schools and at Oxford or Cambridge. They were young together, read one another's works, compared ideas, and developed a mutual understanding of the principles of poetry which were to govern them. They encouraged one another in their contempt for the bourgeois and for social standards based on wealth, snobbishness, intellectual indolence and effete ethical standards. They had read the war-books which came out in the twenties, and blamed a civilization which could produce wars and tolerate their futile sequel in disorganization, exploitation and stupid frivolity. They despised a literature which appeared to acquiesce in the situation or seek escape in the past and in sentimentalism, and was content with a language and metrical forms belonging to an obsolete order and with ideas irrelevant to the present crisis. Developing their own ideas under a common impulse it was not unnatural that their poems should in a certain sense be addressed primarily to one another. They had the same common experience, the same speech and idiom, the same devices of using image and metaphor; if their poems became difficult for the ordinary reader that was partly because they assumed in a reader the experience which their fellow poets had shared with them, and were rather indifferent to the uninitiated. Their use of alliteration, assonance, internal rhymes, half-rhymes and similar devices presented few obstacles, but their clipped syntax and novel image sequences were more baffling; and there were other difficulties inherent in the unusual-ness of the ideas in the poet's mind. They were accused of being unintelligible, and sometimes they were. But the standard was held to be maintained if the poet himself was quite clear about his own meaning; or at least if there were one or two others, of like sensi-bility, who understood. It should always be remembered that a poet does not exist to make statements, but to express a state of mind in some relation to reality; and, I would add, to communicate it. But the last condition may be satisfied if there is an ideal audience of one.

At first the cry seems to be one of despair. Day Lewis apostro-phizes the 'victims of a run-down civilization'. Auden speaks of 'the dingy, difficult life of our generation'. Spender exclaims:

> There is
> A network of railways, money, words, words, words,
> Meals, papers, exchanges, debates,
> Cinema, wireless; the worst is marriage.
> We cannot sleep. At night we watch
> A speaking clearness through cloudy paranoia.

MacNeice speaks of 'the mad vertigo of being what has been',
declares himself 'Jazz-weary of years of drums and Hawaiian
guitar', and rails against those who cannot endure without

> The flotsam of private property, pekingese and polyanthus,
> The good things which in the end turn to poison and pus,
> Without the bawdy chairs and the sugar in the silver tongs
> And the inter-ripple and resonance of years of dinner-gongs.

And A. J. S. Tessimond (born 1902), who is only on the edge of
this group, and not of it, declares not what *he* says but what *they*
say when he writes:

> You say that our civilization is Willesden Green; is Beaverbrook;
> Lyons; halitosis advertisements; cancer and pyorrhœa;
> prize-day, the cheers and avuncular tips for the prudent cheaters;
> pearl-divers diving their lungs out; tin-workers breathing in tin.

It was in this mood of general disgust with the whole trend of
their civilization, this universal disillusion which appeared to
lead only to despair, modified by belief in themselves and their
circle, that they looked for a remedy; and they found it in what
they called Communism; though whether any of them except
Michael Roberts and Day Lewis had ever seriously read Marx
may be questioned. But there was no doubt in the minds of most
of them about their mission (though time and experience, later,
were to change their views). It was only for a few years that the
Communist ideal united them with the conviction of a fixed
social objective. But in the early thirties they announced their
faith in unmistakable terms. In the Preface to the collection of
articles, stories and poems published in *New Country* (1933)
Michael Roberts writes:

> It is time that those who would conserve something which is
> still valuable in England began to see that only a revolution can
> save their standards. It's past the stage of sentimental pity for the
> poor, we're all in the same boat. They can no longer hold aloof
> from politics as intellectuals have done since the institution of a
> nominal democracy. One way or another they must make up their
> minds.

15

And he goes on to associate the revolution which he and his friends desire with the doctrines of a modified Marxism.

> If Marxism seems to us to be tainted with its nineteenth-century origin yet nevertheless to be, in the main, true, if, in the hands of its present exponents, the doctrine seems inelastic and fails to understand a temper which is not merely bourgeois but inherently English, it is for us to prepare the way for an English Lenin by modifying and developing that doctrine.

'We're asking you,' he says, 'to help us abolish the whole class system.' Poetry will be revolutionary. Dealing with a 'new world', it will mean 'more than buttercup lyricism'. The novelist will either write in a way which will show the fatuity of the 'white-collar class', whose 'cultural superiority has vanished' or will 'turn for his subject-matter to the working-class'. He believes that 'the full development of the individual . . . might be possible in a state of social communism'. But how little he has in view the Communism with which the world has become all too well acquainted in recent years is shown by the sanguine words: 'by social communism I do not mean any diminution of mystical loss of personal identity or any vague sentiment of universal brotherhood: I mean that extension of personality and conscious-ness which comes sometimes to a group of men when they are working together for some common purpose.' His real ideal community, one guesses, would be modelled not on the Marxian State, but on the active brotherhood of the modern poets.

Day Lewis, being twenty-nine years of age, writes as one having the whole weight of long experience behind him to a 'young revolutionary', four years his junior, who is 'thinking of joining the Communist Party'. He explains the kind of faith that will be required from him, 'an absolute belief in revolution as the way to, and the form of, new life'. 'The certainty of new life must be your starting-point. Not jealousy, not pity, not a knowledge of economics; not hate even, or love; but certainty of new life.' 'You might as well know that a few of us poets, in our capacity of receiving stations, do detect the vibrations of new life in Com-munism.' The young men who are ready to join the poets must go into the fray realizing that 'they're up against the whole brute force of things-as-they-are'; they must be pioneers, evange-lists, turning to Communism with the religious instinct that has made others turn to the Roman Catholic Church.

W. H. Auden in *A Communist to Others* addresses:

> Comrades who when the sirens roar
> From office shop and factory pour
>   'Neath evening sky

and gives them his assurance

> On you our interests are set
> Your sorrow we shall not forget
>   While we consider
> Those who in every county town
> For centuries have done you brown,
> But you shall see them tumble down
>   Both horse and rider.

And Charles Madge (aged twenty-one) exclaims:

> Lenin, would you were living at this hour:
> England has need of you, of the cold voice
> That spoke beyond Time's passions, that expelled
> All the half treasons of the mind in doubt.

Spender, though only twenty-four years of age, clearly has doubts about the propriety of turning poetry into propaganda. 'Revolution . . . cannot be assisted by censoring the truths of art or artists. Philosophers, statesmen and artists have always been and always will be individualists.' He is evidently uneasy at the dilemma thrust upon the poets who believe in Communism, and is content to conclude that 'by making clear the causes of our present frustration they may prepare the way for a new kind of society.'

One feels that these young poets adopted the cause of Communism not for Communism's sake but as a way out from a philosophy of despair, from the disillusion which Eliot had helped to instil in them, from their 'present frustration', from their sense of being 'up against the whole brute force of things-as-they-are'. Eliot knew that no rearrangement of society would solve his problem of time present and time past; he sought a solution through the Anglo-Catholic Church just as the novelist Graham Greene sought it through Roman Catholicism. The younger poets too were soon to discover that the political cause to which they so eagerly vowed themselves offered no real cure for psychological or moral disorders; most of them at a a later date dropped their Communism. But not before it seemed to offer them a crusading banner under which to prove their faith, to the point if need be of the supreme sacrifice; the civil war in Spain became their Holy Land for redemption. Auden, MacNeice and Spender went in various capacities to Spain, and four other young writers, Ralph Fox, Julian Bell, Christopher Caudwell and John Cornford fought in the International Brigade and were killed. They believed in those days that Communism and democracy were the same thing.

Auden is the shining particular light of this remarkable movement. He has a brain nimble, alert, never-resting; perception, alive and darting; an imagination which sweeps over his world of perceived things with bewildering brilliance; he has humour which turns to satire; passion, which often consumes itself in scorn. In poetry he may be intensely serious or he may be playing a game in the dexterous use of words. His play is grim and his seriousness playful, and you can never be sure where the fireworks will lead you. In much of his work scorn is the predominant note—scorn of shallow emotion, philanthropic pretension, plutocratic display, slickness, trite phrases, borrowed metaphors, sentimentality, secret vice—and these are things which distract his attention when pure beauty is ready to move him. He will not have his landscape blurred 'with old moonlight of romance'. His poet must needs

> Sing of human unsuccess
> In a rapture of distress

At twenty-three he has no patience with anything that is not adult. At thirty-eight, in *For the Time Being*, he makes Prospero say

> I am very glad I shall never
> Be twenty and have to go through that business again,
> The hours of fuss and fury, the conceit, the expense.

But while the strength of his virile verse was devoted to the exposure of sham he became, for a time at least, not without hope derived from the few who shared his 'insight' and 'adult pen'. Thus in a birthday poem to his friend and occasional collaborator, Christopher Isherwood:

> Greed showing shamelessly her naked money,
> And all Love's wondering eloquence debased
> To a collector's slang, Smartness in furs,
> And Beauty scratching miserably for food,
> Honour self-sacrificed for Calculation,
> And Reason stoned by Mediocrity,
> Freedom by Power shockingly maltreated,
> And Justice exiled till Saint Geoffrey's Day.

But he goes on:

> So in this hour of crisis and dismay,
> What better than your strict and adult pen
> Can warn us from the colours and the consolations,
> The showy arid works, reveal
> The squalid shadow of academy and garden,
> Make action urgent and its nature clear?
> Who give us nearer insight to resist
> The expanding fear, the savaging disaster?

In 1937 he was invigorated by his belief in the urgent need for action in the Spanish War. In *Spain 1937* he contrasts Yesterday, To-morrow and To-day.

> Yesterday all the past. The language of size
> Spreading to China along the trade-routes; the diffusion
> Of the counting-frame and the cromlech;
> Yesterday the shadow-reckoning in the sunny climates.

And of To-morrow and To-day:

> To-morrow the rediscovery of romantic love;
> The photographing of ravens; all the fun under
> Liberty's masterful shadow;
> To-morrow the hour of the pageant-master and the musician.
>
> To-morrow, for the young, the poets exploding like bombs,
> The walks by the lake, the winter of perfect communion;
> To-morrow the bicycle races
> Through the suburbs on summer evenings; but to-day the struggle.
>
> To-day the inevitable increase in the chances of death;
> The conscious acceptance of guilt in the fact of murder;
> To-day the expending of powers
> On the flat ephemeral pamphlet and the boring meeting.

Scorn for what he despises can give place to reverence, when he admires. What an admirable appraisement is this, of Henry James:

> O with what innocence your hand submitted
> To these formal rules that help a child to play,
>   While your heart, fastidious as
> A delicate nun, remained true to the rare noblesse
> Of your lucid gift and, for its own sake, ignored the
>   Resentful muttering Mass.

In *In Memory of W. B. Yeats* (January 1939) there is deeper feeling:

> He disappeared in the dead of winter:
> The brooks were frozen, the airports almost deserted,
> And snow disfigured the public statues;
> And mercury sank in the mouth of the dying day.
> O all the instruments agree
> The day of his death was a dark cold day.

In a profound poem, *Commentary,* lamenting this epoch of the 'Third Great Disappointment' in which the Intelligence is so fertile, but 'the Heart more stunted' than ever before, he hears the voice of Man 'mingling with the distant mutter of guerilla fighting': 'O teach us to outgrow our madness.'

That, if any, is the real message of his poetry. If any should complain, as they have done, that his heart is made of stone, that is only because he has looked the Medusa in the face and seen world failure in the 'stunted' heart.

His friends have scarcely attempted to explain how it was that on the approach of the World War he went to the United States and later applied for American naturalization. Since that strange disappearance he has produced a really good book of poems, *For the Time Being* (published in England, 1945), to which I have already alluded, and another book, *The Age of Anxiety* (1947) in which all his inventive skill and rich fancy are used to elaborate a fretful dream of humanity's thwarted existence. One feels that such cleverness is an odd companion for such misery.

Auden is often spoken of as if he were the most obscure of modern poets. Certainly he is often extremely difficult, but a great deal of his verse is simple, direct and lucid.

Of all the poets of this group it is William Empson who is the most obscure. He, like Michael Roberts, John Lehmann and Charles Madge, was at Cambridge; Auden, Day Lewis, Mac-Neice, Spender having been at Oxford. Of all of them he is the most severely intellectual, the least tolerant of romanticism or woolliness or the commonplace, or the facile. If the Sphinx could speak the Sphinx would speak like Empson. Not only with him must there be no word too much, but each word may be called on to fulfil the function of several. He appears to compose his verses as if he were set the task of compressing innumerable quarts into a pint pot. They must have been very arduous to compose, and they are very difficult to read. His poem *The Scales* begins:

> The proper scale would pat you on the head
> But Alice showed her pup Ulysses' bough
> Well from behind a thistle, wise with dread;
>
> And though your gulf-sprung mountains I allow
> (Snow-puppy curves, rose-solemn dado band)
> Charming for nurse, I am not nurse just now.

The commentator will have to remind us of *Alice in Wonderland*, of Alice shrunken, of Ulysses in the Isle of the Phæacians, of Mont Cenis tunnel, of the child's sand-heaps on the shore, and much else. His verses are impressive in sound and texture. They appeal to the ingenious intelligence. I do not suppose it was often intended that they should *move*.

Stephen Spender, admiring Auden as he did, and closely associated with him, is a man of very different temperament. Auden was the attacker of humanity, Spender its defender. He too has modernized his imagery, cultivated spareness, and hardened his metrical forms; but the romantic breaks through; the personal emotion is not concealed; gentleness and pity prevail. It is his feeling for human beings as individuals rather than an abstract conception of justice which makes him side with his fellow-poets in their political views. He is drawn out of himself into the broad highway of humanity's affairs, but is always happy to

retire within himself and express his more personal emotions.
In 'The Prisoners' (in *Poems, 1933*) a poem ends:

> Here are
> Gestures indelible. The wiry copper hair
> And the mothlike lips are dusk and that human
> Glance, which makes the sun forgotten.

And in the next poem he moves out into the broader world of
his compassion:

> They raise no hands, which rest upon their knees
> But lean their solid eyes against the night,
> Dimly they feel
> Only the furniture they use in cells.
>
> Their Time is almost Death. The silted flow
> Of years on years
> Is marked by dawns
> As faint as cracks on mud-flats of despair.
>
> My pity moves amongst them like a breeze
> On walls of stone
> Fretting for summer leaves, or like a tune
> On ears of stone.
>
> Then, when I raise my hands to strike
> It is too late,
> There are no chains that fall
> Nor visionary liquid door
> Melted with anger.

There was enough essential force in Spender to admit of development, and he went on developing before and after the World
War. In the later as in the earlier verse we are aware of the emotional contact between the Spender of the high-way and the poet
attentive to the more sequestered experiences of his individual
life. From this duality there is gain, in that the outer world is
touched by the light of the inner, and the inner receives balance
and proportion. In his better poems every word has its value for
sound as well as sense and plays its part in the cadence, and we are
repaid if we attune ourselves gradually to his manner and mood.
I am least impressed by the poems which I should not be surprised
to learn he esteems the most—those in which he is in philosophic

mood, verses which stand or fall by the truth of their generalizations. Here he does not always escape that 'tyranny of the Universal' which Goethe begged poets to shun; yet even in such
passages the poet in him constantly retrieves the position and
finds his proper expression, as when, in a dissertation on body and
spirit, he writes:

> Without that ghost within, our lives are lost
> Fragments, haunting the earth's rim.

He is at his best in passages which unite emotion and reflection,
or, again, pure perception and reflection, and in either case he
reaches moments of great poignancy and beauty. Within the
first category come the six poems which together form the
Elegy for Margaret. The poet does not fear to watch the gradual
passing away of young life, the desperate conflict of flesh and
spirit, or even the movements of the watchers themselves, and
creates perhaps the impression of dissecting his own grief,
remorselessly, yet with so delicate a hand that he *moves* where
another might have shocked.

> In the corner of the bed you are already partly ghost
> A whispering searching existence almost lost
> To our blatant life which spreads through all the rooms
> Our contrast transient as heaped consoling blooms.
>
> You are so quiet; your hand on the sheet seems a mouse.
> Yet when we look away, the flails
> Which pound and beat you down with ceaseless pulse
> Shake like a steam hammer through the house.

No less poignant, but less subjective, and more interesting
because here the by-way and the high-road meet—the personal
and the impersonal, private sympathy and interest in the widest
life—is the poem written on a verse of the French poet Apollinaire.
Brief quotation would do injustice to this fine poem, which
touches, I should say, the high-water mark of Stephen Spender's
work.

Before the war the name of Day Lewis was frequently bracketed
with those of Auden and Spender, though Spender has recorded
that in fact the three were never all together till they met in
Venice in 1949. The trio were the best known of the 'modern'

poets. In years Lewis was the eldest. He has considerable literary talent, and is a lively critic as well as poet. By study and zeal perhaps more than by innate inclination he accommodated himself to the new style, and used it with much cleverness; usually he avoided the obscurity which marred some of the work of his friends. He has made an excellent translation of *The Georgics of Virgil* (1940).

In speaking of the 'modern poets' there are two women whose names should be included. One is Lilian Bowes-Lyon who, I think, had very little personal association with members of the group, but was in many ways in sympathy with them. Her verses are intensely personal and enriched by her passionate sense of communion with Nature. There was a remote troubled beauty in many of her poems in spite of an obscurity which she vainly strove to avoid.

The second of these is Kathleen Raine. She has been in close touch with members of the group since the days when she was at Cambridge with some of them; but her occasional poems did not become well known until *Stone and Flower* appeared in 1943. She eschews most of the mannerisms of the moderns, while retaining their eclecticism and restraint. Her verses are lyrical—meditative, descriptive, or personal in their emotional import—and reflect her interest in religious mysticism; she is a Roman Catholic. Too much of her verse is simply reflective, and would have been more appropriately written as prose. But in her genuinely lyrical vein the more personal poems have a still, crystalline quality of much beauty.

Dylan Thomas and George Barker were too young to be in the modern movement at its inception, but the former soon found a place near to them, though he, a Welshman, revelled in the romanticism which they eschewed. But his wonderful use of original metres and striking imagery attracted them; his exuberant musical verse dazzled with sound and fury and the racket of elemental, confusing emotions. His is bardic rhetoric, inspired and impassioned, yet sometimes metrically controlled with rare skill. George Barker lacked the erudition which, in every case but that of Dylan Thomas, was looked for in a modern poet. He started imitatively, learnt his lessons, and developed a power which produced some vigorous and moving poems. Some of the tricks he has learnt still obtrude themselves into otherwise original and brilliant verse. His last volume, *News of the World* (1950), shows no diminution of sensibility or skill.

For all their audacity, their mannerisms, their obscurity the 'modern poets' introduced into English poetry an astringency for lack of which, in the twenties, it was threatened with triviality and decay. For years before they appeared on the scene there were some who felt that a drastic change was overdue, and that the 'Georgians' were not satisfying the contemporary need. Perhaps I may venture to quote from an early book of my own (*Personality in Literature*, 1913) to show the reaction of one of the younger readers of that time to the verse which was praised just before the First Great War. I wrote:

> I have heard literary critics speak of romantic or highly imagina-tive novels, saying: 'It is all delicate fancy and imagination; it is not concerned with realities; it is sheer poetry'—as if poetry were not concerned with realities! I have heard people criticize the prose works of Mr. A. C. Benson: 'This is all too musical, and sentimental, and self-centred; this sort of thing cannot be done in prose; it should be done in poetry'— as if nonsense becomes less nonsensical by means of metre or rhyme! This easy-going view of the function of the poetic art has borne an ample harvest of nonsense. I could, were it worth while, name many living bards who consider that any sort of fancy or feeling is good enough for poetry so long as it be prettily or gracefully handled, who would thus degrade poetry to the position of the easiest, as it has for long been the least prized, of the fine arts.

Speaking of 'the querulousness, the vagueness, the mere prettiness' of so much contemporary verse I alluded to the 'solitary position' of Charles Doughty, who 'had expressed him-self in the only way that was natural to him, through an archaic language, the language in which he thought, which lent itself to the hard, vivid, and superbly brutal images belonging to his primitive, barbarian, and as it were primeval theme. To appreciate *The Dawn in Britain* or *Adam Cast Forth* is to long for the hardness and masculinity which have been rare in English poetry for a hundred years; to feel that what poetry needs is more grit and more brain; and to plead for these is to plead for more poetry, for a stronger imagination.'

The 'modern poets', by example and precept, have successfully destroyed respect for the 'all too musical', the sentimental, the

nonsensical in poetry, for querulousness, vagueness, mere prettiness. They cultivated the use of hard, vivid and brutal images;
they have restored masculinity, grit and brains. They administered
a tonic that was needed, though the tonic was bitter. They introduced an educated male intelligence into the practice of the art,
and refined away the dross of loose thinking and metrical verbiage.
They became exacting critics of the contemporary world, the
contemporary scene. In these respects they provided what some
readers at any rate were already hoping for. The form of their
coming could not of course have been foreseen—their new
mannerisms, their complicated imagery, their obscurity, their
anger, their despair, their search for mystical or political harbour-
ages. But these idiosyncrasies are not of the essence of their
movement; these will go, and are already going, but the base
of their building remains. They broke with the tradition and
attempted to start afresh, but when the first mood of violence was
over it became apparent that they had fortified the tradition, in
Eliot's sense of the term, and enriched the material which would
henceforth be part of the English poet's experience. When their
uncommonness could be leavened with a little more common-
ness, their criticism of life with less bitterness, more humour and
more creativeness, they would be justified by their children.
One of these is Christopher Fry.

But at this stage I must say something about modern poets in
that other sense of the term to which I have alluded. For there
were some who never joined the modernist group and were only
partially or not at all affected by their technique, but who none
the less felt the impact of contemporary life, and responded to it
without a violent break with the near past, and with innovations
of their own. Edith Sitwell (born 1887), sister of Osbert (born
1892) and Sacheverell (born 1897), and daughter of Sir George
Reresby Sitwell (the Baronet made memorable in Osbert's
autobiography), was writing and publishing poetry even before
Eliot had become known. Her first book, *The Mother and other
Poems*, was published in 1915, and she has gone on producing
books of poetry from then till now. A volume of Collected
Poems appeared in 1930, and in 1949 a volume of Selected Poems
1920–1947, entitled *The Canticle of the Rose* (published 1949)

which itself was the title of the last of *Three Poems of the Atomic Bomb*. Her active literary life has also included several distinguished volumes of prose.

At first Edith Sitwell was not taken quite so seriously as she deserved to be, partly because she could not bear to be taken too seriously, and partly because she obviously took as much interest in life as in literature; she and her two clever brothers together formed a decorative centre-piece to the artistic society of the twenties, patterned in three shades of intellectual vivacity. But already in her early poems Edith had amazing inventive power added to a musical ear and a trollish fancy. Her delight was especially in the radiant gaiety of things sensed and fancifully associated with a riot of other things, and in the musical succession of sounds into which she could convert them. She was as playful in her clever verses as the modern poets were to be solemn in theirs, and therefore it did not seem to be a very striking innovation that her images were taken from modern life and not borrowed from traditional poetry; and the internal rhymes and dissonances accorded with the jazz tune to which the following, for example, could be sung:

> When
>   Don
> Pasquito arrived at the seaside
> Where the donkey's hide tide brayed, he
> Saw the banditto Jo in a black cape
> Whose slack shape waved like the sea—
> Thetis wrote a treatise noting wheat is silver like the sea;
>   the lovely cheat is sweet as foam; Erotis notices that she
>   Will
>   Steal
>   The
> Wheat-king's luggage, like Babel
> Before the League of Nations grew—
> So Jo put the luggage and the label
> In the pocket of Flo the Kangaroo.

The nonsensical, the impish, the eerie, the fay, the grotesque appealed to the fancy of Edith Sitwell in her earlier phases, but always as something tripping to music, song and dance, olden or modern, flowing 'from satyr-haunted caverns'

> Like the nymphs' music o'er the rocks.

Much of Sacheverell Sitwell's delightful book, *The Gothick North* (1929-30) was about mediæval tapestry, and the reading of it might suggest to anyone how like the work of all the Sitwells is to tapestry or to rich embroidery. Edith Sitwell's early poems shine like a design in many colours woven on a fabric; she describes gaily, and passes swiftly to decorative fancy, mingling the real and the unreal, the whole developing and completing the pattern of her mood. In *Elegy on Dead Fashion* (1926) she actually names the colours:

> Queen Thetis wore pelisses of tissue
> Of marine blue or violet, or deep blue,
>
> The colours most in favour were marine,
> Blue Louise, gris bois, grenate, myrtle green;
> Beside the ermine bells of the lorn foam—
> Those shivering flower-bells—nymphs light-footed roam. . . .

And in *The Nectarine Tree* do we not see as well as hear the laughter and the wind?

> This rich and swan-skin tree has grown
> From the nymphs' amber blood and bone
>
> What laughter falls like rain or tears
> Among my boughs, what golden shears?
>
> Come gardener, and tie
> With your long beard of bass
> (So like the winds' fair hair)
> The pillars of my tree, and win
> The wind to me.

With the passage of time the poet becomes less playful and more serious, though always resisting the solemn. In that singular poem, *Gold Coast Customs* (1929), it is still fancy that predominates rather than imagination, but her humour has become grim and sardonic, and eeriness is intermingled with terror. Edith Sitwell's mood, which had well accorded with the lightness of the twenties, responds to the graver tones of the thirties and the tragedy of the subsequent war years. She was obviously impressed by the poetry of Yeats in his last phase, and read with sympathy and admiration the work of the younger poets. We feel her sympathies broadening, her reflection deepening. Fancy gives way to imagination, under whose influence beautiful images copied from nature yield to more significant images 'modified', as Coleridge put it, 'by a predominant passion'. In becoming aware of things happening in the contemporary world she seemed to become more conscious of the nature of things always happening. Yet she was not of a disposition to yield to despair; and at the same time, while retaining Christian faith, she did not seek escape in Christian mysticism, but still sings: 'Hail to the Sun, and the great Sun in the heart of Man.' In *An Old Woman* (printed in *Later Poems, 1940–45*) she wrote:

> I, an old woman whose heart is like the sun
> That has seen too much, looked on too many sorrows,
> Yet is not weary of shining, fulfilment and harvest
> Heard the priests that howled for rain and the universal darkness,
> Saw the golden princes sacrificed to the Rain-god,
> The cloud that came, and was small as the hand of Man.

There is maturity, but no sign of old age, in the poem entitled *The Poet Laments the Coming of Old Age*. 'Wisdom' she writes, 'is not a hare in the golden sack of the heart.'

> . . . It can never be caught. Though I bring back sight to the blind
> My seed of folly has gone, that could teach me to bear
> That the gold-sinewed body that had the blood of all the earth in its veins
> Has changed to an old rag of the outworn world
> And the great heart that the first Morning made
> Should wear all Time's destruction for a dress.

The *Three Poems of the Atomic Bomb*, the first of which was written on the morning of Monday the 6th August, 1945, are among the most powerful and moving she has written. To quote a few lines would do them injustice. Those and the beautiful *Canticle of the Rose* are enough to assure her readers that a writer who has charmed them so long in many veins can also strike deeper and more significant notes.

Edwin Muir is a Scotsman who has Scottish history and the Scottish scene deeply planted in his mind, and a vein of mysticism in his temperament which indicates his northern Scottish origin;

but it is balanced by fine critical judgment. Educated as a boy at Kirkwall Burgh School, he completed his education by reading, travel, and study of places and people; and escaped from a commercial career by his capacity for journalism and his high talent for literature. With his wife Willa Muir he has translated and interpreted Franz Kafka for English readers and he has written novels and books on Scottish scenes and people. He is also a sensitive and discriminating critic, capable of appreciating and explaining the latest modern poets no less than of exercising his trained judgment in appraisement of the past. But it is as a poet that he especially deserves attention. In a certain sense he is as modern as Eliot; his verse is quite free from facile sweetness or second-hand imagery, though it has no startling novelties and is the reverse of sensational; and it faces the intellectual and emotional issues of the contemporary world. He belongs to the generation into which Eliot was born, of which he has written:

> If a name is required for it, one might call it the lonely or the homeless generation. Those who belonged to it had a keen sense that the individual human being stood alone, and that it was almost impossible for him to step out of his solitude into any sort of communion. . . . Their homelessness made them feel more keenly than others did something which seemed to be happening to civilization; they reflected the sense that civilization was becomingly affrightingly impersonal, that it no longer provided an environment for the traditional life of man, and no longer welcomed it, but seemed to prefer some other kind of quest.[1]

Having alluded to Joyce, Lawrence and Pound, he adds: 'The case of Eliot remains. He was the only one of that unfortunate generation who succeeded in bringing his gifts to fruition, and whose poetry has shown an increasing completeness. . . . Unlike the writers I have mentioned he has rooted himself in a community, the secular community of England and the religious community of Anglo-Catholicism.'

In this passage Muir gives us one of the clues to himself. He too belonged to that generation which he thinks of as 'homeless'. He has a keen sense of the individual standing alone in Space-Time, between the past and the future, in a fluctuating age conscious of its own unrest. And he, unlike so many of the others, has rooted himself in the Scottish community, with an

---

[1] From an essay *T. S. Eliot and his Time* published in *Britain Today* (June 1943).

intense awareness of the Scottish scene peopled with its past; and he also keeps his hold on a faith which saves his poetry, not from bewilderment—which is ever-present—but from hopelessness. The poem *The Labyrinth,* and the book of poems called after it (1949) are full of bewilderment at the labyrinthine ways of life and the imperative quest of the voyager.

> Friend, I have lost the way.
> *The way leads on.*
> Is there another way?
> *The way is one.*
> I must retrace the track.
> *It's lost and gone.*
> Back, I must travel back!
> *None goes there, none.*
> Then I'll make here my place,
> *(The road runs on),*
> Stand still and set my face,
> *(The road leaps on),*
> Stay here, for ever stay.
> *None stays here, none.*
> I cannot find the way.
> *The way leads on.*
> Oh places I have passed!
> *That journey's done.*
> And what will come at last?
> *The road leads on.*

Sometimes, when he faces the contemporary scene, and the 'calamities of an age', he sees punishment for guilt. In *The Narrow Place* (1943), in the poem *The Refugees,* contemplating 'the home-less waiting in the street', he exclaims:

> We bear the lot of nations
> Of times and races,
> Because we watched the wrong
> Last too long
> With non-committal faces.
> Until from Europe's sunset hill
> We saw our houses falling
> Wall after wall behind us
> What could blind us
> To such self-evident ill
> And all the sorrows from their caverns calling?

Sometimes, looking at man, and turning to unchanging nature, he imagines

> That the mountains judge us, brooks tell tales about us.
> We have thought sometimes the rocks looked strangely on us,
> Have fancied that the waves were angry with us,
> Heard dark runes murmuring in the autumn wind,
> Muttering and murmuring like old toothless women
> That prophesied against us in ancient tongues.

His reflective but highly imaginative poetry, beautiful in its measured tones and in the very restraint of its melancholy, is full of perplexed questioning of the where and the whither of burdened but not guiltless humanity, of the incidence of good and evil, of the arduous search for 'the secret place Where is my home'. But there is always love and respect for nature; there is pity; and there is beauty; and occasionally he puts aside melancholy and sad reflection and lets fancy play on some object or living thing that has delighted him, as when he writes of the 'adventurous bird walking upon the air'.

> Where
> In all the crystalline world was there to find
> For your so delicate walking and airy winging
> A floor so perfect, so firm and so fair,
> And where a ceiling and walls so sweetly ringing,
> Whenever you sing, to your clear singing?

Edwin Muir has not the buoyancy, the elasticity, or provocativeness of Eliot, nor so wide a range. He is not a landmark in literary history, nor seeks to be—he is not one of those who would ever run after novelty for novelty's sake. He is too preoccupied in his themes to think of his reputation, beyond the desire which every artist has to write as well as he can, and as honestly. That he owes much to the study of Eliot is obvious, but he has not followed his technique or surrendered himself to his philosophy. He has humanity, as Wordsworth had, but with a humour which Wordsworth lacked. But his is not the gay humanity of Edith Sitwell, which springs from a generous capacity for enjoyment, including enjoyment of trifles; he has none of her nimble versatility. But he has more depth and intellectual consistence. He has sensibility in an extreme, an acute form, kept in its place by judgment. In all his work we are conscious of a certain moral background, a sustained high seriousness, as in Wordsworth—which gives it weight, significance, nobility, without any intrusion of the pompous or the didactic. His poetry is not of the kind which occasionally distils magic words, never to be forgotten, but it is always at a high level, fine, sincere, profitable for the spirit; and it must be taken into account in any estimate of the poetic achievement of this age.

Ruth Pitter had scarcely emerged from her teens when she produced her First Poems (1920). A second volume, *First and Second Poems*, appeared in 1927. But it was *A Mad Lady's Garland* (1934) which convinced attentive critics that the writer was a lyrical poet deserving much more than a word of passing praise. The impression was confirmed by *A Trophy of Arms* (1936), *The Spirit Watches* (1939) *The Rude Potato* (1941, among the most gracious humorous poems known to me) and *The Bridge Poems* (1939–44). There is a beauty moving between the troubled and the serene in *The Spirit Watches*—the piece entitled *The Downward-Pointing Muse* would hold its own in any anthology. But some of *The Bridge Poems* showed further advance, not indeed in sensibility or percipience or metrical aptness, present in all her poetry, but in range and depth of vision.

She is not, in the sense in which the word has been used, a 'modern' poet. She belongs to no clique. She follows no modern fashion. Some of her poems assume a form that was within the reach of poetry long ago, but of these many have a significance which differentiates them from poetry of the past. She is intensely alive in the contemporary world, and sees it through its own eyes. But she is not quite of it. She stands apart, inhabiting a region of her own; and if it has not been as extensively communicated to the reading public as it might have been, that is perhaps because she belongs to no recognizable school, has no trumpeter, and has not been at pains to assert herself.

She has written some lovely poetry, authentic, unmistakable, which in her later work is distilled in experience and projected in language fashioned with fine tact and metrical skill. It has substance, and form; hardness, and fragility; grit, with tenderness and delicacy. In *The Bridge* she writes again and again about natural things—birds, flowers, grasses, trees and water—water especially:

> Water in rain, water in dew at evening
> Falling through clear air, stealing through clean grasses,
> Dwelling in darkness in our Mother's body,
> In secret springs welling and murmuring through her,
> Gathering in brooks and lapsing into rivers,
> Rolling magnificent down glorious tideways
> Deep for the mighty hulls, clean for the salmon,
> Pouring predestined to unfathomed ocean.

But she is aware of water polluted, 'turbid water', water defiled by 'fiery rain' falling, by 'fear and horror', on which none the less the swan rides 'proud and immaculate as winter ermine'. Proud, defiant things, like the swan, the captive crow with 'his monstrous hate', or the fox

> The delicate fox on soft and savage feet

or the big ship coming home with the tide up the estuary are subjects in which she delights. But equally dear to her are the obscure grasses, or the small plant, 'Love's pilgrim and poor suppliant', which

> With a leaf like a small hand
> Signals to you from the sand;
> With a flower like a blue eye
> Propounds love's dreadful mystery.

But at every moment in these poems, while she is describing so intimately the intense life of objects in nature, the reader is aware of the fact that their significance is derived from another life, more passionate, more complex, unbearable if it were allowed to have the last word. But with her the poignancy and terror of human life are never allowed to have the last word. Where some would despair, and others meet despair with mockery, her muse defeats it with beauty; the 'miraculous soul' has its 'secret joy within', and derives unfailing sustenance from without.

> Yes; for the birds were like my dream,
> And the leaves on the tree.

This is not escapism. It is a diversion of life from what is real and unsatisfying to what is satisfying and not less real. Perhaps it is not even a diversion, for one feels that even when she is writing simply of the smallest object she is dealing with a world in which all things are interrelated, where the beauty of a flower challenges comparison with the horror of a massacre, where even in the midst of war things do not lose their values; it seems that for her what Coleridge called 'the beautiful and permanent forms of nature' have their validity none the less because a war is raging over Europe, or because, as related in one grim poem, a crowd of frustrated factory girls may be gloating over the wreaths at a funeral. For them, revelling in the occasion, 'the soul can go for a ride with the rich young dead'. Ruth Pitter can be bitter and hard. She fears nothing, shirks nothing, but triumphantly puts terror and ugliness in their place, and moves on 'into the far secret places' where she discovers beauty and peace, or at least moments of peace. She brings in her own 'coloured glass' to 'exorcise unlove'. Capable, as one must suppose, of the grimmest pessimism and the darkest irony, she emerges amazingly as an optimist —perhaps because she has the persistence to pursue poetry and the poetic vision to the end, ever, as she so admirably puts it,

> Shaping the wonder to a word.

In the years of war she knew and felt the war experience, yet went on writing poetry which, not excluding that experience, transcended it; she continued to be attentive to things of perennial import and express them in strong, simple and beautiful verse.

Roy Campbell was young at the time when Auden, Spender and Day Lewis were young, and deserves mention as a poet with a vigorous and alert mind who was in every way the contrary of those exponents of the new movement. He was right-wing in his views where they were left. Where they despaired of life he plunged into it; where they sought refuge in a Cause, he proclaimed the fact of robust common sense and the excellence of the physical life. He had been a bull-fighter, and he writes like a bull-fighter. There is immense energy and zest for life in his verse which rings with hammer-strokes; and he delights in violent satire at the expense of all that seems to him affected and nonsensical. He is a heady poet, to be read in small doses. A page or two is like a tonic; but pursued too far his verse has the monotony of a bagpipe.

Another zestful writer (quite free from the violence of Campbell) is John Betjeman, whose light lyrical verse, narrative and descriptive, is a gay and spirited projection of the English scene and the common round of English life. His verses are accomplished and lively, his humour impish rather than satiric. Here we have the Victorian tradition in mid-twentieth-century life. And a word must be said of that simple, unaffected poet, Clifford Dyment (born 1914), whose directness and spontaneity have a charm recalling that of W. H. Davies.

There are young poets whose style is stiffened by the reading of Eliot and Auden, but who are no longer under their spell; some consciously or unconsciously reacting against them, others determined by later influences, especially that of the war. It is interesting to find that the kind of poetry that was written by young poets who were on active service in the first Great War tended to reappear in the second; and in some of the writers we hear notes from Wilfrid Owen rather than from Eliot. One of these is Sidney Keyes, killed in action, author of *The Iron Laurel* and *The Cruel Solstice*. Alun Lewis, the Welshman, also a casualty of the war, wrote poetry, but was at his best in short stories. F. T. Prince produced a volume of poems before the war, but the verses written later show him deeply affected by the war experience and nostalgic remembrance of the art and literature which belonged to peace. Laurie Lee, Lawrence Durrell and Bernard Spencer, writing from experience gained in foreign lands or on strange seas, are isolated individuals expressing what they have seen, felt and remembered; it is too soon to know how they will develop under the conditions of more normal life.[1] In the work of Henry Reed there is fine sensitivity and distinction. A number of young poets were brought together in 1941 in the first volume of *The New Apocalypse,* Henry Treece being the leading figure, and among the others, G. S. Fraser, Nicolas Moore, Vernon Watkins and J. F. Hendry. Vernon Watkins is perhaps the most interesting and promising of these. The group, if group it could be called, broke up, and many of its members were scattered over the world on active service.

[1] Since these words were written Lawrence Durrell has produced a long play in verse entitled *Sappho,* which is an imaginative reconstruction of life in ancient Lesbos. The versification is skilful, somewhat in the manner of Christopher Fry, but without Fry's sparkle; the characters are carefully studied. In spite of its form the book has many of the qualities of a novel, in verse, rather than a play.

One or more of these poets may or may not produce something of high importance. But there is at least one poet, not quite so young, but who has only become conspicuous since the war, who can be acclaimed with confidence—the poet-playwright, Christopher Fry (born 1907).[1]

Christopher Fry has brought a breath of fresh air into poetry and into the theatre. Here at last we have poetic drama which the theatre can take to itself and the reader can delight in as poetry —plays pregnant with intellectual ideas, written in swift speakable verse which sometimes has the beauty of fine rhetoric or fantasy, sparkling with relevant wit, gay, tender, exuberant; occasionally he has to pull himself up sharply and stop the overflow of conceits. In the moulding of his verse we can see the obvious influence of T. S. Eliot—but Eliot with how great a difference—how great may be measured by the fact that often he turns to parody of his master in which we can detect affection rather than malice; he is serious enough, but he will not be so serious as to disbelieve in the joy of life or run his head into a blank wall. Also, he has been absorbing the ideas and intellectual gymnastics of recent French writers—Sartre, probably, with critical amusement; Anouilh certainly (he has translated one of his plays); and he may even have shared some of Anouilh's tolerant affection for Alfred de Musset, in whose plays there is sometimes an intellectual fantasy to which we may see distant kinship in *The Lady's Not for Burning* and *Venus Observed*. Anouilh himself, notwithstanding his symbolism and his flights of fantasy, is nearer to the ground than Fry; but when he breaks out into the lyrical or the passionately reflective we can see where it is that Fry has been stirred by him. Monsieur Henri near the end of Anouilh's play *Eurydice* descants on the marks of childhood, youth and maturity imprinted on the visage of old age in some such manner as does the Duke, less solemnly, indeed with gaiety, in Fry's *Venus Observed*. And then, behind all other inspiring influences and more potent, there is that of an older writer who has moved them all—Musset, Anouilh, Fry. This impassioned reflection mingled with Puckish humour, this flow of poetic images which starts from the direct impact of

[1] Author of *The Boy With a Cart* (published in 1939), *A Phœnix Too Frequent* (performed 1946), *The Firstborn* (published in 1946 and performed at the Edinburgh Festival in 1948), *The Lady's Not for Burning* (1949), *Venus Observed* (1950), and *A Sleep of Prisoners* (1951). He is the translator of Jean Anouilh's *L'Invitation au Château*, in English entitled *Ring Round the Moon*.

life, this seriousness and these conceits, this tenderness for the foibles of human nature, where do they spring from if not from the fountain-head in Shakespeare? Prospero waves his wand; the Duke of Altair turns his telescope; and all the wonders of the stars are revealed presiding over the affairs of men.

Christopher Fry has many interests, many moods, and a capacity to excel in all that he touches. Perhaps his danger may lie in his facility. The *Firstborn,* published in 1946 and performed at the Edinburgh Festival in 1948, stands alone in that all is subdued to the necessities of a tragic theme. The characteristic epigrams are not lacking, but where they are impish in the comedies they are ironical here—none better than Fry knows how to adjust the tone to his theme. In this play he does not get so quickly into his stride as usual, and the first Act is not equal to what follows. The subject is the Biblical one of Pharaoh and Moses and the plagues of Egypt, and ends with the tragic death of young Ramases, Pharaoh's son, and the release of the Israelites. The character of Moses, a man who accepts the mystery he does not understand and the mission to which he is called, is powerfully drawn, and Pharaoh himself is an intelligible human being. Aaron, too, is revealed in such words as:

> I've begun to believe that the reasonable
> Is an invention of man, altogether in opposition
> To the facts of creation, though I wish it hadn't
> Occurred to me.

But it is Moses who says ironically:

> They love me from the bottom of their greed.
> Give me the bad news.

or optimistically:

> Good has a singular strength
> Not known to evil.

or in chiding impatience:

> Shall we live in mystery and yet
> Conduct ourselves as though everything were known?

or resignedly at the end when young Ramases dies:

> I do not know why the necessity of God
> Should feed on grief; but it seems so.

The short play, *A Phœnix Too Frequent*, first produced in 1946, is pure comedy, fanciful, mischievous, the grotesque and the charming happily interwoven, except that there is perhaps an excess of the macabre in the final disposition of the corpse. The beautiful foolery and fantastic allegory of *The Lady's Not for Burning* (produced 1948 and 1949) are something new in English literature. The time is the early fifteenth century, the scene in a mediæval market-town. The house of the Mayor is invaded by a soldier, insistently demanding to be hanged, and the beautiful Jennet, accused of witch-craft. Margaret, the respectable mother of truculent sons, is driven to exclaim:

> O peaceful and placid heaven,
> Are they both asking to be punished? Has death
> Become the fashionable way to live?
> Nothing would surprise me in their generation.

But Jennet has no longing for death. She replies:

> Asking to be punished? Why, no, I have come
> Here to have the protection of your laughter.
> They accuse me of such a brainstorm of absurdities
> That all my fear dissolves in the humour of it.

Jennet at the end entreats Thomas to postpone for fifty years his 'curious passion for death', in a scene of felicitous love-making, not the less charming because it is absurd.

While *The Lady's Not for Burning* may be taken as an allegory denying that denial of life which appears to emerge from the philosophy of Eliot, *Venus Observed* is life itself in its gayest aspect exhibited under Prospero's magic spell. It is the Duke who talks like Prospero, Christopher Fry who has imposed the spell. The dramatist is gay when he is most serious, and serious when he is gay. The play begins with 'an act of poetry' when the middle-aged Duke requests his frustrated son to choose him a wife from three handsome women

> All of them at some time implicated
> In the joyous routine of my life. (I could scarcely
> Put it more delicately.) I wish to marry.
> Who am I, in heaven's name, to decide
> Which were my vintage years of love?

Realism and fancy mingle in the entries and exits of the 'handsome women', and Reedbeck (the Duke's unjust steward), and the latter's daughter, Perpetua, who is Rosalind and Miranda in one, and her brother Dominic, and a comic butler and footman. It is under a changing firmament darkened by an eclipse of the sun seen from his observatory that the Duke has arranged the scene; and in this way it is *sub specie æternitatis* that the players behave. The Duke makes astronomy an excuse for philosophy and philosophy an excuse for love. He is tolerant of everything —of his own gay past or the misdemeanours of his steward, who with the best intentions systematically robs him. He makes love urbanely to Perpetua who, challenged to use longer sentences, runs into forty delicious lines, 'wandering, Through shady vowels and over consonants', 'with commas falling As airily as lime flowers,' in the longest sentence ever used by any Beloved in any play, there being, it seems

> no reason
> To draw to any conclusion so long as breath
> Shall last, except that breath
> Can't last much longer.

Which indeed leads the Duke to conclude:

> How nature loves the incomplete. She knows
> If she drew a conclusion it would finish her.

The rhetoric in which the play abounds, sententious and fantastical, is never pushed beyond the point where it may be advantageously broken off with gentle ridicule. 'Would you mind if I reminded you, father, What we were talking about when you started talking?' follows a paragraph in which the Duke has been soliloquizing like Hamlet. And again and again we feel that it is the philosophy of T. S. Eliot which is under the mild censure of parody

> We fall away into a future, and all
> The seven seas, and the milky way
> And morning, and evening, and hi-cockalorum are in it.
> Nothing is with the past except the past.
> So you can make merry with the world, Rosabel.
> My grateful thanks.

Can we not see there a rejoinder to the poetry of despair or renunciation? Christopher Fry is a poet using engaging words and apt images inviting us to look at a world which can be as pleasing as our mood will permit; and that depends on us—or on him when he is writing verse for us. Why despair, when there is always the joy of reflecting, however inconclusively, on the ups and downs of life? There is always life itself, with all the questions it puts (answerable so cleverly), and the images, however evanescent, evoking beauty, and the fact of living, which asserts itself against any Space-Time dubiety. Christopher Fry, gaily, cleverly, triumphantly offers us not despair or renunciation, but life and poetry seasoned with so much philosophy as we may care to add.

'So you can make merry with the world, Rosabel.'

Chapter Seventeen

POSTSCRIPT—1951 TO 1955

AT the end of the half-century literature was felt to be in a state of transition. The pattern—if there was one—was by no means clear. The obscurity was due to causes which are still operative. The human mind is puzzled not only by the problems which beset it in all ages, but by others peculiar to our own time which press persistently and obstinately on daily life. To many it seems that our clever, inventive, restless, much-travelled society is drifting aimlessly in a dim twilight. The intellectual middle-classes, on whom the fate of the best literature mainly depends, have been deprived of leisure and many of the facilities for human intercourse. The novelist, reflecting the contemporary scene, sets his puppets moving at cocktail parties, in the bedrooms of small flats, in aeroplanes, on arterial roads, in Continental cafés; or he finds himself looking for more congenial material in the past; or, abandoning fiction, nostalgically describes his own youth in autobiography. The social philosopher—for example, Bertrand Russell—finds the scene clouded by the irreconcilable conflict between East and West and the near prospect of the extermination of the human race; and this cloud is never far behind the scene even in the lightest pictures of contemporary life. Happy the historian who can immerse himself in the past, or the traveller who describes adventures in the jungle or the ascent of Mount Everest, or even the writer of war-books, which, fitting into the now clear pattern of war, offer something more determinate than the shapeless present. Those who insist, in spite of all, on facing the contemporary scene have to come to terms with a restless, questing, anxious world which has severed its links with tradition and lives from hand to mouth with muddled morals and capricious ideals.

Yet it is the function of the artist to make order out of chaos, and there are no signs of slackening. There are younger writers coming on though no giants are yet visible; and some of those who made their reputations twenty or twenty-five years ago and suffered from the shock of the immediate post-war period seem to have recovered their balance. The prevalent notion that the novel has seen its best days and is doomed to decay is confuted by a considerable number of novelists who have won and deserved attention. Fiction has tenaciously held its own, and if the contemporary novelist who has elected to write about the present refuses to be bound by preconceived ideas of what a novel should be, that is as it should be; for he is working under new conditions on new material to which the creative imagination adapts itself in a new way. An extreme example of innovation in fiction is Wyndham Lewis's *The Human Age*, which I will discuss on a later page. I have already mentioned Koestler's *Darkness at Noon*, George Orwell's *1984* and Mervyn Peake's *Titus Groane* and *Gormenghast*. But there are changes in the spirit and form of fiction no less real because they are not so extreme; these changes arise from the absence of scenes once familiar in this country, the weakening of family ties, the treatment of exotic characters, the exposition of what is in its nature unsettled, and the use of motives which seem to belong exclusively to this moment in the history of man—a usage which, of course, is defective only if the novelist fails to evoke the universal from the particular.

II

Graham Greene, Aldous Huxley and Evelyn Waugh were conspicuous among the novelists who, a few years ago, seemed to be losing their grip. Greene's *The End of the Affair* (1951), although challenging, ingenious, audacious, startling, was only redeemed from triviality by quasi-theological elements which were not very convincing; and his play *The Living Room* (1953) was even more disappointing. But Graham Greene was far too vital to go on wasting his force, and his admirers have been abundantly rewarded by a book compact, balanced, ironical, beautifully written, tense—*The Quiet American* (1955). In this he has gone to the distracted country of Viet Nam for the scene of a tragedy writ small but illustrative of tragedy writ large in the history of the modern world. His narrator, Thomas Fowler, is a special correspondent of a London newspaper, in manner cool, self-possessed, sardonic, determined not to get personally involved in any of the political issues. The villain, Pyle, is only a villain *malgré lui*—an 'innocent', virtuous, God-fearing Bostonian who has adopted all the catch-words about liberty, democracy, self-determination and the book-learnt doctrines that can give a patriotic American an excuse for trying to clean up the world in the interests of idealism and big business. He is an ingratiating, self-satisfied humbug dominated by theories divorced from reality, ignorant of life. Instrumental in getting a crowd of natives massacred by mistake, he can console himself with the thought that 'in a way you could say they died for democracy'. With equally virtuous intentions he falls in love with Fowler's Vietnamese mistress and suggests that he should take her from Fowler and make an honest woman of her. In a masterly serio-comic scene we see him demonstratively 'playing fair'; he proposing marriage to the girl, she puzzled, Fowler ironically listening and interpreting. The little Vietnamese girl is beautifully drawn.   Pyle is an unforgettable character, and the narrator, too, becomes a person almost seen in the round, as narrators seldom are. The plot proceeds faultlessly, sped by the thrills that Greene is so skilled in producing. He unfolds a theme in which stupidity, hypocrisy, avarice, ambition and bombast play their sorry parts. It has been suggested that on this occasion Greene, turning from his favourite theme of religion and sacrifice, has substituted certain problems in morality. But it would be unfair to the artistic character and purpose of the book to describe it as a problem novel. It is full of problems, but they emerge as part of the life which is so energetically, vividly, frankly and sometimes tenderly offered for our inspection. It is Graham Greene at his best.

In 1949, as I have noted, in his film-script *Ape and Essence*, Aldous Huxley yielded to a current of thought which for a short time ran like an epidemic through English literary circles. But soon he submitted himself to a sort of historical rest-cure by preparing and writing *The Devils of Loudoun* (1952), which is not a novel but a piece of exciting history written like a novel. Still troubled by the reappearance of something like the old devil in the modern world it almost seems as if he worked off the malaise by the disciplining exercise of turning to history, sifting the evidence for the guilt of Father Grandier, a priest charged with using obscene power to conjure up devils from Hell and send them into the bodies of all the nuns in an Ursuline Convent.   It is a grotesque, gruesome story which enabled Huxley to purge his mind in the atmosphere of hysteria, sin and mass superstition.

Having done that he has been inspired to return to the writing of an excellent novel entirely free from the incubus of devilry.

The Genius and the Goddess (1955) may be regarded as a piece of case-history. What happens when there is a genius of colossal brain-power, who from *theory* appears to know all about life, not excluding its sex-ritual, but in practice is a child dependent on the love and care of his wife and the energy he can draw from her; when the wife is a divinely beautiful woman (the goddess!) who under stress of emotion confesses that her instincts and the 'flow of life' in her are for ever pitted against 'his huge, crazy intellect' and his 'inhuman denial of life'; when there is introduced into the household of the genius a young man, his assistant, who looks like a Greek god, inherits the principles of a Lutheran minister, and thinks that he worships the goddess from afar as Dante worshipped Beatrice; the situation being complicated by the presence of a precocious fourteen-year-old daughter of the genius who conceives a passion for the Greek god and sees her mother as a rival?

Here is a pretty little situation after the heart of Aldous Huxley, and he makes the most of it. The characters, with the exception of the little girl, who is most skilfully drawn, are described rather than shown; but they play their parts consistently in the frantic drama, which moves swiftly to a tragic end. In this little novel there is no surplusage. It is well contrived, perfectly managed. Perhaps it is even too well contrived. We may feel that these four people are victims of the author's art, neatly arranged like nine-pins to be knocked down—all of them—by a few well-directed balls. But it is an acceptable product of Huxley's brilliant powers.

Evelyn Waugh is another of the distinguished novelists who went through a bad phase soon after the war and has since re-covered. He reached rock-bottom in *The Loved One* (1948), already mentioned, which received much praise in the season of the epidemic of which I have spoken; and his historical novel *Helena* (1950) was characterless and dull. But since then he has proved that the virtue has not gone out of him, and that the quality which shines in him now is not fundamentally different from that which delighted everyone twenty-five years ago. His early skill in making play with light chatter, ludicrous situations, and the posturing of the human inane resulted in cheerful satire on post-first-war society. In *Men at Arms* (1952), and similarly in his latest book, *Officers and Gentlemen* (1955), he has again used all his skill in recording light chatter and the ludicrous behaviour of human beings, but this time in grim illumination of the tragedy of war. He does not flatter the British Army; he does not spare criticism of what his hero Guy Crouchback thinks of as 'the classic pattern of army life as he had learned it, the vacuum, the spasm, the precipitation, and with it all the peculiar, impersonal, barely human geniality'. This is from *Officers and Gentlemen*. Perhaps in that book he goes on rather too long in his exposure of the conversational levities of officers in a London Club, in a training-camp in the Western Isles, and in Crete; but, knowing as we all do what was to happen in Crete, we bear with the fatuities, sensing the tragic climax of evacuation, imprisonment, death. Evelyn Waugh takes the stuffing out of heroes, and leaves something uncommonly like life.

III

Unlike the three novelists I have mentioned, V. S. Pritchett is a rare writer who seems never to have faltered, to be always at his best; and his best is very good. His mind seems to be rooted in realities which are the stuff of literature at all times and not primarily in exceptional times; and perhaps that is why there seems to be so much joy of life in all that he writes—joy in the absurdities of London suburbia in *Mr. Beluncle* (1951), joy in the talk, song, myths and behaviour of the Spanish people in *The Spanish Temper* (1954) and joy in literature in his pungent, sensible critiques. It has fallen to him to show in *Mr. Beluncle* that the London of Dickens still survives in the South-Western suburbs, that there is a recognizable lower-middle-class *milieu* which can easily find room for a person so radiant as his hero, so preposterously complacent, so autocratic in his home, so ludicrously boastful outside. Pritchett has blown life into his comic and half-comic characters and forced his readers to be interested in their behaviour. In spite of the roisterousness of his subject his writing is subtle and delicately expressive. In his hands fiction is a fine art.

Joyce Cary and L. P. Hartley (born 1895) are among the older novelists who have not merely maintained but enhanced their reputations. The former in his recent novels has again and again shown the primitive man which lurks never far below the surface in civilized society. *Prisoner of Grace* (1952), *Except the Lord* (1953) and *Not Honour More* (1955) deal with the same set of people from three points of view, those of Chester Nimmo, the bombastic, half-genuine, half-hypocritical politician representing the Radicalism of the 1920's, Nina, his capricious wife, and the plainspoken, ex-colonial administrator, who is later married to Nina, and knows, still loving her, that she is incapable of resisting her former husband. The reader of these books might find it difficult to know what Cary's style of writing might be, for in each case he adopts the colloquial manner of the narrator, and in so doing shows the character of one man or woman, and his or her attitude to the other characters. The exaggerated strictures on society and public life are those of his narrator, but the exposure of passion, violence and duplicity in human nature is all his own. There is vitality and gusto in every page.

Perhaps the best of Hartley's novels is one that appeared in 1949—*The Boat*—a leisurely story written with gentle irony and delicious humour, telling how a dilettante drifts into the position of protagonist in a village feud. This book was followed by *My Fellow Devils* (1951), *The Go-Between* (1953) and *A Perfect Woman* (1955). Apart from an artificial preamble the second of these is beautifully constructed and moves swiftly to a tragic conclusion. The story is a very simple one; it is that of a girl (in 1900) who is engaged to a Viscount and is passionately in love with a farmer; it is the farmer, not the girl, who commits suicide. The tale is told by a thirteen-year-old schoolboy—a device which dates, of course, from Henry James, and was employed in Rosamond Lehmann's *The Ballad and the Source*. Less skilfully constructed is *My Fellow Devils*, but it deals successfully with moral problems far beyond the range of *The Go-Between*, and succeeds in being at the same time thrilling and subtle. It is the story of a 'too serious-minded' woman, engaged to a serious-minded barrister, who falls in love with a popular film-star and marries him. The actor is as histrionic in his life as in his profession, generous enough, flashy, effervescent, and also, as his wife discovers too late, a crook. The author deals subtly with a perplexing conflict between the heart and the conscience and the clash of incompatible duties. It is a pity that the moral issue involved is rather irrelevantly turned into a religious issue by the heroine's decision to become a Roman Catholic.

17

It is remarkable that R. C. Hutchinson (born 1907), having written many novels, from *The Answering Glory* in 1932 to *The Stepmother* in 1955, and maintained a high standard throughout, should not have received more recognition as a writer of importance. The reason perhaps is that he writes in a manner that has gone out of fashion since the first world war—with the heart, and as if there were an undercurrent of passion swaying the author throughout—never flippant, without extreme cerebral subtlety, with a seriousness which may be painful but never bitter; and never seeking refuge in original sin or nihilism. His *Recollection of a Journey* (1952) well illustrates his range of sympathy and shows his capacity for entering imaginatively into the experiences of foreigners—Poles who were caught in the war between the Germans and the Russians. It is a pitiful story of human misadventure, love and suffering, with no light relief, but never maudlin. It is from the behaviour of his characters, and not his own preaching, that he draws his thesis that 'the human claim to a portion of divinity rests . . . on the genius by which they transcend suffering'.

In writing of Rosamond Lehmann I suggested that it was a sign of her remarkable skill that she had dared to run so many artistic risks and had emerged triumphantly. In *The Echoing Years* (1953) she apparently decided to take a greater risk than she had ever taken before, and challenged danger in every chapter, every page, with disappointing results. The story mainly concerns three people, and begins at the end, so that the two survivors can go back and back into the turgid, troublous moments of their past, and live again in retrospect its passionate episodes. From first to last it is a study of the life passionate, erotically passionate, in all its extremes, and this exclusively, except so far as it is modified by drunkenness. We follow a track of turbulent, grimly serious, hypersensitively analysed life in its erotic aspects. The picture is true only to a limited element in reality, and so not quite true to life as a whole. It is a clever book, full of refinement upon refinement about feeling, yet differing from the author's other work in that the strange and the beautiful do not emerge. It is thrilling, but it is not *moving*. The partial failure arises from the author's excessive daring and the choice of a subject not well suited to her talent.

The work of H. E. Bates has developed considerably since the war. He has become more sure of himself, has acquired more mastery of his technique, and can compose a story, long or short, in such a way as to achieve a high degree of success within the limits imposed by his theme. Yet the results of his work in fiction are still unequal, and this because the themes he chooses are sometimes good, springing from reality, sometimes not good, being something artificially made. This inequality is well exemplified in *The Nature of Love* (1953) which consists of three 'short novels'. In two of these we have, as always, descriptions of nature which are admirable, and we have scenes of physical passion, described with some power; but in both cases the tale of passion is something factitious, and fails to move. Yet in the same volume there is one 'short novel', *Dulcinea*, which comes near to being a little masterpiece. It is simple, very near to earth, telling how a plain peasant girl for money and trinkets gives herself to a coarse farmer, who overcomes his miserliness in the desire to possess and keep her. Disaster comes from her desire to escape to a man she loves. The ingredients of the story are few, but beauty emerges from ugliness, ugliness revenges itself on beauty. It is a terrible and moving story.

Among the novelists who have won recognition since the war is Hugo Charteris, who has imagination of a high order held in check by severe intellectual discipline. In *A Share of the World* (1953), after an unsatisfactory start, he settles down to a story which, in the portrayal of a few characters, is at the same time a criticism of the mental atmosphere in which this generation lives. John Grant the hero may be regarded as a sort of symbolic modern man, tied up in his own insistent consciousness, ineffectually seeking to break away from the 'web' which heredity, memories of youth, and custom have spun round him. A detestable private soldier with whom he had had an unhappy experience in the war keeps on turning up in his later life, playing the part of a spying, unavoidable conscience. The story is mainly concerned with John's brusque, tentative approaches to a girl through whom he believes he could break the web, her resistance to them, their physical drawing together and aloofness, and his tortured feeling of *being alone* when he was most with her. Often the writing seems hung upon the slenderest threads of sensitiveness. Its subtlety is rare and difficult—I think unnecessarily difficult. The savour of the life it shows is acrid but astringent.

Lord of the Flies, a beautiful allegorical story about children, came from William Golding in 1954. Two of a party of little boys, who are stranded on a desert island, have the wit and intelligence to organize their society for survival. Others contest their leadership, and are seen degenerating into bullies and beasts. By a singular feat of understanding and sympathy Golding has treated the boys as boys, yet has succeeded in revealing through them the dual nature of man, the noble and the bestial, the civilizing and the retrograde. A better book than *Animal Farm*.

Alex Comfort (born 1920), has been a prolific writer—of novels, poems, essays and plays—since he was seventeen years old. He has talents many and various. I was especially impressed by his description of the Turkestan desert as seen through the eyes of a determined mathematician, who has made a forced landing in a plane in his efforts to escape from his Russian employers. It occurs in *A Giant's Strength* (1952). The terms used to describe this uninhabited, formidable region, against which the 'homeless' man fights obstinately to survive, are those natural to a mathematician. Behind his struggle with the forces of Nature we see the equally violent struggle of his feelings against the governing powers from which he is fleeing—the 'pig-faces' of the rulers on both sides whose voices ring in his ears, shouting, interfering with a scientist's work, enemies of 'decent human friendship'.

In that book Comfort is dealing with the cosmic forces of nature and the restless human forces that trouble man. William Sansom (born 1912) in his writing himself represents that modern restlessness, rejoicing, it would seem, in incessant movement, skilled in conveying the animated atmosphere of a crowded room, or a fiesta in Seville, or a bull-fight, or cars speeding on the Corniche, and throngs of people some of whom are experiencing the passions that punctuate restless lives. His plots are ingenious. In *The Face of Innocence* (1951) he portrays a woman who fools two men with confessions of lurid amorous adventures in her past which are the more disturbing because she has *invented* them. In *A Bed of Roses* (1954) we see a woman ruthlessly pursued by a bully and a cad whom she has discarded as a lover, and seeking refuge with an honourable wooer, only to discover that she cannot do without her bully. Here the author escapes the risks of melodrama by making the outrageous possible, or at least plausible, and winning attention by his skill in narrative and the painting of scenes. Some of Samson's contemporaries have gone much further than he in emphasizing the restlessness of modern society, showing men and women drifting through life without any aim beyond the excitement of a moment. In *Living in the Present* (1955) John Wain introduces us to a hero, contemplating suicide, obsessed by the 'insupportable ennui and pointlessness of modern life'. In *That Uncertain Feeling* (1955), by Kingsley Amis, we are shown the same pointlessness, the only way of escape being, apparently, into smug propriety—or pointlessness in another form. The principal character is an assistant-librarian in a Welsh city. We meet a similar hero in *Lucky Jim* (1954), who avoids mediocrity only by impudence, pugnacity, an appetite for women and drink, and skill in finding opportunities to indulge his propensities. Amis is a lively writer, achieving effects by crowding as many shocks as possible into a short time. *Lucky Jim* quickly became a best-seller.

Among writers of fiction who were mentioned in an earlier chapter and have maintained their reputation in later books are Sylvia Townsend Warner, F. L. Green, Mervyn Peake, P. H. Newby, James Hanley, and Ivy Compton-Burnett. Of some others—Anthony Powell, Olivia Manning, T. O. Beachcroft, Antonia White and Francis King—I must be content to say that theirs are books which are giving pleasure to fastidious readers. But there is one new writer of whom something more must be said were it only for the fact that he is one of the rare contemporary writers who can hold the reader's attention from sentence to sentence and page to page by the exciting beauty of his style. He is Patrick Leigh Fermor (born 1915).

Fermor is by no means only a novelist. His first book, *The Traveller's Tree*, published late in 1950, is a radiant account of the people and the scenes of the Caribbean Islands. In *A Time to Keep Silence* (1953), describing his experiences when he went to live as a guest in Benedictine and Cistercian monasteries in France, he has not succumbed, as some would have done, to the sensational. He submitted himself to his environment, and recorded his more significant impressions of the life, ritual and faith of the monks among whom he was living. In his account of the ritual there are passages which recalled to me Walter Pater's description of Roman religious rites in *Marius the Epicurean*. Here is the artist at work, rejoicing in visible and audible images, on a religious theme; employing his eyes and ears with judgment, though tending, some might think, to forget the erring humanity of the men portrayed. But may there not be justification for this rare way of describing human beings—through what they seek to be, rather than through what they too obviously are?

After that, later in 1953, came his novel *The Violins of Saint-Jacques*. There are certain elements often expected in a novel which in this book are absent. This is no chorus of ordinary people, no intimately drawn characters, and very little dialogue. There is movement, pattern in movement, increasing tenseness, catastrophe, silence. The design is firm, the execution beautiful. The scenes described (though fantastic and exotic) the passions set in motion (though seeming to belong to an order of life long passed away) are so treated as to leave us at the end with a sense of having been through an exciting and illuminating experience.

The story is told by a French woman who fifty years ago had been the sole survivor from the island of Saint-Jacques in the French West Indies, and describes what happened in that island on the last day before it was destroyed by a volcanic eruption. In this forest country, luxuriant with tropical vegetation, live descendants of negro slaves and a creole aristocracy who cling to eighteenth-century social traditions. Chief among them is the flamboyant Count de Serindan de la Charce, a feudal landlord beloved by his tenants, reactionary, pleasure-loving, tolerant of everything except what is new. The fatal night is that of a carnival in the town and a brilliant ball in the Count's mansion, of fantastic scenes enlivened by French merry-making and African orgies. Beneath the exterior the author has arranged a web of frightening events—the beginning of a feud, the prospect of a duel, the threat of a suicide, and the possible elopement of the daughter of the family with the villainous son of the Count's worst enemy. Raw, sensational happenings these—but why not? Tragedy and romance are made of such stuff.

If I have been just in my appraisals, these samples of the fiction of the last five years serve to show that English fiction, so far from being a declining art, is vigorous and flourishing. In some cases it has taken new forms, seeking in its own way to show and interpret the world we have. If some have jibbed at the formidable task, others are so successfully facing it that they have given to fiction the primacy among the literary arts of today. It can hold its own when compared with the period between the wars, whose importance in the field of fiction has I think been exaggerated. It would not be fair to consider Wells, Bennett, Galsworthy, Conrad and E. M. Forster as representatives of that period, for they all wrote their best or most of their best before the first world war; and James Joyce was Irish. There remain in that period only Virginia Woolf, in the first rank of novelists, and possibly D. H. Lawrence. Today we have Graham Greene and Pritchett very near the first rank; Wyndham Lewis who, though no longer young, has been producing books superior to those he wrote before the war; and others with high qualities who are writing at least as well as in the earlier period, or have emerged since.

IV

Poetry in the last five years is not quite in the same case. There has been nothing comparable with the emergence of T. S. Eliot in the 'twenties or the vigorous outburst of imaginative experiment among the 'young poets' of the 'thirties. The vehement drive of the movement appears now to have exhausted itself, though, in spite of some reaction, its influence upon younger writers is by no means over. T. S. Eliot is still the outstanding poet of this time, though his preoccupation with poetic drama, interesting as it has been for the theatre, has not proved productive of what is most satisfying in his poetry. He has been writing criticism as well as poetry. His published lecture *Poetry and Drama* (1951) was an account of his views on poetic drama in general and his own method in particular.

Of those who were 'young poets' in 1930, Stephen Spender's reputation has stood up well to the test of time. He has not the dash or audacity or nimble metrical skill of W. H. Auden, yet he is nearer to the centre from which radiates the meditative poetry of all times, He is not unable or ashamed to sound the note *sunt lacrimae rerum*; but if these words occur to Auden he, Auden, writes (in *Nones,* 1952):

> Only the young and the rich
> Have the nerve or the figure to strike
> The *lacrimae rerum* note,

lines peculiarly characteristic of the impatient, scornful Auden. In *Nones* there is great power; here are the steely muscles of his imagination; sureness in diction, boldness in imagery; versification varied and springy. In his view of life he has hardened into what at an earlier stage he appeared to be becoming. His scorn of

> The paranoic mind
> Of this undisciplined
> And concert-going age

has not one whit abated, but it is tempered with high spirits and wit.

> I am sorry I'm not sorry . . .
> Make me chaste, Lord, but not yet.

If at times we feel that his unsparing criticism of life is destructive and negative, leaving nothing but sourness and drought, we may be brought up sharply by lines which hint that that is because for him the standards of judgment are high.

> . . . when I try to imagine a faultless love
> Or the life to come, what I hear is the murmur
> Of underground streams, what I see is a limestone landscape.

It is sheer delight to turn to *The Shield of Achilles* (1955). In many of the poems in the book Auden puts aside his intellectual misgivings and, I should add, his obscurity, pouring out reflections that come from the observation of nature in fountains of song that ripple and leap with gaiety not the less gay because it is almost always mixed with mockery. Never has he displayed his metrical skill with more mastery. He does not cease to tilt at the bourgeois and the pedant, but with a lightness of touch which puts them in their place without destroying the likeableness of things to which his selective spirit warms. There is no other living writer using the English language who can write lyrical poetry like this.

Two poets who began to be known in the late 'thirties have since strengthened their position, though they should be mentioned together only by way of contrast. Kathleen Raine is precise even in her mysticism, delicate in her choice of words. In her little book *The Year One* (1952) she showed signs of escaping from a quasi-mysticism which seemed likely to sterilize her poetry, and in coming down to earth she gained in force and attractiveness. The other, George Barker, lacks precision and sureness of touch, and is best where he refrains from philosophy, but there is a streak of true inspiration in his writing which does not fade; he is emotional, alive, rich in striking images—undisciplined, but genuine. *A Vision of Beasts and Gods* (1954) shows him at his best.

Edwin Muir's reputation has well stood the test of an edition of *Collected Poems* (1952). Edith Sitwell's *Gardeners and Astronomers* (1953) has in it zestful verse—full of long lines, rather florid and uncontrolled, torrential, and with the power of a torrent. Robert Graves, prolific in prose and verse, has unique qualities which become more pronounced as he goes on. In his *Poems* (1953) he is more Gravesian than ever—fierce, supercilious, sardonic, powerful—and also neat. He is inclined to be angry about everything, but with refreshing anger. His metrical forms are often beautifully contrived.

The book of *Poems* (1953) by Elizabeth Jennings is a long way from the new poetry of the 'thirties. It was followed by *A Way of Looking* (1955). Her verses, correct, formal, tightly controlled, often express vivid impressions of things physical, and their impact on the emotions; passion and restrained utterance go together. John Betjeman, who was well known for his highly individual books on architecture and places, has won the admiration of a large public with his attractive book *A Few Late Chrysanthemums* (1954), which consists of some skilful light verse and some more serious reflective poems. It is in the former that he excels.

I must be content with a bare mention of the names of Lawrence Durrell, Robert Conquest, Ruthven Todd, Laurie Lee, Robert Gittings, Andrew Young, and Roy Ashwell as poets whose verse will be watched with attention during the next few years.

V

The reception of the piquant, self-revealing volumes of Boswell's journals which have appeared in quick succession is symptomatic of the current taste for autobiography, especially when written while the memory of youth is still fresh. Stephen Spender and John Lehmann, editors of the two new literary journals which have at last arrived to lighten the darkness of the literary scene[1], have both been writing the story of their lives, and both are still in their forties. Lehmann's book, *The Whispering Gallery* (1955),

[1] *Encounter*, edited by Stephen Spender, jointly with Irving Kristol, started December, 1953; and *The London Magazine*, edited by John Lehmann, February, 1954.

is a refreshing, intimate account of places, people and literary enterprizes, starting with a delightful description of the house on the banks of the Thames, where lived an amazing family, which included his father, R. C. Lehmann, long editor of *Punch*, and his sisters, Rosamond the novelist, and Beatrix the actress. What wonder if he lisped in numbers! At Cambridge and afterwards he made friendships with the younger poets and other writers, writing himself and acting the midwife to young talent through the Hogarth Press, *New Writing* and *The London Magazine*.

Stephen Spender's book, *World Within World* (1951), is more inward-looking. It is a series of pictures of a young man, sensitive, self-critical and sincere, set in the environment of a critical period in the world's history. We are never allowed to forget the pressure of his time and generation upon him. The first sentence strikes the note. 'I grew up in an atmosphere of belief in progress curiously mingled with apprehension.' At Oxford we find him coming under the influence of Auden, who impressed him by 'the altogether superior brilliance of his gifts over mine', proceeding, always intellectually, to state in poem or in argument his problem—the problem of 'Man in this Century'. Auden used words drawn from scientific terminology 'as Milton uses names of heathen gods'. But Spender did not yield himself to the ascendancy of Auden, whose early poetry 'gave the impression of playing an intellectual game'. 'I had no confidence in myself as a dominating intellectual force, but a secret and profound belief in myself as someone acted upon by experiences and capable of recording the truth of my feelings about them.' That, I think, is a just account of himself. His response to human life is sensitive, generous, full of pity or abhorrence, and his poetry is a faithful expression of it.

Arthur Koestler is another author who has been writing his autobiography while still in his forties. The first volume, *Arrow in the Blue*, appeared in 1952, the second, *The Invisible Writing*, in 1954. As literature the first is the better of the two, telling of his struggles as a shy child in Buda-Pest, a frustrated student in Vienna, a half-starved aspirant to fame in the slums of Tel Aviv, an elbowing journalist in Jerusalem, Paris and Berlin, a 'rootless vagabond' whose 'seething indignation' led him to embrace Communism as a faith at the age of twenty-five. In the second volume he tells how he released himself from the 'deep, myth-producing forces' which had put him under the spell of Communism, and escaped from the country where it seemed 'the birds had become silent, and the air had lost its fragrance'. 'Why is it,' a Communist woman had asked him, 'that the leaves die wherever we go?' Later, in spite of an amusing awareness of Britain's national defects, the 'rootless alien' succeeded in rooting himself in the country of which he is now a citizen. The first book glows with the intensity of the life he had experienced. The writing of the second is uneven. He is now over-blunt, now highly sensitive. He has a tiresome way of indulging in Freudian analysis, and many passages might have been pruned. In the sum the whole work adds up to an absorbing picture not only of his own life and adventures, but of modern Europe in one at least of its characteristic aspects.

In *An Autobiography* (1954), Edwin Muir, a meditative poet, while not refraining from giving, in his own sensitive way, an introspective account of his spiritual life, is objective in his description of the places, people and events which conditioned his growth and development. The book is written with much delicacy and charm. In *Surprised by Joy* (1955), C. S. Lewis candidly lets his readers into the secret places of his mind, describing the joys of his Christian childhood, the agnostic experience which followed, and his reluctant return to faith in later life.

David Garnett's autobiography, beginning with *The Golden Echo* (1953), is a lively journey among the distinguished friends of his father, Edward, into the choice literary circle of Bloomsbury, and on to the days of his own literary successes in the 'twenties. In *Future Indefinite* (1954) Noel Coward continues an autobiography which he had begun in 1937, and tells, often with unconscious humour, of the many honours which were bestowed on him in many lands. Among autobiographies by older writers I cannot omit to mention *Landfall at Sunset* (1955), by that fine seaman and writer about the sea, Sir David Bone; Sir David Kelly's *The Ruling Few; or The Human Background to Diplomacy*, whose delightful indiscretions were in no way a drawback when he was appointed Chairman of the British Council; and *Uphill All the Way* (1953), a perspicacious, vigorous account of life within the Labour Party by the novelist, biographer, politician, Mary Agnes Hamilton.

VI

'It does not follow,' writes one of the younger historians, Veronica Wedgwood, in *The Times Literary Supplement* (January 6, 1956), 'that the historian will be the better scholar for being the worse artist.' Her own work provides an excellent example of the way in which historical facts can be accurately assembled and brought to life by imaginative understanding and a lively style. Her admirable *Montrose* (1952) has been followed by a much more ambitious work *The King's Peace* (1955), the first volume of a study of the Civil War.

A. L. Rowse, pertinacious, provocative, alive to all things human, goes on from strength to strength, stimulating even those who persist in being irritated by him. He digs and delves in by-ways of knowledge, and moves all the more confidently when he reaches the broad thoroughfares of history. Delightful and 'evocative' (his own word) are his lesser works, such as *The English Past* (1951) and *An Elizabethan Garland* (1953); but impressive on a large scale is his work *The Elizabethan Age*, which began with *The England of Elizabeth* (1950), and was continued with *The Expansion of Elizabethan England* (1955), and will be followed by an account of the 'mind and spirit' of the age. Rowse's work is a good example of the combination in history of the scientific and artistic methods. He has done some original research in collecting new material, but when he has accumulated his facts his imagination steps in and takes charge till a whole age, with all its divisions and sub-divisions, becomes alive with meaning—he sees the living organism of the nation. His studies have made him aware of the 'backwardness' of England in the first half of the sixteenth century, and what fascinates him in the later decades is 'the sudden catching up with a swoop of the national spirit, the soaring, dizzying ascent'. He discovers there 'in embryo the whole subsequent history of our people'. His style of writing is not always elegant; it is always forceful, telling, alive.

Conspicuous among the historical books which can be read as literature are *The Price of Revolution* (1951) by that forthright, challenging writer, D. W. Brogan; *King George V: His Life and Reign* (1952) by the urbane, sweetly reasonable Sir Harold Nicolson, who in this book has shown for the first time his capacity for digesting a mass of historical material and making from it a good full-length portrait; and *Man on His Past* (1955),

by one of the few writers who can interpret history philosophically, Herbert Butterfield. And then, of course, in a class by himself, a master in politics, history and literature, Sir Winston
Churchill, who completed *The Second World War* with *The
Hinge of Fate* (1951) and *Closing the Ring* (1952).

VII

Books of travel and exploration have held a prominent place in
the literature of 1951–55. The interest in such books depends on
several factors—the importance of the achievement described, the
personalities of the chief actors, and the literary quality of the
writing. In V. S. Pritchett's book on Spain the last qualification
matters most. In the books about Everest the first and the second
factors are more important. In the case of Freya Stark and Laurens
van der Post all three contribute alike to the success of their books.
The outstanding event in the recent history of exploration has
been the successful ascent of Mount Everest, and both the expectation of that effort and the victory itself lent interest to books
on mountaineering. Before it, in 1951, came Geoffrey Young's
Mountains with a Difference, in which that intrepid climber gives
exhilarating accounts of his experiences as a climber before the
war, and afterwards, when he had to manage the mountains with
one of his legs missing. A few months later came Eric Shipton's
story *The Mount Everest Reconnaissance Expedition,* 1951, which
admirably disclosed the nature of the problem facing Colonel
(now Sir) John Hunt's party. The achievement itself and all the
planning and team-work that it involved are described by Hunt
plainly and with unadorned eloquence in *The Ascent of Everest*
(1953). Finally, there was Sir Edmund Hillary's *High Adventure*
(1955).

'Time', says Freya Stark in *The Coast of Incense* (1953), 'is a
reality to me. I feel things in movement, proceeding into their
future from their past'. I have already mentioned her earlier books,
mainly concerned with her travels in the East, but her later books
show her making use of all her experience, practical and spiritual.
In *Ionia: A Guest* (1954) she invests the decayed cities of Ionia with
the realities of memory—the imperishable memory of the Greeks
who once flourished there.

If, in all the travel books of Freya Stark, we are never unaware
of the artist, in Laurens van der Post we feel that it is a mystic who

is taking us by the hand and at one and the same time exploring a country (Nyasaland) and exploring his own soul (*Venture to the Interior*, 1952). Towards the end of 1955 this spirited and reflective South African was exploring the Kalahari region in the search for African pygmies and relics of their former culture, and writing exciting articles which will no doubt be the basis of a new book. It is invigorating to turn from his subjective writing to the plain wisdom of that observant, broad-minded, fully-informed woman, Elspeth Huxley, who brings a wonderful balance of heart and head to the problems of Africa. No student of African nationalism and what is called 'Colonialism' should neglect her *White Man's Country* (1953) and *Four Guineas* (1954). For a more intimate account of primitive people, lovingly described, we may turn to Sir Arthur Grimble's *A Pattern of Islands* (1952), which tells of years spent among the people of the Gilbert and Ellice Islands. In *Journey Down a Rainbow* (1955) may be found the combined product of two talented authors, J. B. Priestley and his wife Jacquetta Hawkes, recording from two points of view their experiences in New Mexico. The latter before she became Mrs. Priestley wrote a remarkable book (*A Land*, 1951) on the physical and human evolution of Britain, in which the interests of geographer, archæologist and humanist were beautifully blended.

VIII

T. S. Eliot, as I have indicated, has not ceased to be active in the sphere of criticism; what he writes has the twofold authority of one who is deeply read in books and is also a creative poet himself. The critic who has not that advantage must at least have something of the creative artist within him. Literary scholarship is not criticism, and many books have come from the press in recent years in which the stuffy atmosphere of the lecture-room excludes the fresh air of literature. Yet there are a few living writers whose scholarship is a component element in their rich appreciation of literature. Sir Maurice Bowra (born 1898) is one of these. He is equally at home among the ancient classics and the literature of modern Europe; his breadth and understanding in comparative criticism are well exemplified in *The Romantic Imagination* (1950) and *Heroic Poetry* (1952). Another such critic is Frank Lawrence Lucas, University Reader in English at Cambridge. Deeply versed in Greek literature much of which he has translated and expounded, he is stimulating when he writes about English poetry, and interesting also—so versatile is he—as novelist, poet, playwright. He is a little contemptuous of clever commentators. 'Cleverness,' he says, 'has been the ruin of many writers.' The critic of Shakespeare, he thinks, should be able to imagine himself seated among the groundlings, and the interpreter of Greek drama should constantly ask himself: 'What does this mean, not to the scholar poring in his study, but to a sensible man sitting on a hard seat in the open air of a Greek spring (not always very clement) along with fourteen thousand others?' That is the spirit in which he translates Æschylus and other Greek dramatists (in *Greek Drama for Everyman*, 1954) in verse which keeps to the rules, but not too severely, in language which is in character and is also poetic, with imagery which often brilliantly catches the spirit of the original. When in his critical notes he writes of the ancients he is delightfully free from the awed preconceptions of those who approach a supposedly faultless master. In the same vein, in his stimulating book *Style* (1955), he hits hard at the clumsiness of the pedant, and states the case for the sensible, healthy, energetic writing of English and the enjoyment of literature unspoilt by classroom study. Another critic who belongs to this choice order is Bonamy Dobrée. With much more knowledge than is commonly possessed by professors of English, he applies standards which are fortified by good sense, perception and judgment, well exemplified in his *Alexander Pope* (1951).

Lord David Cecil is not always free from preciosity, but there is taste and fineness of perception in his critical and biographical work. He has not confined himself to literary subjects. His *Lord M.: or the Later Life of Lord Melbourne* (1954) was the concluding volume of a beautifully woven biography of a statesman who completed a romantic career by becoming the adviser and confidant of a Queen. Among the more significant critical works which have deservedly raised discussion in the last five years are Stephen Spender's *The Creative Element*, described as 'a study of vision, despair and orthodoxy among some modern writers' (1953) and *The Making of a Poem* (1955); and Kathleen Nott's provocative *The Emperor's Clothes* (1953), which suggests that the dogmatic religious preconceptions of T. S. Eliot, Graham Greene and others interfere with their experience and blur their vision of reality. Some lively sensible literary criticism may be read week by week in the Sunday papers from Cyril Connolly, Raymond Mortimer and Sir Harold Nicolson.

IX

This age succeeds in retaining on the active list a number of its septuagenarians and even its octogenarians. One of the most prolific and lively writers of the last five years has been Bertrand Russell, who was born in 1872. Having spent the first eighty years of his life in the study and exposition of mathematics, philosophy and the behaviour of mankind, it is as if all that has been no more than a preliminary and that he is now qualified to apply his knowledge in solving the most urgent problems of contemporary life and entitled, for the rest, to relax in intellectual amusements. For relaxation he has written *Satan in the Suburbs and Other Stories* (1953) and *Nightmares of Eminent Persons and Other Stories* (1954), where we find an amazing mixture of the manners of Max Beerbohm, Ann Radcliffe and Bertrand Russell—ironic, darkly romantic, piquant, light-hearted. In *Human Society in Ethics and Politics* (1954) he turns in the second half of the book to a graver question—that of the probable extermination of mankind if the methods of traditional statesmanship are not abandoned. This is not the place to discuss his plan for the salvation of humanity. It must suffice to say that his words are those of a wise, cool-headed, disinterested philosopher whose mind was never more full of energy.

Wyndham Lewis (born 1884) is a youngster in comparison, but he is old enough to make it interesting that he should produce his best book in 1955—and, I would add, perhaps the best piece of imaginative prose written in English since the war. Shortly before it appeared he had prepared the way with two lesser books, *Rotting Hill* (1951), a book of short stories, and *Self Condemned* (1954), a novel. In the first, while exposing the decay in the society of Rotting Hill, he positively revels in the 'rot', becoming more and more high-spirited in his writing, with a kind of thunderous, yet humorous lyricism; and it is noticeable that for all his fierceness he is far gentler to human beings that he ever was in his earlier books. The stories are of unequal quality; some are near failures. In *Self Condemned* he is more consistently successful. Once again there is humour, pathos, and even tenderness in his treatment of individual characters, and his language is subtle as well as forceful and lucid. The hero is a historian who is convinced that 'Man is an uncivilizable animal'; he is shown struggling like Prometheus against unjust powers, the poignancy of the struggle lying in the fact that this Prometheus at last breaks down under the strain of his own unsupportable heroism.

The Childermass, the first book of *The Human Age,* appeared in 1928. Far more important in every way are the second and third books, *Monstre Gai* and *Malign Fiesta,* which appeared in a single volume in 1955. In *The Human Age* Lewis passes from this world to the next—to the existence of man after death, a ghost on the way to Purgatory, Heaven or Hell, a product of his own past and of the designs of the superhuman agents of God and the Devil. It is characteristic of the author that he appears to be as much at home in an other-worldly existence as in this; in the latter his romantic imagination is always peering at something which is grotesquely other-worldly, so that when we get beyond the Earth there seems to be no fundamental change. With him humanity and super- or sub-humanity have always been inextricably involved, the obscene with the divine, the divine with the obscene.

His account of the universe, being a work of imagination and not a metaphysical or theological treatise, is anthropomorphic. All the poets who have led us to non-terrestrial regions have necessarily described shapes such as might conceivably have been seen with human eyes. Homer and Virgil, Dante and Milton were compelled to give human shape and human discourse to their ghosts or angels. Lewis has for his object to do for our time nothing less than Dante did for his; and, I might add, with equal faith—not the same faith, of course, but his own, that which governs his attitude to experience. It is a wild nightmare of a world to which he takes us, but not worse than or so very different from the nightmare he sees on earth. It is because he is so interested in the essential bone shapes of contemporary society that he takes us here to see them writ large in an angelic or demoniacal environment.

It must not be overlooked, however, that the book is a novel, and not only a novel but a thriller, full of action and wild adventure, with rollicking scenes and boisterous naughtinesses, with fighting, tumult, blitz and cosmic eruptions described in words that ring like blows of a sledge-hammer. We can read it if we like simply as an exciting story about James Pullman, recently deceased, who had been a famous author on earth, a very independent, 'unattached' man, 'of the fierce modern genius type, believing not in God, in class, in party, but solely in himself'; and with him the ridiculous Satters, who had been his fag at school, and remained nothing more than a peevish schoolboy all his life. These two at the beginning of *Monstre Gai* have escaped from the temporary selection camp described in *The Childermass* and are seen approaching the Magnetic City, or Third City, to which the important being known as the Bailiff secures their admission.

The Bailiff is a Dickensian character, as alive as any Quilp or Fagin or other Dickensian monster of iniquity—he has a gay wit, a shrill cackle, a plausible tongue, and smells slightly. Pullman takes to him more than he does to the Padishah, the ostensible ruler of the City, 'a supernatural being of great charm, but devoid of the slightest shade of gumption'. Lucifer, it turns out, aspires to the conquest of this city—why he should is not clear, since his representative the Bailiff has enjoyed the reality of power there and the Celestial representative has made so poor a job of it.

From the first Pullman was horrified by the appearance of the residents. They had the 'faces of nonentities'; 'this humanity was alarmingly subnormal, all pig-eye or owlish vacuity. Was this a population of idiots—astonishingly well-dressed?' This 'degenerate, chaotic outpost of Heaven' seemed to be a Purgatory gone wrong. The Bailiff, however, is able to explain the matter plausibly. Heaven, Hell and Purgatory, like the Earth, have been modernized. In the Age of Faith there was a dazzling white Heaven and a good coal-black Hell, but all that is out of date. In the modern age 'we no longer see things in stark black and white'; 'the *Good* and the *Bad* are blurred'. The Devil today 'is a very unconvinced *devil*, and our Padishah . . . is a very unconvinced Angel'. 'I know both,' says the Bailiff, 'so I know what I am talking about.'

Transported with his fag (in *Malign Fiesta*) to the Infernal City, Pullman at first finds it only slightly more repulsive than the Third City, and with his usual fortitude satisfies his curiosity by a tour of inspection of the quarters in which the damned are ingeniously tortured. Satan, however, turns out to be an attractive fiend—as he always has been—in spite of his hatred of the human race and his puritanic loathing of women; and he confides to Pullman that he has decided to resign the post to which God had appointed him—that of administering tortures to the damned. (This is a theological innovation, is it not? Or merely a Devilish lie?) He was bent on new designs against Heaven; he would bring it crashing down by 'arranging for the contamination of the angel nature'. He was going to 'mix it up with the pettiness and corruptions of mankind'. He would even 'force upon it woman—with all her sexishness, her nursery mind, her vulgarity'. And it is only towards the end that Pullman, who has been drifting into active alliance with the Devil, hears with horror of the Deity's message to the evil one: 'This is, up to date, your greatest sin—' the 'humanisation of the angel population'.

There are many inconsistencies in the book—for instance, we are told that no one dies in the Third City, but in the subsequent narrative residents are frequently killed. But in the realm of the marvellous—not the less marvellous because all too human—the inconsistencies are trifles. *The Human Age* may be regarded as an allegory of the conflict—or the diminishing conflict—between good and evil, or a philippic against the increasing depravity of man, or a story of epic proportions about the strange adventures of a daring egoist. The world as Lewis has shown it in other books has always been half-demoniacal, and in this book we only have the reverse of the picture, a supernatural world that is more than half human. To create his future he does not need to go far beyond the present, but he magnifies it and gives us something to dream of o' nights. A fantastic, monstrous, but triumphant feat of creative imagination.

INDEX

[An asterisk (*) put against certain numbers indicates pages where an author is the subject of special discussion.]

For Index to Chapter Seventeen
see over

INDEX TO CHAPTER SEVENTEEN